Lawyers Beyond Borders

LAWYERS BEYOND BORDERS

Advancing International Human Rights
Through Local Laws and Courts

Maria Armoudian

University of Michigan Press
Ann Arbor

Copyright © 2021 by Maria Armoudian

For questions or permissions, please contact um.press.perms@umich.edu

Published in the United States of America by the
University of Michigan Press
Manufactured in the United States of America
Printed on acid-free paper
First published September 2021

A CIP catalog record for this book is available from the British Library.

Library of Congress Cataloging-in-Publication data has been applied for.

ISBN 978-0-472-13256-0 (hardcover : alk. paper)
ISBN 978-0-472-12904-1 (e-book)

ISBN 978-0-472-03885-5 (paper: alk. paper)

Contents

Digital materials related to this title can be found on the Fulcrum platform via the following citable URL: https://doi.org/10.3998/mpub.10038981

Foreword

This book is a story of creativity and hope and lawyers fighting for justice. It is a story of how a relatively small group of attorneys devised a strategy for representing victims of atrocities and human rights abuses across the world. It is a story of how they developed legal theories that never had been tried before to help victims and to prevent violations of rights in the future. It is a story of their victories and also their frustration as an increasingly conservative Supreme Court repeatedly has slammed the courthouse doors closed for such cases.

As the dean of a law school, I also tell my students at commencement about the power they will have as lawyers. I remind them that as lawyers, they will have the chance for tremendous power: to take away lives or to save them; to protect freedom or to compromise it; to protect our environment or aid in defiling it; to help companies do good things or to help them do bad things.

This book tells about both kinds of lawyers. It is primarily about the attorneys who dedicated their lives and their careers to helping victims of human rights abuses. It tells of their enormous ingenuity in bringing suits and fighting as hard as they could for justice. It tells of how they used a statute adopted in the late 18th century, the Alien Tort Statute, to sue on behalf of the victims of horrific abuse in the late 20th and early 21st centuries. But it also tells how corporations fought back, using all their resources to keep such suits from going forward and ultimately to greatly narrow this important law.

Laws are meaningless unless they are enforced. Human rights, too, are merely words on paper unless there are courts to apply them and give them redress. Victims of rights violations deserve to be compensated. And compensation is essential to deter violations for the future. That, of course, is the premise of all liability in the legal system and it is why suits for human rights violations are so important. It is also why what the Supreme Court has done to the Alien Tort Statute in so limiting its use is so awful and so important. If the United States courts are not available for victims to sue, there likely will be no forum in the world.

As I read this wonderful book, I realized that I want all my law students, and all students and prospective law students everywhere, to read it. The lawyers described in this book and their efforts fighting for justice for victims of human rights violations are a model for all of us. It shows that through law we really can make a huge difference. It also shows that even if we fail, it is a fight that is so very important. Maria Armoudian's beautifully written book is a reminder for us all of the power of law and therefore the power of each of us to use it to make the world better.

Erwin Chemerinsky
Dean and Jesse H. Choper Distinguished Professor of Law
University of California, Berkeley School of Law

Preface

Seventy-plus years after "never again," the Universal Declaration of Human Rights, the Geneva Conventions, and subsequent international agreements to end torture and genocide, human rights atrocities have remained a steady fact of life—with little meaningful abatement in sight.[1] These aspirational agreements suffer from political, physical, legal, and societal barriers to realization,[2] leaving millions of victims "below the law"—beyond the law's protection—while their offenders too often remain above it. Obviously, things can—and do—change. History is rife with such examples—through some combination of ideas, human agency, and structures. Thanks to scholars, we know a bit about how and why they occur.[3]

In the complicated realm of realizing international human rights, in preventing or redressing atrocities, I hadn't seen many viable solutions—particularly when violators remained protected by laws of immunity, jurisdiction, sovereignty, or more practical issues around power, wealth, or friends in high places. When I learned about US lawyers, using their tool—litigation—in their own land—the United States—to bring some restitution to victims in faraway lands, I wanted to understand: How had they come up with these ideas? How did they persuade other lawyers, courts of law, or Congress to support unconventional ideas about redress? How did they influence the legal landscape, and how did the work, in turn, affect the survivors and the advocates themselves? What happens in the slow, dynamic process of making—or trying to make—new pathways to justice? This part of lawmaking includes but transcends the institutions. It is the part of law, the painstaking construction of rights and redress that begins in advocates' thoughts and emotions, in conversations between advocates, survivors, and others who might help make change. So, I set out to understand three main aspects in this struggle:

(1) The ideas—classic and new—toward new paths to justice when traditional avenues have failed. How do these develop? From where do they come? How do they move from person to person, through institutions, and over the borders? How do they change in the process? How do they persuade? When and why do they succeed and fail?

(2) The advocates, their thoughts, creativity, strategies, emotions, motivations, and what seem to be unique dispositions or personal characteristics: How did they advance unorthodox ideas against the tide of obstacles and a frequent "no" from the establishments? What propelled them forward to take on these uphill battles that often had few tangible rewards? How did they adjust to the changing political and legal terrain? How did they deal with unusual practical challenges and dangers? How did they view their role, their clients, opponents, the political and legal systems, and the others within it? Did their thoughts, emotions, and dispositions change from the work?

(3) The flow of information: Given vast, legal, financial, and physical, risk-laden obstacles, how did information—about violations, laws, evidence, ideas, forums—move from secrecy or sequestration into courtrooms and beyond?

Using an historical narrative, I traced these ideas, thoughts, strategies, emotions, actions, counteractions and interactions, beginning just before the groundbreaking *Filártiga v. Peña-Irala* to the cases still pending today. I relied on seven types of materials: (1) interviews with advocates, many of which I personally conducted, some in multiple conversations, either in person, or by Skype, or email. I also used archived interviews, including Columbia University's Rule of Law Oral History Project and those published in the media; (2) court records, related legal documents, oral arguments, speeches, and depositions; (3) news articles; (4) archival records from congressional debates; 5) a modified dataset[4] of the Alien Tort Statute and Torture Victim Protection Act cases; (6) academic publications; (7) government and nongovernmental reports. Some scholarship is woven into the body of the book, and some is discussed alongside this book's findings in the conclusion.

I focused mostly on the firsts, the groundbreaking, pivotal, or demon-strative cases that contributed to the field's development or that illustrated the lawyers' thoughts, then contextualized them within broader frame-works of the struggle to pave a new rights revolution. A drawback of this approach is giving short shrift to many important cases, some of which are mentioned while others receive no coverage. Realistically, each legitimate case—of the hundreds filed—could fill a book, or a volume of books with important information.

Finally, because I focused on understanding the ideas and creativity of the human rights advocates seeking to advance international human rights, I did not interview defense lawyers, though I incorporated some of their arguments from their motions, oral arguments, and statements in the media. Perhaps a future project will explore their thoughts, emotions, and strategies. As the field has developed nonlinearly, and in most cases with concurrent developments, the chapters and contents are not exactly in chronological order.

Acknowledgments

It would be impossible to thank everyone who has directly or indirectly contributed to this book. But I certainly could not have done this without, first and foremost, the advocates and historian who generously gave their time to share their experiences, thoughts, and ideas with me. I am grateful and indebted for their time, wisdom, and inspiration: Peter Weiss, Dan Stormer, Paul Hoffman, Gerald Gray, Beth Van Schaack, Marco Simons, Katie Redford, Bert Voorhees, Steven Watt, Judith Brown Chomsky, Katie Gallagher, Beth Stephens, Anne Richardson, Cindy Cohn, Agnieszka Fryszman, Martyn Day, Benedict De Moerloose, Andreas Schüller, Terrence Collingsworth, Scott Gilmore, Matt Eisenbrandt, Almudena Bernabeu, Michael Evans, Kathy Roberts, Susan Burke, Morton Sklar, Dixon Osburn, and their support staff.

I thank my editor, Elizabeth Demers, and editorial associates Danielle Coty and Haley Winkle, my production editor Mary Hashman, and copy editor John Raymond, and the staff at the University of Michigan Press. I thank the two anonymous reviewers for their extremely helpful comments.

I am deeply indebted to my family, friends, and colleagues for their ongoing support over the years: Bernard Duncan for endlessly proofreading, commenting, indexing, transcribing, and encouraging me from the inception of this project to its conclusion; my mother and father, Aghavni and Garabed; Julian Heath and Nicolas Pirsoul for edits, suggestions, humor, and ongoing support; my dear friends for their relentless care: Wyatt Underwood, Dutch Stowe, Ankine Aghassian, Ron Levy, Emanuela Cariolagian, Adrin Nazarian, Michael Shoob, Joe Kahraman,

Ani Muradyan, Denise Robb, Sudd Donge, Jessica Hall, Loucin Mekhjian, Manuel Vallee, Alise Cappell, Serj Tankian, James Robins, Jenny Kildjian, Paul Karon, Jeff and Deborah Kaye, Lisa Kalustian, Corazon Miller, Steve Miles, and Jinee Lokaneeta.

I thank the University of Auckland, Dean Robert Greenberg, and the Faculty Research Development Fund, which provided the seed funding for this book, and all of my supportive colleagues: Simon Thrush, Mike Hurst, Tim Page, Annie Goldson, Kathy Smits, Geoff Kemp, Jennifer Frost, Tracy McIntosh, Jennifer Lees-Marshment, Christine Arkinstall, Melissa Spencer, Barry Milne, Tim Fadgen, Martin Wilkinson, Steve Noakes, Steve Winter, Steve Hoadley, Gerald Chan, Julie MacArthur, Annie Bartos, Julianne Evans, Fabio Scarpello, Simon Holdaway, Sam Smith, and Komathi Kolandai-Matchett.

ONE

Lawyers Beyond Borders

Introduction and Overview

The human rights cases in these pages are among the most unlikely ones slated for victory. The abuses occurred abroad; the victims are aliens, usually with few, if any, resources; the perpetrators are usually powerful, resourced, and well-connected, often members of governments, militaries, or multinational corporations. And the legal and political systems' structures are mostly stacked against human rights abuse survivors.

But this is a book about agency. It's about how, in the face of powerful interests and seemingly insurmountable obstacles, a few dozen avant-garde lawyers navigate a terrain of daunting roadblocks to find necessary tools and forums in pursuit of a slice of justice for those who otherwise would have none. It is about the slow, painstaking process of constructing justice, expanding rights, and developing new legal ground—most of which occurs outside of the courts—in fact-finding, in conversations, in the convergence of historical and modern thinking, and in unspoken understandings between like minds.

It is also a book about a unique type of kinship in the struggle for justice. Bonded by shared values and commitments, these "agents"—mostly human rights advocates—built a modest but relatively cohesive network that informs, strategizes, and supports them in their global quests for justice. This small, globally dispersed cadre work, sometimes together, often separately, toward similar goals—ending impunity and advancing global justice, especially for the disadvantaged.[1] "We're all friends, and they know if they call me and say, 'We're going to take on an oil company,' I'm going to say 'yes,'" explained Cindy Cohn of the Electronic Frontier Foundation. "We tend to have a kind of a shared view of the world and I think a shared view of our role in the world. I think all of us are together because we want to be able to use our intelligence to make things better—and our gifts to make things better."[2] Human rights lawyer Judith Brown Chomsky similarly "litigates with some constellation, some configuration of that [similar] group of lawyers," she said, "people I'm confident that I can work with."[3]

From a vast sea of data, these agents extract vital pieces of information about events, facts, people, institutions, laws, and legal forums, then creatively weave together persuasive legal claims, which can be difficult, given dangers, distances, and secrecy. They "stitch together transnational networks of actors and institutions," connect with "victims in an isolated village in [say] Somalia," and seek redress in hopes of evoking broader effects at home and abroad—for example, a "ground investigation in the home country . . . forensic excavations of mass graves and all sorts of transitional justice initiatives," explained Scott Gilmore, a human rights lawyer at the firm Hausfeld LLP.[4]

In essence, the lawyers use their agency on behalf of people whose own agency has been utterly destroyed—survivors of torture, slavery, massacres, or genocide.[5] Sometimes, the lawyers' intellectual work provides a bit of restitution for the egregious wrongs that their clients have suffered. But the failures are also very real. And just as the agents find ways to influence the structures—the legal system and body of law—their counterparts, the defendants, defense attorneys, some government officials, and judges erect formidable, at times insurmountable hurdles.

Aware of the obstacles that lay ahead in the pursuit of justice, none is a Pollyanna. But they remain convinced that the cases they carefully choose are worth trying, despite the odds usually stacked against their clients. Each win mitigates an injustice for their own clients while paving a potential pathway for another class of aggrieved people to make their cases. And in the process, the possibility of changing global norms emerges.[6] This dual vision of individual wins within the larger possibility of advancing global human rights impels this core of lawyers forward. To some extent, these goals have inched toward reality. But a "victory in court can mean very little; it can be fleeting . . . with evolving jurisprudence," admitted Katherine Gallagher of the Center for Constitutional Rights (CCR). Still, "in the best circumstances," they are "part of something much bigger than the litigation."[7]

In the US, the number of these types of international human rights-related redress cases grew from the one in 1979 to approximately 400 at the time of this writing.[8] While the first cases laid the groundwork for other survivors to come forward, the growing case numbers did not translate into a parallel growth in wins, perhaps in part because of the field's specialization. But perhaps also because of the required tenacity, versatility, creativity, optimism, and comfort with difficult, complicated, and sometimes dangerous scenarios. "You have to be an optimist to do this kind of work," human rights lawyer Paul Hoffman told the panel of justices on the Ninth Circuit Court of Appeals.[9] Matt Eisenbrandt agreed. "You are continuing . . . because you think they're important and because you think that there is some utility in doing them . . . even if you might have lost a number of cases along the way."[10]

By all accounts, the advancement of international human rights has been an uphill battle—even for the experts, its pathway, particularly in the US, growing narrower in the twenty-first century. And while some aspects of human rights litigation in the US are nonpartisan—for example, when individuals from "pariah" countries commit egregious violations[11]— the equation changes when the accused is either a powerful corporation, a government ally, or the government itself. In these instances, advancing human rights redress is constrained by politics, ideology, partisanship, practicality, and ideas about justice, on the bench, in the legislatures, and executive offices, such as the White House, which often weighs in on the litigation. In more controversial cases, these advocates have fewer friends in either governments or courtrooms, for political and practical reasons. But the struggle is continually changing.

Born from the merging of ideas—old and new—and the enterprising spirit of innovative lawyers, the pathway to justice for profoundly injured people from other lands has expanded and contracted, then shifted to other jurisdictions. These dynamics from the field's birth, expansion, and retraction to its current state are highlighted in the following chapters. While international human rights litigation in US courts was born in part by the advocacy of attorneys Peter Weiss and Rhonda Copelon, three additional sets of lawyers—and a therapist—developed the next phase. The third phase is taking shape now.

Where It Began

The idea that aliens can find justice an ocean away from the site of their abuses can seem foreign itself. But the idea came into US legal consciousness in two different eras. In the modern era, it arose from the trailblazing attorney Peter Weiss of the nonprofit Center for Constitutional Rights (CCR).[12] But Weiss was more or less channeling some of the earliest philosophical and American thought when he unearthed an eighteenth-century statute called the Alien Tort Claims Act or, more recently, Alien Tort Statute (ATS), which was woven into the country's first Judiciary Act. At the time of the first Congress, early US lawmakers, such as Alexander Hamilton and John Jay, agreed that egregious international torts could be litigated in the United States' federal judiciary and would create uniformity in the law of nations and peace within the fledgling country.[13]

To Weiss, the statute's concise language seemed perfectly suited for trying international human rights abuse cases in US courts, as they fulfilled the statute's requirements: they were civil wrongs and violated the law of nations.[14] Representing a Paraguayan father and daughter, Joel and Dolly Filártiga, targets of Paraguay's military dictator, he and Copelon used the ATS to sue Americo Peña-Irala, the man who tortured to death Joel's son and Dolly's brother, Joelito Filártiga, in Paraguay.

When Peña-Irala traveled to New York, Dolly followed, with hopes of confronting him for his crime.[15] But Weiss offered more than a confrontation. His advocacy helped secure Peña-Irala's deportation and a $10 million judgment against him in the Filártigas' favor. Although the Filártigas never collected the court-ordered compensation, the case gave the family a sense of emotional relief, closure, and a bit of agency (see more in chapter 2).[16]

Soon, other idealistic litigators, including Paul Hoffman, David Cole, Michael Ratner, Beth Stephens, and Jennifer Green began using the statute to bring international human rights cases, building a rights fabric via US courts for those harmed abroad. While CCR lawyers Cole, Ratner, Stephens, and Green developed the field from the East Coast, Hoffman did so from the West Coast, while teaching law, litigating at a private law firm, and volunteering for the American Civil Liberties Union (ACLU). The new ATS ruling gave Hoffman the necessary nexus by which to connect his interest in human rights to his work in the US courts. Once he became legal director of the Southern California ACLU, Hoffman used the ATS to try building an international human rights portfolio there.[17]

While Hoffman is but one of a few key agents pushing on the legal boundaries to shape the body of law, case by case, his work transcends the courtroom. His network, voluntary service, and intellectual contributions helped develop organizations that work to advance the law, which, in turn, assist the nonprofit organizations and community organizers in their quest for human rights protections.[18]

The birth of a San Francisco-based organization called the Center for

Justice and Accountability (CJA) is one example. The idea of creating a nonprofit organization exclusively to litigate international human rights cases in civil courts emerged when a therapist named Gerald Gray heard Hoffman's Bay Area talk about his case, *Abebe-Jira v. Negewo*. In that case, Hoffman and Stephens represented three young women, tortured in Ethiopia, who fled to the US and Canada. For EdgeGayehu Taye, the US ceased being a refuge when she reencountered the man who, in Ethiopia, had bound, gagged, hung her upside down, and beat her. As fate would dictate, the torturer and his victim had both found jobs at the same Atlanta hotel.[19] In part because of their legal action, the man was eventually deported, relieving her from regularly reliving her traumas.[20]

Sitting in the audience of Hoffman's talk, Gray reflected on what a win could mean for torture survivors whom he was counseling. Similar to the Ethiopian women's experiences, Gray's clients were forced to relive trauma and terror each time they reencountered their abusers in the US, the country supposedly providing refuge. Under such circumstances, Gray's goal, to help them heal and recover, was all the more remote.[21]

Gray approached Hoffman, then board chair of the nonprofit human rights organization, Amnesty International USA with his idea: perhaps a nonprofit organization dedicated to representing human rights abuse survivors in court could help restore agency to victims, relieve them from encountering their abusers, hold their perpetrators accountable, and deter future atrocities. Through his human rights network, Hoffman and another Amnesty International colleague secured seed funding for what became the CJA.[22]

The new organization developed cases that added new contours toward advancing human rights: judgments in favor of victims and precedents for future cases (see chapter 3). But suing individual tormentors who happened to come to the US, one-by-one, was a slow, limited way of protecting human rights in the face of mass scale human rights abuses under authoritarian regimes, sometimes supported by transnational corporations profiting from exploiting rich, underexplored lands. Remedying these situations would have much greater impact, according to Chomsky. In contrast with individual "wrongdoers," in which "other people will take their place . . . you haven't advanced the human rights in any significant way, whereas if corporations can be convinced that they can't do that, it has a much greater effect. It affects other corporations, and of course, the [defendant] corporation. Shell in Nigeria is more powerful than Nigeria. Its income is more than the GDP of Nigeria."[23] But addressing these injustices required another strategy, one that could challenge much bigger, more resourced and powerful defendants. That was the plan of three young lawyers and a Burmese democracy advocate who sought to help local villagers who were tortured or enslaved to build a pipeline.

Corporate Torts

Around the same time frame as the CJA's founding, three University of Virginia law students traveled to Thailand to document the effects of globalization on poor countries in Southeast Asia, and to study the promise-versus-peril of large land-and-water-altering projects such as dams and deforestation. Their discoveries, the relationships they built, and the culmination of their ideas developed another trajectory in the field of human rights.[24]

Globalization had opened new frontiers for transnational corporations to expand their sources of profit. But with some resource-rich regions under authoritarian regimes, the route to those profits meant partaking in the plundering of poor, disadvantaged people's lives, lands, and livelihoods. Pleading for the end to the destruction was sometimes met with brutality—including enslavement, torture, prison, or death—with no means of recourse in their own countries. Local courts, legislatures, and executive branches were often politically incapable, disinterested, or beneficiaries of the situation. Burma (now Myanmar) was one of those places. The military regime controlled the country's political apparatus, leaving those who were being brutalized with nowhere to go except into hiding. So they fled to the forests along the Thai/Burma border.[25]

Those circumstances and a fresh look at the ATS by the law students—Katie Redford and Tyler Giannini—became the basis of EarthRights International, a new nonprofit that would represent the Burmese victims. Rather than primarily suing individual violators, as CCR and the CJA had done, EarthRights focused on the corporations partnering with the regime (and their executives). The oil giant Unocal of California was one of those companies.[26]

No human rights victim had successfully sued a corporation using the ATS. But the students-turned-lawyers persuaded CCR and leading civil rights lawyers to join them for the cause.[27] And in two cases, *Doe v. Unocal* and *Roe v. Unocal*, this combination of lawyers sued Unocal in both federal and state courts.[28] After years of court battles, in 2005, the oil company compensated victims with approximately $30 million,[29] funds that could never bring loved ones back from the dead nor truly repair the damage.

But the funding went a long way to rebuild communities.[30] *Doe v. Unocal* signaled a breakthrough for the profoundly injured to recover some sense of justice from companies profiting from their ruin. A day in court in a land far away was a long and circuitous path toward justice, but it was justice nonetheless (see chapter 4).

The experience of the Burmese people was reminiscent of the struggles of the indigenous communities around the Niger Delta in Nigeria, a region plundered by oil exploration in partnership with the Nigerian government. But three similar cases took different turns. In the first, *Wiwa v. Royal Dutch Petroleum*, the company paid the injured plaintiffs $15.5 million to compensate for their losses and suffering. In the second, *Bowoto v. Chevron*, a jury found in favor of the oil company (see chapter 4). The third, *Kiobel v. Royal Dutch Petroleum*, created one of the biggest modern legal obstacles for foreign human rights abuse survivors seeking justice through US courts. The decision came years after Esther Kiobel fled Nigeria, eventually to the US, where she found asylum but not justice.

Justice, No Justice

In Nigeria, the indigenous Ogoni people, subsistence farmers and fishers, relied on the land and sea to survive. The region was resource-rich with abundant oil and fertile soil but capital-poor with no substantive infrastructure, hospitals, electricity, or sewer systems.[31] Oil money supplied roughly 80 percent of Nigeria's revenue, a reality that skewed government decisions in favor of fossil fuel industries, to the neglect of human needs. That was the source of the troubles for Ken and Owens Wiwa, Kiobel, and their fellow Ogoni people.[32]

The saga began in 1958, when a multinational oil corporation, Royal Dutch Petroleum (Shell), began drilling, building, piping, flaring, spilling, and dumping through the heart of Ogoniland. The building and piping uprooted and destroyed the Ogoni people's planted fields. Their flaring blackened the air by day and illuminated the skies at night.[33] Their spilling and dumping of toxic waste killed the fish and ruined drinking water and crops.[34] In a 12-year time frame, some 1.5 million gallons of oil spilled in the region, leaving the Ogoni people with little means by which to survive, much less thrive.[35]

Community leaders, including the Nobel Prize–nominated Ken Saro-Wiwa and Esther Kiobel's husband, Dr. Barinem Kiobel, a Nigerian commissioner, organized the Movement for the Survival of the Ogoni People.

They drafted the Ogoni Bill of Rights and organized demonstrations with up to 300,000 Ogoni to call for an end to the destruction. Their requests and demands went ignored, while bulldozing of planted farmlands and crops and the poisoning of land and water continued. Unrest grew; groups clashed. And Shell-backed military units responded with raids, rapes, beatings, massacres, and the destruction of nearly 500 homes, according to court records. Some 30,000 Ogoni people were displaced.[36]

Ogoni leaders, including Saro-Wiwa, Barinem Kiobel, and John Kpuinen, were imprisoned, tortured, and deprived of food, water, and bedding. So Esther Kiobel took food to the prison. Guards seized her, stripped her naked, and beat her with a high-tension wire, according to her complaint.[37] A year later, the Nigerian military's Special Tribunal formally charged nine Ogoni leaders, including Saro-Wiwa, Kiobel, and Kpuinen, with murder and sentenced them to death by hanging.[38]

Shell eventually abandoned the drilling but left unmitigated pipelines spilling, leaking, and blowing out. Contamination continued spoiling farmlands and water resources, while terror, trauma, and grief remained for the Ogoni people.[39] With evidence that Shell materially supported the military units that had tortured and killed their loved ones, the Wiwas, Kiobel, and their coplaintiffs filed lawsuits against the parent and local corporation, Shell Petroleum Development Company of Nigeria, in the Southern District Court of New York (the Wiwas in 1996 and Kiobel originally in 2002). Causes of action included summary execution, crimes against humanity, extrajudicial killing, torture, rape, arbitrary arrest and detention, forced exile, wrongful death, and property destruction. Others joined Wiwa and Kiobel as plaintiffs, claiming torture, public whippings, clubbing, and exposure to chemical agents. The Dutch oil company, they said, conspired to intimidate them into silence and drive them from their homeland.[40]

Before *Wiwa v. Royal Dutch Petroleum*'s trial, Shell agreed to compensate the plaintiffs $15.5 million to settle the lawsuit (see chapter 4).[41] But Kiobel's case, knocked back by the Supreme Court, never reached trial on its merits. Three courts each ruled differently but none in ways that might help her: the Southern District Court of New York dismissed all but three of Kiobel's claims, allowing her to sue for aiding and abetting torture, crimes against humanity, and arbitrary detention. The Second Circuit Court of Appeals ignored the district court's reasoning and instead rejected Kiobel's claims based on a different question—corporate liability—opining that corporations could not be held liable using the ATS.[42] Kiobel's lawyers appealed.

Although the Supreme Court acknowledged serious allegations—that the corporation "enlisted the Nigerian Government to violently suppress" the burgeoning demonstrations and aided and abetted arbitrary arrest, beating, raping, and killing—it restricted the ATS's application to cases that sufficiently "touch and concern the territory of the United States."[43] Kiobel and victims like her lost their standing to sue unless they sufficiently demonstrated a US connection to the wrong (see chapter 7). With a dead end created by the ruling, all looked bleak for a swath of foreign victims who had pinned their hopes on the US courts for justice.

Though her US-based remedies were exhausted, Kiobel took her complaint to the Netherlands, Shell's home country, and finally got a day in court (see chapter 8). While Kiobel persisted abroad, in the US, lawyers for a group of tortured and terrorized Indonesian villagers pried the federal court doors back open years after the court had confined their case to state claims. The return was born of an unexpected discovery, a memorandum from ExxonMobil's US headquarters that made the US connection.

The Torture Memos

The long, tortuous path for persecuted Indonesians seeking redress continues at this writing. Nicknamed the "petro-city," the Aceh region happened to be on a large natural gas field.[44] In 1971, Mobil Oil contracted with Indonesian oil and gas company Pertamina and the Indonesian government, then a military regime under General Suharto. In exchange for "blank shares" in Mobil Oil Indonesia, a subsidiary of Mobil Oil Corporation, Suharto's military units provided security for the company, according to court records.[45]

Oil money contributed between $2 and $3 billion annually to Indonesia's national revenue, transforming Aceh from a poor province into a fast-growing economy. But uneven distribution of jobs, contracts, and wealth built resentment among locals, who built an independence movement.[46] Suharto turned Aceh into a "military operational area" with an occupation of 12,000 military troops to keep "order."[47] With torture, massacre, and disappearances, the military units crushed the independence movement then continued committing atrocities. Soldiers stripped some victims naked, dragged others with cars, drove over them, or shot them in sensitive body parts such as the genitals or neck. By 1998, more than 3,000 had been tortured, and another 3,000 were either disappeared or killed.[48]

In 1998, the post-Suharto government officially lifted the military area status, but the troops remained, triggering another separatist movement. By then, local residents learned of Mobil's funding, its employment of soldiers as security, and provision of facilities where atrocities were committed.[49] With no recourse in their own country, 11 Acehnese survivors sued ExxonMobil Corporation in the United States District Court for the District of Columbia, complaining that the company was aiding and abetting the battery, torture, burns, electrical shocks, arbitrary detention, and the deaths and disappearances of their loved ones.[50] One plaintiff, John Doe III, detailed his ordeal: soldiers working for ExxonMobil thrice shot his leg, smashed his skull, broke his kneecap, and burned him with cigarettes. After his hospitalization, they tortured him for another month, according to the complaint.[51]

For 16 years, the villagers' legal fates moved from district court to circuit court and back to the district court, while the courts shifted their legal basis from federal law to state common law, restored federal claims, and finally assigned Indonesian law to the case. The district court deferred to the State Department, which warned of a "potentially serious adverse impact on significant interests of the United States" and "a significant risk of interfering in Indonesian affairs." The court dismissed federal claims, maintained state claims, such as assault, battery, and negligence, and restricted document discovery, stating, "Exxon will not be required to produce documents from its Indonesian operations unless it receives all 'necessary authorizations' from the Indonesian government."[52]

That narrow window was enough to uncover evidence that Exxon executives decided from their US headquarters to hire known human rights abusers. More than a decade after the initial filing, the circuit court reinstated the ATS claims, based in part on Exxon's awareness of "atrocities committed by . . . Exxon's dedicated unit . . . while Exxon profited from the operation of its Aceh facility."[53] As of this writing, it is one of the corporate case survivors of the post-*Kiobel* standard (more in chapter 7).

In another *Kiobel*-affected corporate case, *Doe v. Chiquita*, Colombian torture survivors took multiple actions, including suing the individual corporate executives for their decisions and actions that evidently enabled their suffering. And in the "war on terror," because the court dismissed lawsuits against the government, individuals and for-profit corporations were the remaining avenue for the survivors' redress (see chapter 7). These are a few cases shaping the contours of the law, the legal remedies available for survivors via the US legal system. While informative in understanding how rights are constructed, they simultaneously tell another story, one of systemic political and legal complications that push many attorneys away from human rights litigation. Lengthy, complex litigation processes, requisite emotional wherewithal, economic disincentives, and cognitive agility have culled the field to a core of dedicated, tenacious, creative lawyers with the means to navigate the legal, political, and practical mazes. Under the Donald Trump administration, circumstances became even more difficult.

The Trump Era

From its inception, the Trump presidency began building ideological hurdles for human rights cases with antialien rhetoric and high-level ideological appointments in government and courts with palpable effects: "On the one hand, really no one likes trafficking or slavery. But on the other hand, this kind of upswing in the acceptance of racism and bias against migrants, that does affect our case[s]," explained human rights lawyer Agnieszka Fryszman. "Those biases come out, and you've got to think about how you're framing your case."[54]

When Exxon's former chief executive, Rex Tillerson, moved into the US's top diplomatic position, human rights lawyers wondered about the fate of cases, such as *Doe v. Exxon*, asking, "What does that all mean? How will that play out? And what is the judge going to think? But then the judge denied [Exxon's] motion [to dismiss]," said Fryszman.[55]

In addition to the "anti-immigrant, antipoverty" rhetoric, human rights lawyers worry that Trump changed the legal fabric of the US by "encouraging . . . this concept that there is no rule of law and . . . no facts," added human rights lawyer Morton Sklar, who fears the rhetoric will affect juries' decisions.[56]

The political environment has additional hidden effects. A growing civil rights crisis at home, for example, whittles the time and attention of the core human rights lawyers away from international human rights. Already "hopelessly overextended,"[57] limited time and brainpower dictate hard choices, which means fewer available options for representation for victims.[58] "How much time am I going to spend on international human rights litigation in the Trump era, versus other more direct existential threats to civil liberties in the community?" asked Hoffman. "I've always done both, and I'm just not sure yet about that because—and we have some cases that we're going to still do—but whether I would initiate new [human rights] cases in this era, you know, I'd have to think twice about that."[59]

On the heels of "an important and highly satisfying case against the ex-president of Bolivia," Beth Stephens concurred: "I'm less likely to work on international human rights litigation because I think there are other things right [here] now that are . . . pressing . . . there are so many awful things going on right now."[60]

While political and legal obstacles are undoubtedly daunting, they are the tip of untenable piles of complications of a human rights practice. These pragmatic and economic problems can drive others away from the field.

Practical Constraints

Years of complex litigation and unreimbursed costs are financial risks that sole practitioners can rarely take. Larger law firms must fit high-risk human rights cases among a larger caseload of higher probability wins to support these riskier ones. Most human rights specialists work in the nonprofit sector in organizations such as CJA, EarthRights International, CCR, the ACLU, the Electronic Frontier Foundation, International Rights Advocates, and the World Organization for Human Rights, sustained by charitable grants and donations. For small NGOs, grants "were never enough to pay anything. I never earned more than $30,000," explained Sklar, director of the World Organization for Human Rights.[61]

Nonprofit lawyers sometimes enlist pro bono help from large plaintiff-oriented firms, as is the case of CJA. The private practice lawyers divide their time between human rights and less risky cases, sometimes doubling as law professors.[62] "You couldn't earn a living doing this, and . . . it's very wearing," explained Judith Brown Chomsky. With "nobody depending on my cases to [financially] deliver," Chomsky is able to donate her time and brainpower.[63]

These practical realities have made the goal of "keeping and continuing to develop a sophisticated bar" much more difficult. "If there were big paydays out of these cases, you'd see very good lawyers flocking to them. Everybody's got to eat, so you've got to get [lawyers] who [are] both very smart and willing and able to work for very little," explained Cohn. "There are kids graduating from law school every year who would love to do this work if they can find a way to make it so they could still pay their loans. . . . If we could unlock the money, we could unlock a lot of that talent."[64]

Each type of defendant—corporation, individual, or state—brings its own distinct problems. With deep pockets and armies of defense lawyers, multinational corporations fight primarily not on the merits of the cases but by overwhelming opponents in a sea of procedural motions. In *Doe v. Unocal*, for example, "There were so many ways [that they tried to] get us out of court," recalled Anne Richardson, counsel to the Burmese plaintiffs.

"You could teach a law school class based on this case because there was every [available] motion [used in it]. So many motions that happen in any case happened in this [one] case, and you could trace all of the various efforts that they made to throw it out. And it just kept chugging. And it went through three different defense lawyer firms. And we just kept going and going and not getting thrown out."[65]

Exxon, another "huge and well-funded defendant" is similarly aggressive, according to Fryszman. "We're way outnumbered in terms of the lawyers they have versus the lawyers we have. It's sort of like standing in front of a fire hose. It's really terrible. . . . They totally over-paper us and over-lawyer. These companies are really well-funded, and they're pretty much determined to crush you with motions and aggressive litigation tactics."[66]

With individual defendants, the problem arises at the other end: even when the victims win, defendants often flee, leaving judgments unpaid and uncollectible. Without restitution money, an expelled tormentor or an official acknowledgment of injustice is still a type of victory for survivors: having faced their bully and potentially removed him from the country, they enjoy greater freedom.[67] But for the attorneys, litigation costs often go unreimbursed, unless, like in the rare case of a lottery-winning Haitian army high command member, officials enforce the judgment.

In that case, survivors Marie Jeanne Jean and Lexiuste Cajuste sued Colonel Carl Dorélien, held responsible as a mastermind of their suffering in Haiti. After the violent coup ousting Haiti's elected president, Jean-Bertrand Aristide, paramilitary units shot dead between 3,000–4,000 of his supporters. In one massacre in the Raboteau neighborhood, paramilitary members killed Jean's husband. For his advocacy, Cajuste, a union organizer, was arrested, detained, and tormented in prison.[68]

When Aristide returned to power, Dorelien fled to the US, where he won $3.2 million in the Florida lottery. In 2005, in ruling for Jean and Cajuste, a judge ordered Dorélien to pay $4.3 million in damages for torture, extrajudicial killing, arbitrary detention, and crimes against humanity. Of those funds, CJA lawyers representing Jean and Cajuste recovered $580,000, funds used to support fellow survivors and Haitian refugees.[69]

Alongside these risks and costs, human rights cases also present unique challenges in fact-finding.

The Trouble with Fact-Finding

Obviously, human rights abuse victims are not from safe, secure neighborhoods. Representing them means entering their world to understand

the events and their contexts—the complicated, traumatic, often dangerous business of gathering evidence, hiring translators, and finding witnesses, many who naturally mistrust outsiders and go silent out of fear
for their lives. "It's not like, say, a police abuse case where you can call up
people, interview them, go to the scene, and it's a fairly straightforward
investigation," explained Marco Simons, general counsel at EarthRights.
"Most often we won't speak the same language as most of the relevant witnesses. And if [we] speak the same language, they probably won't have easy
access to telephones and email. So just having a conversation with your
client or a witness involves multiple rounds of trying to set up communication through go-betweens and interpreters and, frequently, trips to the
region."[70] That means years of costly investigation, usually before filing an
official legal action.

"I've never seen a major human rights [case] come through without at
least, bare minimum, four or five years investigating," added Gilmore. "It's
painstaking and an incredibly difficult process."[71]

In *Doe v. Unocal* and its companion *Roe v. Unocal*, for example, the plaintiffs and witnesses were in hiding in makeshift refugee camps in the jungles
at the Thai/Burma border, recalled Richardson, co-counsel on the case. To
meet with them, their lawyers traveled through Thailand or met them in
Bangkok. "None of us was allowed to go into Burma because they probably
would've arrested us on sight," said Richardson. "They would've figured
out who we were, and not let us in or not let us back out if we got in."[72]

Lawyers then worked to protect deeply vulnerable clients "in ways that
wouldn't elicit any suspicion about who they were," Richardson recalled.
"A huge amount of energy went into preserving their anonymity" to protect them from either the Burmese or Thai government.[73] This required
ensuring safe ways for the refugees to respond to discovery requests and
to appear for depositions. "We required that all the depositions happen in
Bangkok, which was a location that everybody could get to. So I went to
Bangkok to defend depositions."[74]

In *Doe v. Chiquita*, Simons described "fact-finding in rather dicey parts
of Colombia . . . Just the logistical, practical challenges of putting a case
together are pretty significant."[75] Human rights attorney Terrence Collingsworth also worked in Colombia during "the height of the civil conflict
there, before the [paramilitary] AUC turned itself in. [It] was a very, very
harrowing experience. . . . I was forced to go to areas that were combat
zones . . . and hope for the best," he recalled. But he added, "The bigger
problem is my Colombian team are dealing with death threats. . . . He
[could become] another Colombian lawyer joining the long list of activ-

ists who have been killed there, and it would be hard to pin responsibility for that on any one individual."[76] Collingsworth also faced dangers in Aceh, Indonesia where the civil conflict nearly caught him in cross fire (see chapter 8).[77] Lawyers representing "war on terror" torture and rendition survivors faced a barrage of obstacles to safely meet with their clients (See chapters 5 and 6).

Even normal process-service faces case-killing complications. If process-serving a foreign state, such as Syria, the law specifies, "You have to go to DHL, and then they have to go to the Syrian palace and ring the doorbell, and after three failed attempts, they all say, 'oh, nobody's here.' Then, you have to go through diplomatic channels," explained Dixon Osburn, one of CJA's former executive directors.[78]

Security often obstructs process-service to heads, quasi-heads, or former heads of states. Representing Bosnian rape survivors, Stephens discovered that Radovan Karadžić was in the US attending a United Nations meeting for a day, leaving little time to prepare, file the complaint, and serve papers on the Bosnian-Serb leader before his departure. "We got the complaint done at about four o'clock, [and] one of my colleagues agrees to taxi it down to file it in the Southern District of New York," she recalled. Arriving at "about five o'clock and thirty seconds, the clerk is . . . ready to lock the clerk's office," but allows him to file. He "taxis it up to the hotel where [Karadžić] is staying, and the private investigator is sitting in the lounge in the lobby and says, 'I saw him go into a private dining room' . . . Karadžić comes out. The [armed] investigator walks up to him and says, 'I'm serving you . . .' And the minute he steps up, the security people put their hands on [Karadžić's] back and whisk him into the elevator, and the papers are lying on the floor." They wondered, "Was that enough?"[79]

Representing parents of a humanitarian worker shot dead by Israeli forces, British human rights lawyers "had tried to serve [former Israeli prime minister Ehud Barak] in France, and he had gotten wind of it and didn't get off the plane," recalled civil rights lawyer Dan Stormer. But Barak's four US speaking engagements gave lawyers "four shots" at process-service. "We had to buy tickets [to the talks]. And in order to buy one ticket, we had to buy . . . all of them. . . . [The process-servers] go four hours early to the first event . . . and they sort of lie in wait, and it turns out [Barak] was already there. He had come much earlier. . . . And so it didn't happen."[80]

At the second event, "police security, the hotel security, personal security" blocked service. "So we're starting to panic. . . . At around midnight, I'm waiting for the call. I'm starting to get really worried, and I'm coming up with these wacko approaches . . . [like] I'll go, and we'll rush the stage," laughed Stormer. But the process-servers "came up with this incredibly novel approach, which is virtually unheard of in the world of [process] service, which is, they called up the venue and they said, 'We want to serve Ehud Barak. Will you take us to him? We don't want to disrupt the proceedings.' . . . And they said, 'Oh, sure.'" At a 9 p.m. speaking break, they approached Barak. "The process-server hands it to one person, who hands it to security, who hands it to Barak. Barak takes it and reads it and says something like, 'Thank you for not disrupting proceedings.' And they leave."[81]

Stephens served Guatemala's former minister of defense, General Hector Gramajo, at commencement proceedings at Harvard. Initially, "We didn't want to serve him at graduation [and] we were afraid we would lose him. We were afraid he'd leave the next day," she said, adding, "The result of serving him at graduation was a fantastic photograph."[82]

Cumulatively, these political, legal, and practical conditions help explain why victims have few options for counsel, and partly what has stunted another rights revolution. But while local litigation as a means of advancing international human rights was born in the US, the US is now only one part of the global quest for justice. Working with US lawyers, Canadian, British, European, Asian, and Latin American lawyers have established similar strategies to represent the aggrieved in their own courts. The legal systems in each country offer different types of opportunities for justice. Using the principle of universal jurisdiction for the most heinous acts, EU lawyers simultaneously push civil and criminal cases[83] while in Canada and the United Kingdom, human rights lawyers primarily use common law.[84]

The following pages tell remarkable stories of survivors who have endured harrowing experiences and advocates who use the law to help their recovery. Collectively, the individual stories construct a larger thesis about the global struggle for human rights amid intertwined forces of politics, economics, agency, law, and lawlessness with human lives in the balance. They expose the system's underworld and "overworld" that enables human rights violations to occur, the forces that prevent their resolution, and the transient nature of rights—how they develop and how they revert—an ongoing struggle between advocates, plaintiffs, defendants, and the structures and values they seek to shape.

Throughout the book, subthemes arise—the role of serendipity alongside dynamic, strategic action in the battles to shape the contours of the law, the powerful role of judges, their often contradictory reasoning, and the contest between the ideal and the practical in the decisions made by all involved in the struggle. Finally, while the advocates struggle to change the law and assuage damage, the dynamic interactions between client and counsel affect both—sometimes healing, realizing, recovering, fulfilling, and sometimes retraumatizing or vicariously traumatizing (more in chapter 9).

TWO

The Seeds of a Rights Revolution

Seventeen-year-old Joelito Filártiga had committed no crime. But being the son of an outspoken doctor had consequences during the Alfredo Stroessner Matiauda regime of Paraguay. Dr. Joel Filártiga's criticisms and his work providing healthcare to impoverished Paraguayans made him and his family a target.

Police abducted the teenager in Paraguay's capital city, Asuncion on March 29, 1976.[1] The next morning at approximately four a.m., his 20-year-old sister, Dolly, was awakened by a knock on the door. "There was a small problem" with her brother, she was told, before being escorted a few doors down to the home of Americo Noberto Peña-Irala, inspector general of police in Asuncion. There, she discovered her brother's mutilated body in a pool of blood with marks of whips, knives, and electric shock to his penis. His cause of death—heart failure.[2]

"Here you have what you have been looking for, for so long and what you deserved. Now shut up," Peña-Irala said to Dolly.[3] "Take your brother's body, because we'll throw it away if you don't," she recalled to the *Washington Post*'s Carla Hall.[4]

"Tonight, you have power over me," she replied. "But tomorrow, I will tell the world."[5]

The Filártigas had faced ongoing harassment: Joel, the father, was jailed and tortured;[6] Dolly, as a child, was "taken from my father . . . He was in jail. People would say they are going to kill us," she recounted at an Antioch Law School talk. "The police come to your house. They take your father; they come [for] you."[7] After Joelito's death, Dolly, her mother, and their lawyer were arrested; the latter was shackled to a wall and later stripped of his law license, dashing hopes for justice in Paraguay.[8]

Peña-Irala traveled to New York with his common law wife, her niece, and their son. In an event of serendipity, a letter addressed to them mistakenly arrived at the Filártiga's home, revealing Peña-Irala's whereabouts.[9] Dolly and Joel followed.

With Amnesty International sponsorship, Dolly made good on her word, speaking to Americans about Paraguay's human rights crisis. While her father, Joel, returned to Paraguay, she remained in the US, cleaning houses to sustain herself while searching for the man who took her brother.[10]

A young scholar, Richard Alan White, helped Dolly locate Peña-Irala. An advocate, Richard Michael Maggio, reported him to the Immigration and Naturalization Service, which arrested him, and ordered him deported.[11] That meant legal action against Peña-Irala needed quick resolve—before his ejection. Swift action could only happen through established friendships, grounded in a common ethos. An international trademark attorney moonlighting as a human rights lawyer[12]—Peter Weiss—was the nexus that led the transformation of human rights redress, starting with the case for Dolly Filártiga.

International Human Rights Redress in US Courts

Weiss and a small team at the nonprofit Center for Constitutional Rights (CCR) were prepared to stay up all night to draft and file a groundbreaking human rights case. Shaped by the events of the Holocaust on one hand and great philosophical ideals on the other, Weiss, a refugee, had already dedicated his professional life to representing those whose lives, bodies, and spirits were crushed by human rights violators. "I lost a grandfather, and uncles and aunts and cousins in the Holocaust," explained Weiss. "That's the aspect that kept me in human rights."[13]

The convergence of those extremes—the horrors of the Holocaust and high ideals about law, morality, and justice from Aristotle, Plato, and Cicero—sent Weiss searching for legal tools to advance human rights. "Aristotle . . . said, some laws were used as laws of nature and should govern societies wherever societies exist . . . which is as good a definition of universal jurisdiction as you would want," explained Weiss. "The way Marcus Aurelius put it . . . I'm paraphrasing. He said, people everywhere have the same kind of reason, and that reason, if properly applied, produces certain norms which should govern any society. And that's what universal jurisdiction is."[14]

The idea of universal jurisdiction, that some crimes are so serious, heinous, and threatening to the international community that states are morally obligated to prosecute them, is "not all that new," Weiss asserted.[15] As part of international law, it is part of "the constitution of the world."[16]

While violations mounted in most quarters of the globe, "I just hung onto that approach," he said. That led him to recognize the potential of a 200-year-old, mostly dormant law, the Alien Tort Statute (ATS), to advance international human rights, helping victims harmed abroad, from in his own country, the US.[17]

The Laws of Nations

"I really don't know" who discovered the Alien Tort Statute, admitted Weiss. But he remembered the call from a friend at Amnesty International who introduced him to the Filártigas.[18] "I was sitting in what I call my straight office, which was basically international trademarks [law]," recalled Weiss. "And I said, 'What's up?'"[19]

On the line was Gerhard Elston, then director of Amnesty. "And he said, 'A Paraguayan torturer is about to be deported from the United States, and he has been identified by Paraguayan refugees [as] from the dictatorship in Paraguay, and we have his address,'" Weiss recalled. "He put me in touch with Dolly Filártiga."[20]

That was the necessary information for Weiss to try his theory of the ATS as a tool of universal jurisdiction. Its bare-bones, 33 words granted aliens access to US courts for civil wrongs that violated the law of nations: "The district courts shall have original jurisdiction of any civil action by an alien for a tort only, committed in violation of the law of nations or a treaty of the United States."

"We decided, 'well, yeah . . . There's an ATS case because this Paraguayan police official . . . the inspector of police in Asunción was . . . identified as a multiple torturer," explained Weiss. He quickly "called a staff meeting" at CCR.[21]

Founded by a group of scrappy civil rights lawyers, CCR had, for more than a decade, pushed the boundaries of legal doctrines to help forgotten and marginalized communities. Working with the civil rights movement to end segregation and to realize the promise of the Universal Declaration of Human Rights, CCR lawyers long tried seemingly impossible cases to stretch the law toward greater justice.[22]

But the Filártigas' case posed unusual complications: it was "foreign cubed"—meaning it featured a foreign plaintiff, foreign defendant, and foreign locations of the wrongs—which Weiss's CCR colleagues reminded him. "People kept saying, 'I don't understand what you're talking about. You've got a Paraguayan plaintiff and a Paraguayan defendant, and it's something that happened in Paraguay. Why do you want to waste your time?'" he recalled. "But fortunately, at that period of CCR's work, when people came in with a case that they wanted to bring, and that seemed correct from a legal point of view, but difficult to win, the Center would agree [to pursue it]. So we had three of us against a larger number, who, if it had been up to them, might not have brought it. [But] the three of us persuaded the others, who said, 'It sounds crazy but do it anyway.'"[23]

Within 24 hours, Weiss and three CCR colleagues—Rhonda Copelon, John Corwin, and Jose Antonio Lugo—completed the legal complaint and sent a process server to Peña-Irala at the Brooklyn Navy Yard, where he awaited deportation.[24] Their complaint accused Peña-Irala of wrongful death in violation of the laws of nations and US treaties. The tricky part, jurisdiction, they claimed, arose from combined legal texts from their own country and international agreements: the US Constitution, federal statutes, the United Nations Charter, the Universal Declaration of Human Rights, the UN Declaration on the Protection of All Persons from Being Subjected to Torture or Other Cruel, Inhuman or Degrading Treatment or Punishment, the American Declaration of the Rights and Duties of Man, and customary international law. To compensate the Filártigas, they requested $10 million plus interest, costs, and disbursements.[25]

While sympathetic, Judge Eugene Nickerson dismissed the lawsuit based on a narrow reading of the ATS and its jurisdiction. But he delayed Peña-Irala's deportation for 48 hours to permit the Filártigas time to appeal the decision. In another all-nighter, Weiss and his colleagues filed the appeal and asked to delay Peña-Irala's deportation for long enough to take his deposition.[26]

The next year, a panel of the Second Circuit Court of Appeals concluded that despite foreign plaintiffs, defendants, and site of the violation, the ATS granted the Filártigas—and others like them—access to US courts when the tort violated laws of nations. "There can be little doubt that this action is properly brought in federal court," wrote Irving Kaufman for the court. "The international community has come to recognize the common danger posed by the flagrant disregard of basic human rights and particularly the right to be free of torture. . . . From the ashes of the Second World War arose the United Nations Organization, amid hopes that an era of peace and cooperation had at last begun. . . . For purposes of civil liability, the torturer has become like the pirate and slave trader before him . . . an enemy of all mankind. Our holding today, giving effect to a jurisdictional provision enacted by our First Congress, is a small but important step in the fulfillment of the ageless dream to free all people from brutal violence."[27]

Remanded to the district court, the Filártigas won a $10.4 million judgment, money they could not collect, as Peña-Irala was deported to Paraguay.[28] But the Filártigas' emotional win also offered profound implications for international human rights. Over the next several decades, *Filártiga v. Peña-Irala*'s victory reverberated, signaling hope for potential redress for similar sufferers who had fallen below the law and for advocates seeking to construct legal protections for them.

Filártiga's Effects

Paraguay was one of many countries ruled by dictators or overrun by terror groups. Over the next decades, victims of human rights violations or their surviving families from Chile, Argentina, El Salvador, Guatemala, Peru, Honduras, and Colombia would find and sue their abusers in US courts. They would share the path with victims from Ethiopia, Liberia, Haiti, the Philippines, Bosnia, and Somalia. Their cases inspired new laws, lawyers, and nonprofit organizations, both in the US and abroad, expanding the strategy for otherwise forgotten survivors. But in the immediate aftermath of *Filártiga*, the meaning of the largely untested ATS remained unclear.

A few lawyers began testing the statute for adjudicating common torts, such as libel, breach of contract, and fraud. For the most part, the courts dismissed those for not violating the "law of nations," falling short of the statute's requirement. Courts also rejected a 1981 human rights lawsuit against the Libyan Arab Republic, three Palestinian organizations, and the National Association of Arab Americans for the "coastal road massacre" in Israel, which killed 37 people and wounded 76.[29] Because the three-panel DC Circuit Court of Appeals couldn't agree on reasoning, the ruling failed to establish precedent, leaving an opening for *Filártiga*'s progeny. "We dodged a bullet with the split decision," admitted human rights lawyer Beth Stephens.[30]

The promise of *Filártiga* and confusion arising from a smattering of dismissals inspired two members of Congress to strengthen the body of law. Led by a Greek American congressman from Pennsylvania, Gus Yatron, the Human Rights Subcommittee of the House Foreign Affairs

Committee began holding hearings to understand "where torture is being practiced, who is practicing it, and what can be done to stop it."[31]

Yatron had already pressed to condition foreign aid on human rights reforms for countries that were using torture, abductions, and slayings, including Turkey, El Salvador, and Nicaragua.[32] He had criticized the Reagan administration's covert operations in Latin America and sought to redirect land reform toward supporting peasants.[33] And he called on the administration to cancel a trip to the Philippines due to widespread political repression and human rights violations.[34] "The significance of much that we do in human rights is difficult to measure, but you keep doing it because it is important, because it may save lives," he said during a reelection bid.[35]

At a May 15, 1984 hearing, "The Phenomenon of Torture," Yatron, the 56-year-old Chair of the Subcommittee on Human Rights and International Organizations, declared his goal—to abolish torture—before taking testimony from torture survivors and human rights organizations.[36] Leading the testimony, Amnesty International's deputy director, Larry Cox, described the state of the world—98 countries still used torture to control and suppress dissent, to intimidate and gather information—and offered examples: a young Argentine woman endured beatings, burns, and shocks to her most sensitive organs; Syrian officials forced heated metal skewers into their victims' anuses. Chileans doctors used medical knowledge to keep their victims conscious, so as to inflict the greatest degree of pain; mutilated bodies were publicly displayed as warnings to others. "Torturers go on torturing," Cox concluded, because they are successful.[37]

Helsinki Watch executive director Jeri Labor detailed torture in Turkey. For legally representing 4,000 fellow Kurds "being tried for political crimes," Kurdish lawyer Huseyin Yildirim was arrested and detained in Turkey's Diyarbakir Prison, "possibly the most horrifying hell-hole in the world," Labor said. In Yildirim's 40 days of torture, he recalled being "thrust repeatedly, naked, into flames . . . suspended from one or two legs from the ceiling . . . [a] cord [attached] to my penis and pulled the cord by means of a pulley attached to the ceiling." His "fingers, teeth and jaw broken by blows with a metal bar and my broken teeth afterwards brutally extracted." He was "dragged across a large room knee-deep in sewage" while being "beaten . . . [by] 50 officers with sticks." His own pain was met with witnessing others' torture, including ten murders, two who were burned alive. "I am only a lawyer," he concluded.[38]

Turning to Yatron's key question—"What can be done to stop it?"—Amnesty presented a 12-point program against torture, providing the basis for the future Torture Victim Protection Act (TVPA): working on the side of the survivors, it sought to facilitate healing, prevent torturers from entering the country, and grant survivors a private right of action to sue their abusers in US courts. The measures would affirm, clarify, and expand the *Filártiga* ruling, giving judges jurisdictional certainty, if doubt arose.[39]

The US Senate's June 26, 1984 companion hearing—"Practice of Torture by Foreign Governments and US Efforts to Oppose its Use"—similarly reflected the "worldwide problem" of torture. Torture is "not limited to a few countries," acknowledged Foreign Relations Committee chair Charles Percy.[40] Mirroring Yatron, Percy asked why torture "occurs with such alarming frequency" and how they might "curb this terrible human rights abuse."[41]

Amnesty International, the Lawyers Committee for Human Rights, and Helsinki Watch argued for universal jurisdiction over the crime of torture, asylum for victims, and outlawing the conditions that enable torture and secrecy. That year, Congress adopted a joint resolution, signed by President Reagan, to develop a global effort to disrupt torture and for US ambassadors to investigate reports of torture.[42] The following December, the UN General Assembly adopted the 1984 Convention against Torture and Other Cruel, Inhuman or Degrading Treatment or Punishment, which called upon states to prevent torture within their own territories and forbade transportation of people to countries where they might be tortured.[43]

In the 99th Congress, Yatron and colleagues introduced the first iteration of the Torture Victim Protection Act, HR 4756 into the House and S2528, authored by Senator Arlen Spector, in the Senate.[44] Both bills failed.

While Yatron was working to expand access to US civil courts, another notorious human rights abuser landed on the shores of the USA. In February 1986, after his 20-year authoritarian rule, former Philippines president Ferdinand Marcos fled to Hawaii.[45] Within a month of his arrival, survivors of his reign filed lawsuits against him, including a class action, a case against his daughter, and, eventually, his estate, in US courts—for torture, summary execution, and disappearance of loved ones.[46]

Terror and Trauma in the Philippines

Marcos came to power in 1965. His second term, won four years later, would have been his last, had he abided by the Philippines' constitution. But in 1972, Marcos declared martial law across the country. A year later, he ordered ratification of a new constitution, quadrupled the size of the military, placed its members in the key institutions under his control—corporations, media entities, and government.[47] His sweeping arrests and mass incarceration of political opponents[48] landed 70,000 students, leftists, farmers, and journalists—suspected opponents or sympathizers of separatism or communism—in detention. Thirty-five thousand people suffered torture and 3,257 lost their lives, according to historian Alfred McCoy.[49] Officers "broke" community leaders—priests and professors—using physical and psychological torture.[50] They interrogated victims while shocking their genitals, simulating drowning, suffocating, and forcing victims' heads in excrement-filled toilets.[51]

Mariano Pimentel, Jose Maria Sison, Agapita Trajano, Fluellen Ortigas, Ramon Veluz, Jaime Piopongco, and Celsa Hilao were among thousands who suffered and eventually sued Marcos and his family in US courts. Soldiers broke Pimentel's arms and legs "then buried him alive in a sugarcane field," his lawyer told the investigative publication *Civil Beat.* Local children found and dug him out of the ground, he reported.[52] Military members blindfolded, handcuffed, and repeatedly battered Sison, forced water into his nose, and locked him in solitary confinement where for approximately eight years, he was regularly shackled to his cot in a small hot room with no natural light.[53] His brother, a member of Marcos's economic staff, disappeared in 1971.

Two surviving mothers, Trajano and Hilao, sued Marcos for their children's deaths: Trajano's 21-year-old son, Archimedes, was arrested at a university forum where he challenged Imee Marcos-Manotoc, the president's daughter, about her leadership appointment. Guards seized, blindfolded, and tortured him to death, according to court records.[54] He died after more than twelve hours of torture, according to his mother's complaint filed against Marcos and his daughter, Marcos-Manotoc.[55] Hilao's daughter, Liliosa, a student leader and journalist at her university paper, was also arrested and detained. Witnesses found her frothing at the mouth, her battered body sprawled on a prison camp floor. She died after hospitalization.[56]

In early 1986, political winds began to change in the Philippines, raising hope for justice. Mass protests, burgeoning Philippine NGOs, and the Catholic church forced Marcos's ouster, giving rise to new leadership. Corazon Aquino, the widow of assassinated Senator Benigno Aquino Jr., ascended to the presidency on February 25, 1986. She led reforms for civil and human rights, peacemaking efforts with insurgencies and separatists, and established human rights investigations. But repeated coup attempts on her presidency hampered substantive justice for the abused. Hope fell once more.[57]

News coverage of Marcos's reign reached across the Pacific into the USA, where it sparked the interest of litigators. In a "jump of faith," Pennsylvania-based lawyer Robert Swift boarded a plane to Manila "to seek clients" among the "thousands of people who had been subject to abuse," he told David Giles of an American Bar Association publication, *Litigator*.[58]

Swift approached SELDA, an organization of survivors[59] formed a year before Marcos' ouster, explained the ATS, and offered to shoulder litigation costs, to be reimbursed should they win.[60] Without proper redress in their own country, litigation would at least establish a historical record of the atrocities, a win in itself for some of SELDA's members.[61] The Ford Foundation funded SELDA's historic documentation project.[62]

Within a month of Marcos's February 1986 arrival in Hawaii, Swift and two additional legal teams—Sherry Broder and Jon Van Dyke of Hawaii, and Melvin Belli and John Hill of California—sued the former dictator in the federal district courts of Pennsylvania, Hawaii, and California, collectively representing thousands of survivors. Swift's class action, the first of its kind, represented approximately 9,000[63] victims and family members; the other two legal teams represented individuals and smaller groups.

Fearing that Sison's far-left politics and "lighting rod" status could harm SELDA's class action, Sison and Piopongco filed a separate lawsuit.[64] Through human rights advocate Ellen Lutz, they met civil rights lawyer Paul Hoffman, then legal director for the Southern California ACLU. Representing Sison, his mother, brother, and Piopongco,[65] Hoffman sued Marcos and Philippine General Fabian Ver in Hawaii.[66] It was one of his early efforts to integrate international human rights into the agenda of American nonprofits, such as the ACLU, which had traditionally focused on defending domestic liberties.

International Human Rights and the ACLU

A sense of duty, formed in childhood, guided Hoffman's efforts to develop human rights law in the US. His relatives, "whose entire family had been wiped out in the Holocaust," would "talk about it every time we'd go over there," he recalled. "The pain was a shared family pain, and so I was taught that one of the things you're meant to do in life is make up for that, carry that, speak for them."[67]

While studying at the London School of Economics, Hoffman's teacher described his experiences living in Uganda under dictator Idi Amin. "He was a Ugandan Asian who was on the death list for Amin," Hoffman recalled. "And so I spent the year with him cataloguing all the people [who] were being killed."[68]

As a young lawyer, Hoffman knew then "that's what I wanted to do . . . [so] I went around the country looking for places." He found work at a Los Angeles private law firm "that let me do a lot of ACLU cases pro bono. . . . I probably did 20 cases in five years."[69]

The litigator, law teacher, and organizer collaborated, brainstormed, and began developing legal dimensions for the human rights movement with other early international human rights advocates. "In 1978, which is when Paul Hoffman and I started working together, there was no such thing as international human rights [litigation]," recalled Washington, DC-based human rights lawyer Morton Sklar. "There wasn't any way to get international human rights into the US . . . and Paul and I, and Paul Martin at Columbia [University] joined together to put on training programs to get lawyers and judges here in the US to understand what these human rights things were all about and why they should be used here [in the US]."[70]

In 1982, while litigating and teaching law in Los Angeles, Hoffman founded the Legal Support Network for Amnesty International USA and, as its first national coordinator, matched volunteer lawyers to victims of rights violations who needed counsel. Over the next two years, he joined Amnesty's board and became legal director of the Southern California ACLU.[71] Through the organizations, he would attempt to wed disparate bodies of law, in part by building an international human rights program at the ACLU. "[It] was a bit of a struggle," he admitted. "National tried to clamp down on me. But we never paid attention to national anyway."[72]

The attempted restriction on Hoffman's efforts was probably tied to the organization's historical roots. Since its 1920 founding, the ACLU had worked to protect rights and liberties within US borders. It defended free speech after World War I and during the McCarthy anti-Communism era, and fought against the World War II internment of Japanese Americans. But the organization's decentralized structure left room for local chapters to veer from one another.[73] Ramona Ripston, then the director of the Southern California ACLU, supported Hoffman's desire to build an international human rights division. "Ramona let me do anything that national wouldn't clamp down on me," Hoffman recalled.[74]

The Marcos lawsuit was among the early international human rights cases for the civil liberties group. And at the time, the odds looked unfavorable for the survivors. No survivor had successfully sued a head of state; the

ATS's resuscitation had barely been tested; the TVPA had not yet passed the Congress; and the Supreme Court's "act of state" doctrine argued against judging other governments for acts committed within their own borders.[75]

With that legal terrain, perhaps it was no surprise that the district courts dismissed the Marcos lawsuits—except Trajano's case against Marcos-Manatoc, Marcos's daughter. Her status fell outside the "act of state" doctrine's boundaries, and she failed to appear in court. On May 29, 1986, the court entered a default judgment in Mrs. Trajano's favor: "Trajano was tortured, and his death was caused by Marcos-Manotoc, a fundamental human rights violation and a tort in violation of the law of nations under 28 USC section 1350." It awarded Mrs. Trajano $4.16 million plus attorney's fees.[76] For the remaining cases, Filipino survivors appealed to the Ninth Circuit Court of Appeals.[77]

Meanwhile, another group of survivors—from Argentina's Dirty War—made a discovery: in the junta's aftermath, the commanding general, Carlos Guillermo Suarez Mason, responsible for their woes had fled Argentina to California, in the same country where Argentine survivors had found refuge. Using the ATS, Alfredo Forti, Debora Benchoam, and their fellow Argentines found and sued Suarez Mason in a California federal court for charges including torture, murder, and prolonged arbitrary detention.[78]

The Dirty War Comes to California

In 1975, Argentina's government declared a "state of siege" and authorized its military to suppress "terrorism" in the country. The following year, military commanders toppled the government, and ruled the country as a dictatorship. By the Dirty War's end, the junta had tortured and killed between 12,000 and 30,000 people—among them, students, trade unionists, journalists, artists, and others suspected of opposing the dictatorship's plans. Many "disappeared," never to be seen again.[79]

Suarez Mason commanded "Zone One," encompassing the national capital and Buenos Aires province. His Secret Operational Order 9/77 directed raids, abductions, and secret detention centers where approximately 5,000 people were interrogated, tortured, or disappeared, according to press reports.[80]

At the time of their ordeals, Forti and Benchoam were 16 years old. On February 18, 1977, Forti, his four younger brothers, and their mother boarded an airplane in Buenos Aires bound for Venezuela where his father was working as a surgeon. Members of the Air Force boarded the plane, seized the family, and delivered them to the "Pozo de Quilmes" detention center near Buenos Aires. Six days later, security forces blindfolded, tied, and released the five brothers on a street in the capital region. But their mother, Nelida Azucena Sosa de Forti, disappeared, according to press reports and court records.[81]

At 3 a.m. on July 25, 1977, masked, plainclothed security men burst into Benchoam's home where she and her family were sleeping. They abducted, cuffed, blindfolded, and incarcerated her and shot her 17-year-old brother, Rubin.[82] For four years, Benchoam remained in prison without charge, surviving sexual assault and brutal conditions. When her brother's remains were returned, his face was deformed, his cause of death, internal bleeding from bullet wounds, a death that soldiers called a "mistake" of the Dirty War. Benchoam believed his activism in high school had made him a target.[83]

Upon Argentina's return to democracy, its president, Raúl Alfonsin, ordered the arrest and prosecution of nine military officers involved in the juntas between 1976 and 1983. Five commanders and two former presidents were convicted and sentenced. But Suarez Mason fled to California where, for three years, while arrest orders pended in his home country, he lived as a fugitive. In January 1987, on a tip, the US Marshals Service international operations arrested Suarez Mason at his Foster City, California apartment where he was entertaining guests.[84]

Represented by CCR and private lawyers,[85] Forti and Benchoam filed one of three lawsuits against Suarez Mason for his role in their abductions, torture, arbitrary detention, false imprisonment, assault, intentional infliction of emotional distress, and cruel, inhuman, or degrading treatment. Forti complained about his mother's forced disappearance, Benchoam about her brother's death by summary execution. Together, they requested $40 million in damages.[86]

Five additional survivors of the Dirty War followed. Horatio Martinez-Baca, a lawyer who had served as secretary of state for Mendoza Province in Argentina, was imprisoned for four years, suffered torture, including battery from his head to the soles of his feet until he fell unconscious. "They put a wire around my penis and a nail into my gums," he told Paul Ciotti of the *Los Angeles Times*. Attached to a 12-volt battery and rheostat, wires sent electrical shocks to his mouth and genitals while interrogators demanded information.[87]

"All your life you burn your eyebrows in a university studying constitutional principles, the Code of Hammurabi, the Magna Carta, Norman barons, Alexis de Tocqueville, the Bill of Rights and then you are thrown in jail without the minimum rights of your life, deprived of everything, without knowing what this is all about, just because you [object] consciously and honestly and in good faith to the military takeover. You are not a communist or a Marxist. You are a nice, stupid [person] who believes in democracy," he told Ciotti.[88]

At the urging of US Senator Edward Kennedy and the US State Department, Martinez-Baca won his freedom. Air Force officers seized him from the motorcade vehicle and escorted him to the plane, where the Pan American pilot demanded his release: "This is American Property. Dr. Martinez-Baca is a free person here," the survivor recounted to the *Los Angeles Times*. Then 40 years old, Martinez-Baca moved to Oakland, California to find he was across the Bay from the fugitive home of Suarez Mason, known to prisoners as "the lord of death and life."[89]

When Martinez-Baca learned of Suarez Mason's arrest, he returned to the law books to understand his legal remedies. A team of lawyers—CCR's Weiss, David Cole, Michael Ratner, and eight private lawyers—agreed to take Martinez-Baca's case.[90]

In court, Martinez-Baca confronted his abuser, detailing the horrors he had endured, before Rabbi Marshall Meyer described findings in his official investigative capacity. Representing himself, Suarez Mason refused to answer questions posed by Martinez-Baca's lawyers and rose to argue with a witness but was silenced by Judge Samuel Conti.[91]

Suarez Mason's was "an enterprise of terror," decided Judge Conti, who ruled that the general must pay $21 million in damages to Martinez-Baca.[92] The judgment, argued Martinez-Baca's lawyers, was another stitch in the legal fabric begun by *Filártiga*. It sent a message to human rights violators: should they enter the US, they could be held accountable for their crimes.[93] The large verdict could serve as "an enforcement mechanism for violations of international human rights."[94]

Two widows and a surviving mother and sister—Susana Quiros de Rapaport, Maria Teresa Pinero de Georgiadis, Maria Elena Perez de Antonanzas, and Norma Antonanzas de Barrosa—filed a third lawsuit. Their husbands, son, and brother died in Suarez Mason's custody, ostensibly for carrying literature challenging the junta's legitimacy.[95] While their cases advanced, Congress reintroduced the TVPA.

The Congressional Record

On March 4, 1987, Yatron and more than 100 cosponsors reintroduced the TVPA as HR 1417 into the 100th session of the House. Later that month, a fellow Pennsylvanian, Senator Arlen Specter (R), followed, introducing a companion TVPA (S 824) in the Senate.[96] The bills would "establish clearly a federal right of action by aliens and United States Citizens against persons engaging in torture or extrajudicial killing, and for other purposes," affirming the ATS, the *Filártiga* decision, and expanding jurisdiction to US citizens. Explicitly authorizing US courts to adjudicate human rights cases, violators acting "under the color of law of any foreign nation" faced civil liability; their victims would have civil remedies when none were available in the countries where the violations occurred.[97]

The TVPA is "a practical way to allow . . . a few important lawsuits, every year and to make it clear to torturers throughout the world that the United States is not a place to come, and for those who come, that there may be a judgment entered against them in suits brought by their victims," explained Michael Posner, founding director of the Lawyers Committee for Human Rights, at the hearing. Perhaps if "other countries will do the same . . . by the end of this century or early in the 21st Century, we will be at a point where, throughout the world, people who commit torture and other gross human rights violations will know that there is no place to go," he said, and "there is a remedy for their victims regardless of where they turn."[98]

A "small measure" toward fixing an enormous problem, the TVPA would also fulfill part of the Torture Convention's requirements—providing a means of civil redress for torture victims without alternatives, according to witnesses at the March 23, 1988 committee hearing. With an explicit grant from Congress, it would simultaneously abate confusion in the courts, which had ostensibly led to dismissal of the human rights case *Tel Oren v. Libyan Arab Republic*.[99] "The Protection Act would preclude resort to the judge-made 'act of state' doctrine, pursuant to which US courts have declined under some circumstances to examine the legality of some official public acts of foreign sovereigns within their own territories," wrote the Human Rights Committee of the City of New York's Bar."[100] Its tailored language ensured the most deserving and appropriate cases would be adjudicated, said supporters.

The following month (April 18, 1988), the US government under Ronald Reagan signed the Convention against Torture, and Other Cruel, Inhuman or Degrading Treatment or Punishment, which came into force the following year (June 26, 1989). Declaring equal and inalienable rights as the "foundation of freedom, justice and peace," the Convention required states to take "effective" measures to prevent torture, and with no exceptions or justifications, to take torturers into custody, cooperate in criminal proceedings, and ensure torture victims obtain redress, including compensation and rehabilitation.[101]

Some members of Congress argued to maintain sanctuary for "human rights abusers" under some circumstances, using Marcos as an example: "We must not lose the opportunity of allowing people to come here if doing so will be in the interest of our country and theirs. I am thinking of someone like President Marcos, who might accept sanctuary as a condition of relinquishing power," argued Congressman Gerald Solomon.[102]

The House overwhelmingly passed Yatron's TVPA legislation. But both his and Specter's TVPA bills died in the Senate. A persistent Yatron reintroduced the bill, now numbered HR 1662.

Eight days later, on the other side of the country, a San Francisco court ruled in favor of the surviving Argentine women whose families had died in Suarez Mason's custody. With no defense made for Suarez Mason's "torture-killings," on April 11, 1989, Judge John Vukasin ordered the former general to pay the deceased's family members $60 million, the largest international human rights award to date.[103] Additional judgments expanded the general's aggregate debt to his victims to approximately $89 million.[104]

Meanwhile, in Washington, the House again passed the TVPA (HR 1662), with 362 ayes and four noes, and Senator Specter again pressed for passage in the Senate. "It is time the Senate acted on it," he insisted at the Senate's Judiciary Committee Subcommittee on Immigration and Refugee Affairs.[105]

While maintaining that "we are wholly opposed to torture," the George H. W. Bush administration pushed back, arguing that the TVPA could interfere with "complex and multifarious foreign policy" and create "frictions and tensions" with other countries, which "would haul our officials into court" on "specious charges," according to Assistant Attorney General John O. McGinnis. It might empower aliens to file "inappropriate" lawsuits for acts with "no connection to the United States" and "determine the timing and manner" for claims against "foreign countries and their officers."[106] These matters should remain with "persons who are responsible for the conduct of foreign policy," the presidency, not the courts, nor the Congress, he said, adding that the ATS is "extremely ancient."[107]

"Older than the Bill of Rights?," retorted Specter, then added, "Age is not necessarily a disabler."[108]

The State Department followed, expressing fear about "political opponents" bringing "nuisance or harassment suits . . . for publicity purposes," or leaving US personnel "to defend against expensive and drawn out proceedings." The Department's David P. Stewart, assistant legal advisor, argued that victims should pursue justice in the countries where the abuses occurred.[109]

"Go back to Iran and sue?" countered Senator Paul Simon. "Go back to the tender mercies of Colonel Qadhafi and sue in Libya?"[110]

Opposition to the bill was still too fierce. Citing "overburdened federal courts" and lawsuits that "have absolutely no connection—neither parties nor subject matter—to the United States," opponents again defeated the TVPA. But with narrowed parameters, the next iteration finally passed both houses of Congress. In its final form, the TVPA explicitly authorized US courts to adjudicate cases of torture or extrajudicial killing occurring under "authority or . . . color of law." But it required survivors to first exhaust remedies where the wrongs occurred, placed the burden of proof on the plaintiffs, and added a ten-year statute of limitations. On March 12, 1992, President Bush signed the bill into law.[111]

Six months later, after winning on appeal, the plaintiff survivors of the Marcos regime went to trial, where those who could attend detailed their traumas, and witnesses or advocates testified for victims who could not.[112] Absent was the dictator, Marcos, who had died in 1989. The court's consolidation of the cases, however, created conflict between the private and NGO advocates. Swift switched "his plaintiffs, because the original plaintiffs [from SELDA] were political," recalled Hoffman. "He wanted to separate his people from our people," particularly Sison, a high-profile Communist leader. Perhaps he "thought that [the separation] was going to help [his case]."[113]

Though representing different clients, Judge Manuel Real restricted trial participation to only one lawyer at a time, which resulted in "big fights," particularly during cross examination when Hoffman believed his client Sison was "redbaited" and left without adequate defense. "When it was Swift's responsibility . . . Swift would stop objecting when he [defense counsel] was redbaiting. And we got into a big argument about that."[114]

In September 1992, the jury found Marcos, his associates, and family members liable for human rights abuses.[115] The nearly $2 million judgment grew with a $100,000 daily sanction between 1995 and 2005,[116] reaching $353 million.[117] The landmark case—the first ATS litigation against a former head of state, the first international class action human rights lawsuit to include disappearance as an ATS human rights violation—settled for $150 million.

Because the Marcos family had hidden and scattered their assets under aliases and shell company names in tax haven countries, such as Panama, Liechtenstein, and Switzerland, the judgment took years to collect.[118] Opposition from the US and Switzerland on collection efforts made compensation more difficult, according to Swift.[119] In 2011, years after they initially filed, victims began receiving compensation.[120] Ultimately, "everybody won. . . . Nobody was left out," said Hoffman[121]

With wins in court and Congress, momentum appeared to be on the side of the survivors, portending the potential of a human rights revolution through civil action. By offering its legal system as a path to justice and its shores as a refuge, the US was poised to lead another iteration of its rights revolution.

For the next three years, human rights violators from Haiti, Ethiopia, Bosnia, and Guatemala found themselves sued by the people whom they had tortured—using the ATS, the TVPA, or a combination of both with lawyers from CCR—with Beth Stephens, Michael Ratner, Jennifer Green, and David Cole taking lead roles. Many abusers left the US, either voluntarily or by force. The cases inspired new organizations, including the Center for Justice and Accountability and EarthRights International, which then spawned international NGOs with similar goals—using litigation to help victims heal, bring abusers to justice, and prevent future human rights violations.

THREE

Litigation as Recovery

The Birth of the Center for Justice and Accountability

The upheavals in Latin America and the Philippines and congressional hearings on torture in Washington, DC corresponded with an awakening in San Francisco. Therapist Gerald Gray stumbled across shocking information: psychologists—fellow mental health practitioners with professional duties to heal and support—had designed torture programs in Latin America. "I discovered by accident, reading an article about torture in Latin America," he recalled. It was "a public health article [that] talked about a plague, which was new in Latin America. It's a metaphor. It's not a physical plague. It [is] about the spread of torture. And in the course of talking about it, the editor or the writer indicated that people from psychology were seriously involved in developing torture because they knew about vulnerabilities, which were psychological, which the military really hadn't studied."[1]

The realization "absolutely froze me because I realized that I had enemies in my profession, who were putting people into my waiting room. And I was trained to get them out," Gray explained.[2]

The shock was of a magnitude that Gray could recall, more than thirty years later, vivid details of the moment. "I can tell you the time of day, the place where I was when I was reading it—afternoon on a sunny day, breeze moving the curtain in my living room," he said.[3]

The discovery prompted two investigations—one into the scope of the problem, another into available treatments for torture victims. Gray's calls to human rights and therapy organizations led him to two torture treatment centers, one in the US, another in Denmark, ostensibly insufficient for the scale of need. "I thought, well, if psychologists are involved in torture, we'll work on the other side of it; we will work with the people who have been tortured. And I decided to establish Survivors International in San Francisco . . . a torture treatment program," he recalled. "We saw our first cases in 1990. That year we saw twelve people. The next year, 35 people. The year after that, 70 people. . . . Now, years on, they've seen thousands of people."[4]

In 1995, the San Francisco General Hospital phoned Gray with a referral. A Bosnian torture victim had asked for therapy, an unusual request from a refugee. "I knew something was up, because nobody asks for therapy that quickly. People will come to us because they have to be seen for an evaluation for political asylum," Gray explained. "They usually ask for social work first. They want medical care. They want a roof over their heads. They want an income. And maybe they'll trust you enough then to come to take therapy."[5]

San Francisco was far enough from Bosnia to serve as a fine refuge if not for the presence of the man's torturer. "He'd been shown photographs of house parties in his community in San Francisco," recalled Gray. One photo showed a clear shot of his former neighbor, who had tortured him in his home country.[6]

Counseling, in this scenario, seemed futile. "If victims [are] running into their torturers in a situation where they either [have] to flee or fight," they are not "getting sanctuary in this country. And if these torturers were hiding in these communities, and the communities knew about it, then our treatment would be incomplete, because people would still be afraid," explained Gray.[7]

It also made deadly scenarios possible. "I feared that my patient would hunt down his torturer and kill him,"[8] recalled Gray. "All his symptoms were acute: rage, fear, paranoia, sleep disturbance, increased startle response, and so on."[9]

Fellow therapists suggested that these types of encounters were relatively common. "About half of the centers had had this experience. None of them had reported it, and none of them was trying to do anything about it," he said.[10]

Gray's discoveries coincided with a Bay Area talk by human rights lawyer Paul Hoffman about three Ethiopian women, refugees who had fled their country after torture and terror. In their new home, Atlanta, Georgia, one survivor encountered—by coincidence—the man who had tortured her in Ethiopia. Working with Hoffman, then legal director of the Southern California ACLU, and CCR's Beth Stephens, the women had sued their torturer in Atlanta for wrongs committed in Ethiopia. Hoffman's talk and their legal victory gave Gray the idea to establish an organization dedicated to legal redress for survivors and accountability for their torturers.[11]

Red Terror in Atlanta

A clerk in Ethiopia's Ministry of Forestry and Wildlife, 18-year-old[12] EdgeGayehu Taye was uninvolved in the political turmoil of Ethiopia's "Red Terror." But she could not convince the Addis Ababa official Kelbessa Negewo. In February 1978, revolutionary guards came for Taye. They stripped, hung, and beat her for hours, lashed her with plastic cables, poured water onto her wounds, and imprisoned her for three years.[13] Once released, Taye paid Somali nomads to smuggle her out of Ethiopia.[14]

The previous month, guards arrested and detained 17-year-old Hirute Abebe-Jira and her 16-year-old sister.[15] Negewo and the other guards stripped, bound, gagged, and hung Abebe-Jira upside down, whipped, then beat her to the souls of her feet, she said in court pleadings. They stuffed a blood and vomit-soaked stocking into her mouth and threatened her life, should she not reveal information that she did not have.[16]

Two months later, it was Elizabeth Demissie, a 17-year old student, and her family for whom they came. Six months after a first arrest and release, armed men rearrested, detained, and tortured Demissie, her sister, and father. Returning Demissie to her cell, they took her 15-year-old sister Haimanot, who died in custody. Their father was later found dead in an alley.[17]

Fleeing Ethiopia, the three women settled in Atlanta, Georgia, Ontario, Canada, and Los Angeles, California, respectively. Thousands of Ethiopians did the same, roughly 5,000 of whom made their home in Atlanta, the city where Taye found work waitressing at the Sheraton Colony Square hotel.[18] There she spotted Negewo, a few feet away, working at the same hotel.[19] He too had moved to Atlanta and had found work as a bellman.[20]

Taye called Abebe Jira and Demissie, who flew to Atlanta to see for themselves and concurred with Taye: he was their torturer.[21] Through a friend in the Atlanta mayor's office, Taye called the CCR, where Stephens had been working on international human rights cases.[22]

Stephens had joined CCR via Nicaragua where she lived after law school. CCR "had done a lawsuit on behalf of the family of a US citi-

zen killed in Nicaragua, and I did the investigation on the ground," she
recalled. "One part of my assignment was to do more Alien Tort Statute
cases. At that time, in 1990, there had really only been three."[23]

Stephens and Hoffman found local counsel in Georgia and sued
Negewo in the Federal District Court for the Northern District of Georgia.[24] In court, Negewo, representing himself, claimed the action was part
of a movement by the Ethiopian People's Revolutionary Party to "get me
here," according to a report by *New York Times* journalist Ronald Smothers, who attended the trial.[25] G. Ernest Tidwell of the Northern Federal
District Court in Atlanta, Georgia was not swayed. On August 20, 1993,
he ordered Negewo to pay $500,000 in reparations to each of his three
victims.[26] Negewo appealed. Three years later, the Eleventh Circuit Court
of Appeals affirmed the decision. The judgment "felt good" for Abebe Jira.
"I am standing up and facing him. I don't have to be afraid of him," she
told the *New York Times*. "Maybe finally he will have to pay for making so
many lives miserable."[27]

What little of the judgment the women could collect, they donated
to the ACLU,[28] affirming Gray's assertion: "Usually people don't go after
money, although money is part of what's on the counter. They want other
things, getting justice. They got rid of him. He fled. He hid, so they didn't
have to see him every day. He hadn't gone entirely unpunished. They faced
him. That made them feel less afraid of him."[29]

The confluence of events—the article about psychologist-designed torture, the Bosnian torture survivor who had encountered his abuser, and
Hoffman's talk about the Ethiopian women's victory—formed the foun-
dational idea of a dedicated nonprofit organization to represent victims of
international human rights violations in US courts. In the best scenarios,
the new NGO would simultaneously support survivors' recovery and fight
impunity—"track torturers and bring them to justice under this [US] law,"
said Gray.[30]

The formal legal process, the courtroom, and official acknowledg-
ments of the wrongs perpetrated on them might help victims reclaim lost
agency, a principal injury during trauma, Gray thought. A form of "civilized revenge," litigation might also avert a cycle of violence between foes
reencountering one another. But most victims have had no access to the
legal system. The NGO might fix that.

Gray called Hoffman, then chair of Amnesty International USA, about
his idea. Well placed to persuade the established human rights organization to support a fledgling nonprofit, Hoffman agreed to request seed
funds from Amnesty to launch the organization under two conditions: he

needed three survivors ready to take action against their violators, and the new organization must find other funding after Amnesty's seed grant.[31] "So I set about trying to find three cases," Gray recalled. Through his relationships with fellow health care professionals, two Latin American plaintiffs came forward, Zita Cabello-Barrueto from Chile and Juan Romagoza from El Salvador; the third, a Bosnian refugee, from a random phone call.

Zita Cabello-Barrueto: Winston Cabello, an economist in Chile, was among more than a thousand Chileans who had disappeared during the Pinochet regime. No one knew his fate—until 1990, when bodies began being exhumed. Only then did his family learn that Cabello had fallen victim to the notorious "Caravan of Death," which had tortured, killed, and dumped approximately 75 people for "disloyalty to the dictatorship." Cabello's body bore marks of "a gash, a wound from his ear down through his throat . . . [and] gunshot wounds from the feet all up through the body," according to court records.[32]

Gray met Cabello's sister, Zita Cabello-Barrueto, through a Chilean doctor "who had worked in torture treatment in Los Angeles" and who "himself had been tortured," Gray recalled. "He was [former Chilean president Salvador] Allende's personal physician. He knew me and he was willing to talk to the community" about civil actions in US courts.[33]

Families of the disappeared, like Cabello's, tend to experience amplified trauma. Swings of heightened anxiety vacillate with peaks of hope that their loved one will return, then turn to hopelessness when other disappeared persons are found to be dead.[34] Survivors' guilt, feelings of impotence and self-reproach, particularly for parents who could not protect their children, compound trauma, giving way to their higher mortality rates.[35] Cabello's father "stopped talking, never played the guitar again," said Cabello-Barrueto to the *San Francisco Chronicle*. His "spirit died with my brother."[36] (He died before their civil action concluded).

Cabello-Barrueto's own grief and trauma left her wanting "to never wake up again. If I woke up, then it would be real," she explained to Anne O'Neill of the *South Florida Sun-Sentinel*. "It felt like I lost half of myself when Winston died. I lost the trust I had in people. From that moment on . . . I stopped believing in the good in people."[37]

For Cabello's family, Chile's amnesty laws made matters worse. Protecting junta members from prosecution left victims without legal recourse or a means of processing grievances in their home country—a formula that leaves human rights victims with lasting symptoms—devastation, depression, rage, despair, and deep mistrust, the latter a frequent torturers' goal, according to Gray.[38]

In the US capital, however, another crime opened the channel for Cabello-Barrueto's redress. "Caravan of Death" member Armando Fernández-Larios had struck a plea bargain with US law enforcement for his role in the assassination of former Chilean ambassador Francisco Letelier and his assistant, Ronni Moffitt. For his cooperation and guilty plea, Fernandez-Larios received a reduced sentence and continued entrée to the US.[39] He settled in Miami, Florida, bought a condominium, and operated two businesses, according to the *Miami New Times*.[40]

Cabello-Barrueto had heard the name, Fernando-Larios, whispered as her brother's killer from a friend of the man's psychiatrist. Another acquaintance mentioned him as a potential interviewee for a documentary she was producing about events in Chile. His role in the "Caravan of Death"—evidenced by a 1998 Chilean investigation—coupled with his presence on US soil enabled Cabello-Barrueto's legal action as one of CJA's first clients. (Cabello's family eventually won an $8 million verdict).[41]

Juan Romagoza, Neris Gonzalez, and Carlos Mauricio: Guatemala-born psychologist Mario Gonzalez was counseling friends and family members who had survived torture. As his home country, Guatemala, became further mired in violence, Gonzalez fled with his wife and children and made Chicago their new home. Through word of mouth, Guatemalans and Salvadorans, and later survivors from across the globe, found their way to the Kovler Center where he had begun working.[42] Through Gonzalez, Gray met traumatized Salvadorans, including torture survivors Juan Romagoza, Neris Gonzalez, and Carlos Mauricio. Romagoza, a Salvadoran surgeon and resident in a free cardiac clinic at the University of El Salvador, witnessed terror before being tortured himself. Security forces had stormed into his clinic, kidnapped one of his patients, and gunned down another. After Romagoza founded a free clinic for torture survivors and the impoverished, he too became a target. Soldiers abducted Romagoza and for 22 days tortured him with electrical shocks to his ears, tongue, testicles, anus, and edges of his wounds until he lost consciousness, according to his testimony. They reawakened him by kicking and burning him with cigarettes, hung him by his fingers tightly wired to the ceiling, sodomized, water-boarded, and hooded him with an asphyxiating toxic substance.[43] They hung him upside down, immersing his head in water and locked him in a coffin for days at a time.[44]

Upon release, a starved and permanently injured Romagoza weighed 70 pounds and could not walk on his own. Nerve damage ended his surgery career. After a period in hiding, Romagoza won asylum and citizenship in the US,[45] eventually becoming a CJA plaintiff in a case against General

Carlos Eugenio Vides Casanova, head of the Salvadoran National Guard and later minister of defense, and General Jose Guillermo Garcia, for interrogating and presiding over torture, according to the plaintiffs' complaint.

Eight months pregnant church-worker Neris Gonzalez had taught reading and mathematics to campesinas when National Guard members abducted her from a local market. For three weeks, guards repeatedly tortured and gang-raped her, forced her to drink blood and to watch others' torture and mutilation.[46] Memory loss left her with only one recollection of her release—lying among corpses in the back of a dump truck. At the dumpsite, Gonzalez gave birth. Her newborn's cries led local villagers to find and rescue her, but her baby died from in utero injuries. Gonzalez sought help for flashbacks and anxiety attacks at a torture treatment center in Chicago and later joined the lawsuit.[47]

A professor at the University of El Salvador, Carlos Mauricio witnessed "bodies being dumped in the streets after being cruelly tortured" before becoming a victim himself.[48] As he left his classroom, a special unit of the army cornered, kicked, and beat him with rifle butts, then blindfolded, handcuffed, and dragged him into a car, he recounted to broadcasters of "Making Contact" radio. While blindfolded and handcuffed, Mauricio recalled being led over corpses, "the smell of death," and screams of torture before enduring eight days of severe beatings.[49] Transferred to an underground, hidden cell, he witnessed a woman holding the hand of "a young boy . . . through the bars." The boy had "no food for . . . weeks probably . . . She gave him something to eat. . . . The only edible thing she got, she gave to her son. It was the only moment that I cried," he told the broadcasters.[50]

With broken bones, permanent damage, and emotional numbness, Mauricio was released with a warning to leave his country. Eventually arriving in San Francisco, a trauma counselor told him about the lawsuit against Casanova, encouraging him to join the case. Initial reluctance to reveal his suffering gave way to his decision to "join the case . . . to find some healing for the trauma," he said. "I wanted to come and tell the military that they were responsible for the genocide against the Salvadoran people."[51]

CJA's clients, Romagoza, Gonzalez, and Mauricio, pressed the case against Garcia and Casanova, who had moved to Florida and gained permanent US residency. They eventually won a $54.6 million judgment against Casanova who was deported from the US.[52]

To meet Hoffman's condition on asking Amnesty International for seed funds, Gray still needed a third case. *Mehinovic v. Vuckovic* arrived "out of the blue," he said.[53]

Kemal Mehinovic: Gray received the call without warning. An American woman phoned, querying him about his work, then eventually introduced him to a Bosnian government official who wanted to make public the fates of the Bosnian people through the media. The official referred torture survivor Kemal Mehinovic.[54]

A local baker in Bosanski Samac, Bosnia, Mehinovic opened his door in May 1992 to find two Serb policemen, who dragged him from his house, beat him with brass knuckles on his front steps, and continued torturing him at the local police station, according to his legal complaint. For more than two hours, they hung him upside down and beat him with batons and a baseball bat on his most sensitive body parts. While he writhed in pain on the floor of the "interrogation" room, Nikola Vuckovic took over, repeatedly kicking Kemal's genitals and face, leaving him disfigured and damaged, according to his complaint.[55]

For two years, Mehinovic and his kinsmen languished in a concentration camp, enduring routine beatings, humiliation, starvation, and physical and mental torture. After losing everything in the Bosnian War, he found refuge in the United States, landing in the state of Utah in 1995. An odd turn of events enabled him to sue his torturer. About three years later, a Bosnian friend phoned. Vuckovic had been spotted in Georgia. Mehinovic and three kinsmen sued Vuckovic in an Atlanta court where Judge Marvin Shoob found him civilly liable for torture, cruel, inhuman, and degrading treatment, arbitrary detention, war crimes, crimes against humanity, and genocide. The survivors were awarded damages totaling $140 million, $10 million for each plaintiff and $25 million each for punitive damages.[56]

CJA's Birth

With three plaintiffs, Hoffman approached Amnesty International, which allocated seed money to launch the CJA. "I think we gave them $400,000 and Amnesty's name and resources," recalled Hoffman, adding, "They were never formally connected."[57]

Financial support then flowed from the United Nations' Voluntary Fund for Victims of Torture and from lawyers and clinicians, half of whom were from the Jewish community. Both groups understood Gray's logic: "The argument [was] that getting justice was therapeutic, and supporting this program was supporting mental health," he said. They "knew in their bones the meaning of chasing down these people. . . . Long-time, well-established professionals" from the Jewish community helped support "the refugee communities [who] didn't have money. The Jewish community in this country did. They've been here a long time; [they were] well-established professionals."[58]

Within two years, Gray "raised a million and a half dollars. It was a lot easier to raise money for this project than it was for treatment," he said. "I think the reason is this: when people look at treatment . . . mental health or homelessness problems, any expression of mental health problems in general, it looks endless. It's bottomless. There's no cure. . . . But if you look at the possibility of civilized revenge, or getting justice, a lot of people understand that in their bones."[59]

Alongside Gray, experts in human rights law and trauma clinicians joined the CJA's board: Hoffman, CCR's Beth Stephens, Ralph Steinhardt, Reverend William Schultz, Cosette Thompson, and trauma counselor Mario Gonzalez.[60] Shawn Roberts was appointed the CJA's first legal director, and Beth Van Schaack its first full-time staff attorney, joining as a half-time lawyer, a "sort of" office manager and a legal director, "and that was it," Van Schaack recalled.[61]

When Van Schaack left to join an international law firm, Morrison Foerster, she continued litigating full time for *Romagoza* on a pro bono basis. The firm spent "definitely more than a million dollars on this case, just in terms of staff, attorney time, travel to El Salvador, interviewing witnesses, expert testimony, everything that, you know, defending against motions to dismiss, the appeal, everything—quite a big investment," she said.[62]

That collaboration with private law firms became CJA's model, benefiting the nonprofit with skilled volunteer litigators and financial support while helping private firms meet pro bono obligations and train young lawyers. "It gives their junior lawyers a way to get advanced trial experience," explained Van Schaack. "The young people enjoy it. They get deposition time, trial time, etcetera. And then of course the firm gets the benefit of having a big pro bono practice."[63]

The "perfect model" wedded the "experienced trial lawyer who has resources coupled with the human rights lawyer who understands the subject matter and who has the client relations piece, where they really work with those people," she added.[64]

The idea stuck. "You get great litigators who know evidence law . . . procedural law, who know everything about the local judge, who know all that kind of stuff, discovery, whatever. And we know everything about the facts, everything about international law, everything about ATS/TVPA law," added Kathy Roberts, who later served as a CJA legal director.

"Because the cases are very expensive, they have to be big firms, or at least they have to be willing and able to pay expenses. . . . We bring a case that is possibly ten years of litigation. That possibly will involve flying countless witnesses from multiple continents to come stay at hotels, interpreters and depositions, and maybe foreign depositions. There's a lot of costs."[65]

Through disparate interactions, young lawyers gravitated to the organization, each bringing unique skills that shaped it further. Roberts found the organization after completing her PhD in philosophy. Searching for a way to pursue "the intellectual stuff" while being "of service," she began law school where, in her first year, torture survivor Carlos Mauricio and then-CJA legal director Joshua Sondheimer "came to my human rights law class. I was fascinated and immediately set out to try to figure out how I could get an internship with this remarkable organization," she recalled. After four years of legal practice, Roberts joined the CJA, eventually becoming its legal director.[66]

While working on asylum cases for US law firms, Spanish immigration attorney Almudena Bernabeu met Salvadoran counselor Felix Kury, who provided trauma expertise to "legendary immigration lawyers."[67] First and secondhand knowledge informed Kury's practice and connections. El Salvador's violence had taken the lives of his friends, and the terror and torture had debilitated his clients. In the 1970s, amid the escalating crisis that spawned a civil war in his home country, Kury moved to the US but maintained close ties to his countrymen through counseling and an organization he cofounded, El Comite de Salvadoreños Progresistas (Progressive Salvadorans), which published reports of human rights violations in El Salvador through its newspaper, *El Pulgarcito*.[68] In 1989, gunmen raided the Central American University and massacred his friend, Ignacio Martin-Baro, and five additional Jesuit priests, "men of peace, men who defended the poor and didn't carry weapons," Kury said to Marisa Gerber of the *Los Angeles Times*.[69]

Kury told Bernabeu about the fledgling CJA: "He said, 'You know . . . these gringos have put together an organization. . . . These guys are talking about litigation." But there seemed, to Kury, to be lacking "political [teeth]," recalled Bernabeu. "I think you should go and talk with the gringos," he had concluded.[70]

Initially, the model seemed incomprehensible. "I had no idea about how you could do anything in court for these kinds of people in these kinds of situations," she recalled. The laws "made no sense to me, because we don't have such torts [in Spain]."[71] With deep knowledge of El Salvador's crises and language skills, Bernabeu joined the CJA as a volunteer investigator.

"I had been taking the declarations for asylum applications and for the amnesties that were passed in the '90s from, I think, over 800 Salvadorans," she explained. "I would have a whole map and understood the war and . . . the different groups. . . . And they [the CJA] . . . were in need of a Spanish speaking lawyer."[72]

Through tips in newspapers, phone calls, and "knocking [on doors]," Bernabeu helped build CJA's cases by tracking down witnesses and plaintiffs. She discovered "solidarity within organizations in San Francisco with some Hondurans, and they gave me the tip of important human rights organizations back in Honduras in [a] case, who are still doing victims' work. And then I called this woman, Mary, who I will never forget . . . [who helped locate] most of my plaintiffs in that case," she said.[73]

Although Scott Gilmore "never intended to practice law," he soon found it "irresistible" as he discovered its promise. "I was serving as an intermediary between therapists and social workers and refugees who had survived horrific human rights violations," he recalled. "And what really stood out to me was that standing on the other side of this transaction was the person that inflicted all this trauma on them. And nowhere in this cluster of service providers was anybody trying to address the perpetrators, and in particular, the impunity. The perpetrator was continuing. . . . My former clients had been abused by government officials, nonstate actors, rebel fighters, many of whom were continuing to commit atrocities."[74]

The translator and writer-performer made the career change that eventually led him to the CJA. "For many, the traditional model of being a human rights lawyer is as a shield, to protect your clients from the predations of a repressive government. For me, I really wanted to be the sword. I wanted to track down and pursue the human rights violators. . . . I really went into the law with that in mind. I started working as a human rights investigator and researcher and doing human rights policy in Washington before I actually was a lawyer. So I very intentionally became a lawyer knowing I wanted to do this type of work."[75]

In 2012, when American war correspondent Marie Colvin was killed while reporting on the siege of Homs, Syria, Gilmore analyzed her death as a possible war crime, presented the analysis to the American Society of International Law and the potential case to CJA's then executive director, Pamela Merchant.[76] "Reporters without Borders arranged for me to meet with the Colvin family. They explained to me that they wanted to seek justice," Gilmore recalled. "They wanted to uncover the truth of what happened to Marie Colvin. If it was indeed a targeted killing, they wanted to hold the Assad regime accountable."[77]

The case presented the possibility of going "after current atrocities," said former CJA executive director Dixon Osburn.[78] The facts supported a rare ability to sue a sovereign state in US courts—"an American" killed by a "state sponsor of terror," the exception carved out by the Foreign Sovereign Immunities Act. It could also "instigate a criminal investigation, either in the home country or by some third country or by an international court," added Gilmore.[79]

"Then the question was, 'Did the regime actually murder her?,'" said Osburn.[80] A six-year investigation uncovered "eyewitness testimony, defector testimony, who observed the planning of the attack, Syrian government documentation revealing a policy of launching military operations against 'those tarnishing the image of Syria in the international media,' and audio and video recordings of the attack," explained Gilmore.[81] The Colvin's $303.6 million win against the Assad regime became part of cross-border efforts to resolve the Syrian human rights crisis[82] (more on this in chapter 8).

While continuing litigation in US courts, the CJA broadened its focus, looking globally for solutions. For example, "We represent over a hundred Cambodian Americans before the courts in Phnom Penh," said Osburn. "We're really the only NGO outside of Cambodia that's representing civil parties."[83]

That model began at the CJA in the early 2000s when Bernabeu joined the effort in Spanish courts to prosecute Guatemalan officials for torture and killing in what became known as the "Guatemalan Genocide Case."[84] In 2008, alongside the Spanish Association for Human Rights, the organization used universal jurisdiction to take another case to the Spanish courts—a case against the former president of El Salvador and 19 former members of the military for the massacre of six Jesuit priests, a housekeeper, and her daughter.[85]

The organization also pursues uncovering hidden "truth[s], because atrocities had not been recognized for what they are," developing precedents, and strengthening "rule of law" and "confidence in the democratic institutions, the same institutions that betrayed victims and survivors in the beginning," explained Osburn. "That's our theory of change, and we're always trying to see how many of these dots we can connect as sort of a holistic approach."[86]

While its role is evolving, CJA's original mission—to facilitate healing for survivors of atrocities—still serves as its foundation. Though long-term effects are unclear, anecdotes suggest promise with some caveats.

Litigation and Recovery

"They'll never be the same," admitted Van Schaack about survivors of torture and other grave human rights abuses. "You can't undo what's been done."[87]

By all accounts, human rights abuses—particularly torture—are among the most debilitating and traumatizing experiences.[88] Guilt, shame, terror, alienation, a distorted sense of reality, and feelings of abandonment debilitate and devastate to varying degrees.[89] At the heart of the psychological injury is total "lack of control, complete lack of agency," said Gilmore.[90] "You're being forced to reveal your kind of innermost secrets through the infliction of pain. And that's one of the most traumatizing aspects of it. And so for many of my clients, having the opportunity to bring the case and have agency, be an active agent of change means that they are setting the wheels in motion. They are triggering the justice mechanism. They are testifying through the lawsuit, calling witnesses to testify, forcing the defendant to answer for what they did. That is an incredible rehabilitative step for many of my clients . . . the restoration of feeling like they have control. And they are an agent. They have their own sort of renewed sense of humanity."[91]

The effects are tricky, inconsistent, and often unpredictable, affecting victims differently, according to experts, including Gray.[92] So is the healing process and the use of litigation as a path to recovery. "It's limited but can be very big . . . to overcome helplessness," explained Gray. But he added, "It's not for everyone. . . . Some people back out, reasonably. . . . And some go forward."[93]

Distinct from criminal prosecutions where victims play limited roles, civil litigation transforms victims and survivors into plaintiffs who are "fighting back and being acknowledged," which is "very valuable," sometimes even without a win, said Stephens.[94] By "seizing justice, and seizing the role of plaintiff," they restore agency, added Van Schaack. The plaintiffs are "actually in control. It's your claims. It's your lawyer. They represent you. . . . She [the plaintiff] looks at the person [her violator] in court, and she testifies."[95]

That contrasts with cases in which survivors are merely witnesses, said Van Schaack. "It's very different when you can't j'accuse," she explained. "You can't point the finger at the person whom you feel is responsible and get them to answer for themselves. So in my Salvadoran case, both of those defendants took the stand and tried to defend their actions. And we were able to cross-examine them and basically show that they knew what was going on . . . and that included a massive regime of detention and torture that our clients got sucked into."[96]

Decision-making about key questions is a vital part of the agency-giving process. Survivors decide, for example, "How do you want to frame it? What claims do you want to bring? What part of your story is important? What part do you not want to make public? All of that sense of control can be very valuable to people as part of a healing process," explained Van Schaack. "You're telling your story; you're talking to a jury; you've got a judge. The proceedings are about you. You're controlling the proceedings, working through your lawyer."[97]

Osburn agreed. "The first part of it is really rooting our work in the experiences of the victims and survivors. . . . They're the ones [who] need to drive the process. And what is justice and accountability for one person or one group may not be the same idea . . . for another group."[98]

Studies to date suggest litigation's varied influences.[99] But "on balance, trials have a psychologically positive effect on victims when they lead to public discussion of the abuses they suffered, breaking a former silence," according to one study.[100] Anecdotally, some plaintiffs report transformations: Martinez-Baca's opportunity to "serve my incarcerator and torturer [Suarez Mason] with a suit" was his greatest satisfaction, he said at a press conference. But it didn't erase the trauma: "You still have the ex-prisoner mentality—your life stopped in jail. It was the most important thing in your life—the most terrible and the most unforgettable."[101]

Mauricio exhibited exuberance "a couple of weeks after they had won" their case, recalled Roberts, who met him at the University of California, Berkeley. Mauricio and Sondheimer "walked in about four feet above the floor . . . [Mauricio] told us in really shockingly, for me at that time, it was shockingly intimate detail, about how he had been kidnapped and tortured, and what that recovery had been like . . . and what it meant to him to be able to confront those generals who were responsible and see them on the stand and say, 'You! You are responsible! It was obviously a hugely transformative and positive experience for him," she recalled, adding, "It's arresting to have someone come and tell you how they were tortured with joy. But it's because of this process that he had just come through."[102]

Mauricio's wife affirmed these effects to Van Schaack. "Like a year after the case, she [Ruth] said, 'I have an entirely new husband because of that case. It was transformative for him. He became more confident. He was more at peace. He was more excited about what he was doing,'" recalled Van Schaack. "All of this was . . . after being powerless."[103]

Fair adjudication as the victim confronts their abuser is what lawyers like Benedict De Moerloose of TRIAL International believe is "the strongest moment" for survivors. With "authorities listening to them and controlling the alleged perpetrators . . . they say in his face, 'you know, I have been tortured.'" De Moerloose recalled a trial in which his Algerian client "was speaking, and then the defense minister [the accused] wanted to interrupt him . . . and the prosecutor, a woman, says, 'It's not your time to speak,' and this for him was huge. It was him now in control."[104]

Observers, such as journalist Lisa Lambert of the *San Francisco Weekly*, said the process transformed Cabello-Barrueto from a "mild-mannered teacher of Latin American studies into a cross between Columbo and Capt. [*sic*] Ahab," adding that her "low-key style" masked her "steely determination."[105]

While Cabello-Barrueto acknowledged the change, crediting "the power of hope," others found the trial as "a grieving period. It was closure," ostensibly reverberating with other Chilean survivors. For example, Letelier's widow reportedly remarked, "'I'm so happy you could do it, because I couldn't.'"[106]

The trials' end can bring relief, according to lawyers, including De Moerloose and Martyn Day. De Moerloose's torture survivor client said, "'I am so relieved. I can close on part of my life. . . . I can go on with my life now.'"[107]

The fight may offer vicarious healing for "whole communities" who are traumatized. "It may be an individual who was killed or tortured or whatever, but they represent something that's a trauma for their whole communities," explained human rights lawyer Judith Brown Chomsky.[108] In these cases, the victory "can have trigger effects for their communities at large, in particular if it's for . . . a well-known incident that really resonated in its horror," said Gilmore. "To see that incident be adjudicated in a court of law and for there to be a finding of guilt or liability, that kind of vindication resonates," which Gilmore thinks can empower them to spur transitional justice efforts in the home country.[109]

That seemed to ring true for Victor Jara's family and community, according to Osburn. "Joan, his widow, who was 88 at the time, flew in, and his two daughters flew in, and for them, it was this final coming together of everything they had been working towards for four decades . . . that is something that has reverberations back in Chile," which "wants this perpetrator extradited."[110]

It helps that "not everybody has to go to court. Three or four people go; they face their torturers," added Gray. "I know there have been reverberations in countries of origin. . . . I can't say that we've prevented torture, [but] I think we've been part of recovery from torture for a lot of people. And though we will never catch all the torturers, it is clear we will catch some—and none of them will ever know who is next."[111]

Litigation also has downsides. Forced to revisit excruciating experiences, survivors may be retraumatized, dissociate, or have flashbacks, and can transfer those effects to their service providers. Suleiman Salim, a survivor of the CIA's rendition and torture, flashed back and dissociated during a deposition (detailed in chapter 9). Still, by the case's conclusion, Salim changed for the better, according to his lawyer, Steven Watt. "When I speak with him on the phone, it's like a weight has lifted. He sends me pictures of him fishing. . . . He's getting his life back in order. He's a really beautiful person . . . and his PTSD symptoms are leveling out now, so when we talk, it's about good things. I can tell, his voice has changed; he's much more together; he's brought the two [dissociated] Suleimans together."[112]

FOUR

The Burmese Connection

On the eighth day of the eighth month of 1988, students, Buddhist monks, and other citizens of Burma rose en masse to protest the oppressive military dictatorship that took power in their country by coup d'état. Forty-one days later, another regime seized power and crushed the movement, jailing, torturing, and killing thousands of democracy activists.[1]

A poor country, rich in natural resources, Burma's government sought economic partners to help extract natural gas from its southern peninsula, a region that had, for generations, been home to subsistence farmers who grew cashews, rice, and groundnuts. Economic globalization, the regime's enabler, opened the region to multinational companies, including France-based Total and California-based Unocal, keeping them flush with cash, while the regime relied on forced labor, torture, and environmental destruction to build the Yadana pipeline project.[2]

Newspapers and NGOs, including Amnesty International and the Free Burma Coalition, released detailed reports of the regime's human rights abuses. But no solutions to alleviate the suffering had materialized. With no recourse in their own country, and no survival options on their traditional lands, many fled to the jungles just inside Thailand, out of the regime's reach but far from their intergenerational homes and farms.[3]

Questions about globalization's promise and peril drew interest from scholars, NGOs, students, activists, and lawyers, some seeking to remediate damages for the aggrieved. This combination—local and international—shaped potential remedies for the Burmese survivors and others similarly harmed, connected in part by three University of Virginia law students—Katie Redford, Tyler Giannini, and Mark Bromley on a summer school project.

In the summer of 1994, Redford, Giannini, and Bromley travelled to Southeast Asia as part of a globalization research project, documenting human rights issues arising from "opening markets" in poor countries. Large, controversial projects—clearcutting rainforests and building giant dams in countries like Indonesia and Thailand—were said to alleviate poverty. But they were also poised to upend ecosystems, rural villages, local livelihoods, and destroy wildlife.[4]

The students' summer assignment—human rights issues in the logging industry—eventually led them to Ka Hsaw Wa,[5] a democracy activist, who after being tortured in a Burmese jail, also escaped to Thailand's jungles. Ka Hsaw Wa continued striving for a democratic Burma, documenting the experiences of hundreds of refugees who suffered similar fates—torture, rape, or enslavement.[6]

Through Ka Hsaw Wa, the students met the survivors hiding in the jungle and listened to their stories: facing untenable choices—to "buy" their freedom or be forced to work as "pipeline porters"—they fled their traditional lands.[7] "I preferred to escape than be treated worse than an animal," explained one survivor.[8] Some who remained slaved on the project until they could no longer work, and were then shot dead, according to a government defector.[9] "If we refused, they said they would kill us," recalled Jane Doe,[10] who eventually sued the California oil company, Unocal.[11] When soldiers arrived at their home, her husband fled, leaving her and their infant girl behind. A soldier struck Doe "with his gun. I fell and hit my head on a stone and lost consciousness," she recounted to documentarians. Regaining consciousness, she saw her baby engulfed by fire: "I grabbed her and fled to the jungle. We were escaping to the border. Three days later I reached a camp hospital. . . . Two days later, my baby died," she said.[12]

Doe's ancestral home, burned to the ground, cleared the way for energy extraction from the Yadana gas field that lay beneath. The combined clearing and forced labor would generate mass profits for the regime and oil companies. But for the Burmese who had lived there, "Everything is gone. . . . We lost everything."[13]

The troubles gave rise to local militia groups with plans for rebellion and sabotage,[14] a strategy that the students sought to dissuade. Perhaps, instead, they could give the law a chance, using the 200-year-old Alien Tort Statute, which had been used by torture survivors against their individual abusers. But it had not been successfully tried with a corporate defendant.

Returning home, the students made plans. After law school, they would form an NGO to represent the Burmese survivors. Redford began studying "how to sue oil companies for doing human rights abuses overseas" as her law research paper. "I called Beth Stephens at CCR as part of the research because her name was on all these [ATS] cases," recalled Redford. She told Stephens about her plan, "this case that we wanted to bring when we graduated and became real lawyers."[15]

In charge of CCR's human rights docket, Stephens's cases included landmarks, such as representing Bosnian victims of rape and sexual violence against former Republika Srpska president, Radovan Karadžić, who was later convicted of genocide, war crimes, and crimes against humanity. "Without realizing the potential," that case, though against an individual, perhaps laid the groundwork for the corporate cases, according to Stephens. Because "international law says only states can commit . . . some of the [human rights] violations," while other violations "don't require state action," the lawyers argued that the "unrecognized political leader . . . was acting in concert" with a state. "I think my memory is that it was Paul Hoffman, who said, 'Hey, you know, your two theories that say that you can go against non-state actors, that means you can go against corporations.'"[16]

Stephens, Jennifer Green, and Judith Brown Chomsky, had also tried litigating against a manufacturer supplying tear gas to Israel, using common law, not the ATS. Thus, while accustomed to powerful opponents, she was still reticent to oppose a multinational corporation with near unlimited funds that could consume an NGO's limited resources, Stephens said.[17]

Perhaps this case was different, argued Redford. While the tear gas company was supplying to Israel, "no one was calling Burma an ally in any strategic, political situation, or [suggesting] that they were just a misunderstood democracy that was being called a dictatorship," she recalled.[18]

Despite reticence, Stephens invited a future call, should Redford advance the case. "I'm sure she was just like, 'Who the hell is this kid?'" laughed Redford. "I am sure she was just being nice and thinking we would never call back, but I did."[19]

The real discouragement came from Redford's law professor, Jack Goldsmith, who roundly criticized her work. "He told me we couldn't do this," she recalled. "He was like . . . this will never happen; you can't do this; it's unconstitutional; it's a terrible idea. [Then, he] spent the rest of his career fighting against everything we do."[20]

Redford, Ka Hsaw Wa, and Giannini nonetheless formed EarthRights International with the Burmese refugees as their first clients and published a report of their findings, titled *Total Denial*. That report inspired Marco

Simons to "go to law school . . . for the specific purpose of working on these kinds of cases," he said. The case formed the basis of his law school admission essay, and he later joined the EarthRights team.[21]

"Everybody recognized at the time that this [pipeline] was really going to be the economic lifeline for Burma's military regime," Simons explained. "Before the gas pipeline came on board, the military regime's hard currency reserves were probably less than a hundred million dollars, which is incredibly low for a nation of 50 million people. They were on the verge of economic collapse. And it was the natural gas deals that were keeping them afloat for another fifteen years."[22]

The Labor Lawyers

Economic globalization had also altered working conditions for laborers, both in the US and abroad, shifting the focus of their lawyers, such as Terrence Collingsworth, who had traditionally worked for unions in the US. "Most of the problems were now globalization issues and not union issues in the US. And the union issues in the US were shrinking because of off-shoring, but to the extent that they needed lawyers, they already had good lawyers. So I decided to start focusing on the international aspects," he said.[23]

Through international fair labor campaigns, Collingsworth learned about the crises in Burma. "I had an old friend [U Maung Maung] through the union movement who was the head of the federation of trade unions of Burma (FTUB), which was operating in exile in Thailand," he recalled. Maung asked Collingsworth and another attorney, Jon Bonifaz, to represent workers "forced to work on that pipeline for Unocal and Total."[24]

Collingsworth and Maung approached Unocal's chief legal officer, Dennis Codon, for independent inspection, as a start to a remedy. Codon stopped responding, according to Collingsworth, prompting his decision to pursue more aggressive legal recourse.[25]

By this time, "more traditional avenues" of advocacy, such as documentation, reports, and trade submissions seemed futile to Collingsworth. "We tried negotiating. We worked on those codes of conduct issues and appealed to the government to change the laws," none which worked, he said.[26]

Outspent and outlobbied by multinational corporations, Collingsworth's efforts were "derailed by the fact that the companies had a lot more power than we did. If we had to have their consent to any actions we were taking, we were going to get nowhere. And so we were flounder-ing around trying to figure out how we could get a stick to start really getting leverage. And the only thing we could come up with sort of fell in our lap."[27]

Courts might provide that leverage, he thought. With no precedent, both teams—the EarthRights lawyers and the labor lawyers (Collingsworth and Bonifaz)—filed separate ATS lawsuits against Unocal, Total, and the Burmese government's own oil company. A judge joined the lawsuits, and an eight-year battle began, with shifting strategies and courtrooms, mov-ing from federal to state court, before the case finally concluded.

Building a Team

Redford called Stephens again, asking CCR to join the case. While the legal theory was sound, Stephens worried that CCR "just didn't have the resources." But her Jennifer Green, presented a "quite brilliant" idea to spread the workload across "a network of lawyers," Stephens recalled.[28] While Stephens was on leave, Green "forged ahead and managed to put together legal teams" that were ultimately successful. She was "crucial to that development," Stephens said.[29]

CCR could provide ATS expertise, brief-writing, district court argu-ments, and "big heavy motions and appeals," recalled Anne Richardson, co-counsel on the case. For an experienced litigator and a law license in California where they would file the complaint, "Paul [Hoffman] was the obvious choice."[30]

The former chair of Amnesty International USA and a Human Rights Watch committee member, Hoffman knew the woes of the Burmese people and the struggles of their allies to help alleviate their distress: "They tried to use all the other available tools, like pressure. There were approaches made by NGOs like Amnesty and Human Rights Watch to the CEO. All of that was blown off. They went to shareholder meetings and protested. That was blown off. They did a human rights report and publicized that. That was blown off, and so there was no way to stop them. They would just say, 'Yeah we understand. We are not really involved, and you know we can't stop SLORC [the military junta, the State Law and Order Restora-tion Council] from being SLORC. You know, we drill in difficult places.'"[31]

But circumstances made Hoffman reticent. It "was too big of a case because I was pretty much solo at that point," he acknowledged and sug-gested the NGOs call civil rights and employment lawyer Dan Stormer, he said. Novel strategies, risky cases, and blazing new trails in civil rights were Stormer's forte.[32] He had won large verdicts for poor, aggrieved Americans harmed by a system that treats those "outside the norm poorly," Stormer said. His legacy included creating new legal pathways for victims of sexual harassment. "In the '80s with sex harassment, we were one of the first employment law firms to do those cases, and we had great results. And ultimately lots of other lawyers started doing them," enabling him to shift focus, Stormer said. His law partner, Barbara Hadsell, "led the way in slum-housing litigation, and [then] other lawyers started doing that," so she could move on to other areas of law.[33] But international human rights abuse cases had not yet landed on Stormer's agenda. "I just didn't know how [to do them]," he said, adding, "There are so many other civil rights issues that are out there. You can't learn everything or do everything."[34]

At the time when Hoffman called Stormer, civil rights law had matured. With civil rights buttressed by many lawyers, Stormer was open to exploring a new challenge. "I look for cases where there is a need. . . . There's a compelling need for this [human rights] litigation to be brought. . . . They were torturing, killing, conscripting, maiming, destroying villages," he said, adding, "Unocal along with Total and a company that supposedly was created in Burma [were] . . . conscripting people . . . for two, three, four weeks at a time. They were destroying villages. They were doing what conquerors do, women being raped, men being tortured, people forced to work, villages destroyed, people displaced."[35]

Though he didn't yet know the human rights field, "we had counsel. They were young and inexperienced, but they knew the law. And they were able to educate us as the process went on," recalled Stormer.[36]

Stormer's associate, Anne Richardson, was similarly focused on "traditional civil rights cases—employment discrimination cases, whistleblower, police abuse . . . [not] international human rights law," she said. But as "a moment came along," she pressed the firm to take the case: "When you listen to a story on the radio, about something awful that's happening somewhere, you just wish you could do something about it. So here was a moment where people said, 'Here's this horrible thing that's happening over there, [and] this is an American corporation. Will you join our team and let's try and do something about it? . . . It's like, wow. There's an amazing opportunity, and we have a big team. We thought we could spread the responsibility."[37]

Daunting risks, enormous stakes, a powerful, politically connected, fierce opponent, a case that could drag on for years, and prohibitive costs that could bankrupt a small firm like Hadsell Stormer were big concerns.

"[We had] discussions about the pros and cons, the risks. How much it was going to cost? How long it might go on for? Could we afford to do this? What else were we going to do to make sure that we could?," Richardson recalled. The reality was, "We didn't think we had a shot at it. We thought we were most likely going to lose, because there were so many uphill battles." But the firm took the leap, "putting their own line of credit on the line."[38]

The Courts

Doe's lawyers lost their first motion—to stop the pipeline, based on the doctrine "that says you can't enjoin somebody from doing something if it's going to happen anyway," explained Richardson. Unocal's lawyers argued that even if it ended its pipeline construction, "a Japanese company or another company that wasn't bound by US law would just go in, and the joint venture would still continue."[39]

Unable to stop Yadana and the abuses that accompanied its development, Doe's lawyers sued for reparations. "There was no other alternative," said Hoffman. "At that point, there was really no relief other than money."[40]

So it began, the roughly eight-year ordeal, pitting 14 impoverished Burmese nationals hiding in a Thai forest against a multinational corporation with billions in annual revenue.[41] The case drew broad attention from both human rights and corporate observers, scholars and advocates. Human rights advocates hoped it signaled a way to stop the abuses, while corporation allies expressed concern about a flood of claims and accusations about violations for which the companies may have had side roles.

Over the lifetime of the case, the NGOs and boutique firms representing Doe faced three different large legal defense firms that barraged them with challenges, many of which were unrelated to Doe's claims. Ostensibly to confuse, exhaust, drain, or legally outwit opponents, the motions required Doe's counsel to expend scarce resources. For example, Unocal's legal team argued that the court had no jurisdiction, that the company had nothing to do with the abuses, that refugees' claims were fabricated, and that the plaintiffs had sued the wrong entity.[42]

The company also changed its arguments. In 2002, for example, Unocal spokesperson Barry Lane acknowledged that the human rights abuses were "very well documented," but denied the company's involvement to Lisa Girion of the *Los Angeles Times*. "There is no evidence showing our participation or our solicitation to get this to occur, or that we benefited from it," he said.[43] In 2004, however, Unocal lawyer Dan Petrocelli, of the law firm O'Melveny & Meyers, argued that Doe had fabricated her story. Presenting a Thai publication's photo and story of a woman whose baby survived scalding water, he argued, "It's the same person, the same shirt, the same piping—the same baby!"[44]

The courts vacillated, depending on the judge and the motions. While the court denied Unocal's motion to dismiss the lawsuit on subject matter jurisdiction, it dismissed claims against the two other defendants—the French oil company Total and Burma's SLORC.[45] Total "didn't have enough conduct in the US to get jurisdiction over them," while immunity laws protected SLORC, even if it was acting "more like a private party. There are exceptions [to immunity protection] when they are doing work that's more like a private company would do," explained Richardson. "It's a very well-established doctrine, but the court held that it didn't apply to our case."[46]

Doe lost on class certification and racketeering claims, the latter of which had been presented as "an enterprise involving a French oil company, the American oil company, the Burmese and the Thai . . . engaging in criminal acts," argued Richardson. "They raped people; they killed people." But these entities did not contain "enough of a link to the United States" to be held liable for racketeering in a US court.[47]

Crucial to the litigation was the question of Unocal's liability for the abuses. Written evidence established company knowledge of the violations. In a memorandum about Burma's "reign of terror," its consulting firm had warned Unocal executives, "The local community is already terrorized. . . . Potential profits will need to be unusually high to justify the high political risks."[48]

Before the liability question could be answered, a new judge, Ronald Lew, replaced Richard Paez, who was promoted to the Ninth Circuit Court of Appeals. "Grieve now and start writing the appeal brief," a colleague warned Stormer about the change.[49]

The prediction was right. Despite finding "egregious human rights violations have occurred and are occurring now," Judge Lew dismissed the case, deciding that the plaintiffs had not demonstrated Unocal's participation, control, or influence on the violations.[50]

The survivors' advocates appealed to the Ninth Circuit Court of Appeals and sued in state court, with the latter case relying on common law torts, such as "wrongful death, assault, battery," and unfair business practices, according to Stormer. "It is an unfair business practice to rely upon rape and terrorism as a function of your business," he argued to the UPI press agency.[51]

The appellate court reinstated the case while Doe's lawyers pressed the state case. Unocal responded by trying to move the case, first to Bermuda, where its subsidiary, the Unocal Myanmar Operating Co., had incorporated, then to Myanmar (formerly Burma), and finally argued to apply Burmese law, which required "community service."[52]

California district court judge Victoria Chaney denied Unocal's motions, ruling that neither Bermuda, nor Myanmar, was the appropriate forum, nor was Burmese law applicable. The company's subsidiaries could not function in Bermuda, and Myanmar lacked an effective rule of law, she opined:[53] "Even in the unlikely case that these (Myanmar) statutes authorized the violent and oppressive behavior at issue in this case (which Defendants repeatedly and reproachably liken to 'jury duty'), this court would refrain from applying the Village and Towns Acts for public policy reasons," she wrote, adding that case law supported her refusal to apply foreign laws that were "so offensive . . . prejudicial to recognized standards of morality."[54]

One trial focused entirely on Unocal's complicated corporate structure, during which Chaney granted Unocal's request to limit testimony about the case's facts.[55] "They [Unocal's lawyers] said, 'you know, Unocal is this parent company. You didn't sue the subsidiary of the subsidiary of the subsidiary,' which was a shareholder in the joint venture," recalled Richardson. "We had an entire trial over whether or not these subsidiaries were alter-egos of the big company, which is an extremely hard standard to prove. You do have to prove that there is . . . a bad reason for having these separate corporate identities. And they were very up front that it was for tax purposes, which isn't against the law."[56]

Unocal won that round along with Judge Chaney's praise. "Mr. Petrocelli, your law firm has done a dynamite job," she remarked.[57] But the win ostensibly helped Doe's counsel demonstrate liability, according to Stormer.[58] "The defense they used for the alter-ego theory basically proved our agency and our vicarious liability theories," explained Stormer.[59] In essence, the subsidiaries "were all agents of the other parent company," part of a joint venture, added Richardson.[60]

"Unocal knew or should have known there were human rights abuses," Chaney concluded,[61] supporting a trial for the Burmese survivors.[62]

Other Unocal wins ultimately helped Doe's case, according to Stormer. "Everything that looked bad turned out to be good," he said. That included a time when "we were able to turn [a] dismissal or remand to our advantage."[63]

Chaney set a jury trial for June 2005, a time that corresponded with important company matters, including a pending merger with another oil company, Chevron. These factors likely influenced the company's decision to settle the case, according to Stormer and Richardson.

Two months before the jury trial in March 2005, the company agreed to compensate the survivors with an undisclosed sum, which observers estimate at $30 million.[64] Those funds helped rebuild a damaged community, including "infrastructure projects for all kinds of wonderful [activities] for training, education, all these great things," according to Richardson, who served for three years on the fund's board, making the hard-fought win for the plaintiffs and their counsel meaningful: "So many hours we spent on it. I calculated half my working time in eight years was spent on this case," recalled Richardson.[65]

What Did It Mean?

The first ATS lawsuit for human rights violations abroad to settle with a transnational corporation in the US, *Doe v. Unocal* signaled a means to remedy damages for some of the world's least powerful by some of the world's most powerful actors. While Doe's government, which controlled institutions within Burma's borders, enjoyed immunity, the case suggested that other entities—such as corporations profiting from or participating in the human rights abuses—might be held accountable for their parts in the violations and be liable for compensating victims.

The first ATS international human rights case to join a network of law firms from civil rights, labor rights, and NGOs for human rights and the environment, the case created a model and an enduring network that continued in different iterations after *Doe v. Unocal*'s conclusion. Using the ATS, state law and courts to advance international human rights, *Doe v. Unocal* demonstrated an alternative to federal courts for international human rights abuse survivors.

The case also established the fledgling NGO EarthRights International as a human rights leader, which Redford suggests was against the odds: "We were told by all the 'experts' that we couldn't do it, and that's because no one had ever done it. The more experienced people were like, 'it's impossible.' And so we were of the mind [that] someone has to do it first, and then other people will do it. And that's, of course, what happened," she recalled.[66]

Perhaps the nay-saying created EarthRights' purpose: "to bring the cases that no one else will bring, either because it's not a money-maker, or it's too risky, or . . . there is no precedent. We will bring those cases. We can't do every case, but maybe we can do the trailblazing cases, and then others will follow," she explained.[67]

With this mission came the dual approach—to seek relief for their own clients while simultaneously supporting broader communities and movements, according to lawyers Redford, Stephens, and Chomsky. "All of our clients understand that their case is . . . representing broad communities who might not be named but who are suffering in the same way that they are suffering," explained Redford, adding, "As a small organization, [we] want to have as much of an impact as possible with [our] limited resources."[68]

Doe v. Unocal and its offspring offered focus and real-world arguments for activists—both in the field and in shareholder boardrooms, suggested Redford. The activists could, for example, argue, "'This is bad for our shareholders, being sued for rape, torture, and crimes against humanity,'" she explained.[69] EarthRights' next case would push the law's boundaries even further.

Beyond Doe

Oronto Douglas, lawyer for Ken Saro-Wiwa, the slain Nobel Prize–nominated Nigerian writer and television producer, approached Redford at a conference in Ecuador. "He and a couple of [Saro-Wiwa's] other lawyers were at this conference that I was at . . . called Oil Watch. And it was this network, this attempt to establish a global network of advocacy organizations and legal organizations that were trying to hold the oil companies accountable for widespread human rights and environmental abuses," recalled Redford. "Oronto was like, 'Why can't you sue Shell?' And I was like, 'Yeah, why can't we?'"[70]

Douglas presented evidence for Royal Dutch Petroleum's role in human rights abuses and Saro-Wiwa's execution, information that Redford took back to the *Doe v. Unocal* team. "If any case is going to potentially expand [the Unocal case], this could be it," she said, adding, "There was a global movement to save Ken's [Saro-Wiwa's] life and then the Ogoni Nine."[71]

The movement to save Saro-Wiwa's life had failed. The playwright, poet, and community leader's life was cut short when, in November 1995, he and eight colleagues were hanged by the country they had served and called home, their bodies dumped into an unmarked grave.[72] Their deaths ended a local chapter meant to restore living conditions for a community ravaged and ruined by oil spills, waste, gas flares, and terror.[73] Ruination of land, air, and water left the Ogoni people with little chance of survival, which, to Saro-Wiwa, was tantamount to genocide.

Letter-writing, pleading, and protests had little influence with either Nigeria's government or Royal Dutch Petroleum. The community's efforts to persuade were met with terror, massacres, and torture that crushed the movement.[74] Saro-Wiwa went public, generating global media attention, which ostensibly contributed to his demise, according to human rights lawyer Judith Brown Chomsky: "The reason why the oil companies and the government in Nigeria went after Ken Saro-Wiwa was because he took what was going on in that obscure part of the world and put it on the front page of the papers. It was in people's living rooms through their television and the documentarians who were based in Great Britain. They made a tremendous difference."[75]

Three survivors—Ken Wiwa (II), Owens Wiwa, and Blessing Kpuinen, widow of executed youth leader John Kpuinen—turned to the lawyers at EarthRights, CCR, Hoffman, and Chomsky—for representation in US courts. On November 8, 1996, they sued Royal Dutch Petroleum (Shell) in the US District Court for the Southern District of New York for summary execution of their family, crimes against humanity, torture, cruel, inhuman, or degrading treatment, arbitrary arrest and detention, wrongful death, assault and battery, and intentional and negligent infliction of emotional distress.[76] With the ATS granting standing, survivors asserted that the company violated international law, Nigerian law, and US federal and state laws. Additional survivors later joined the suit.

A second lawsuit targeted Shell executive Brian Anderson, who had reportedly met with Dr. Owens Wiwa three times during Saro-Wiwa's detention. Dr. Wiwa had requested his help to battle false charges against his brother. Anderson allegedly proposed a quid pro quo—to help if Saro-Wiwa ended the campaign and retracted his claims of environmental damage, according to the complaint and media reports. Anderson denied this account.[77] While Saro-Wiwa's fate awaited, the company officially stated, "It is not for a commercial organization like Shell to interfere in the legal processes of a sovereign state such as Nigeria."[78]

After Saro-Wiwa and his cohort were hanged, the company claimed it had tried to help. "Shell attempted to persuade that government to grant clemency; to our deep regret, that appeal—and the appeals of many others—went unheard," it said. "We were shocked and saddened when we heard the news."[79]

The Dutch oil company used legal tactics that were similar to those of Unocal, arguing primarily on procedural issues, rather than the substance of the case, prolonging the case and draining resources from the human rights advocates. It motioned for dismissal based on the forum, jurisdiction, and due process, and claimed the victims failed to either meet standards of law or to show that Shell had worked "in concert with the Nigerian government with respect to each human rights violation."[80]

Company documents, however, revealed that Shell's executives had, in writing, requested the aid of Nigerian security forces, financed their weapons, including semiautomatic rifles, bullets, pistols, hand grenades, ammunition, and gun apparatus, and asked for them to be "expedited as we are now under severe pressure," according to memoranda signed by Shell Petroleum Development Company of Nigeria's Security Advisor, V. A. Oteri. "We wish to use the opportunity to thank [*sic*] for your continued interest and support of our operations," he wrote on Shell letterhead.[81]

Presenting a report by a magistrate judge, Henry Pitman, the company persuaded the district court's Judge Kimba Wood that England was the case's appropriate forum. But for the Ogoni people, an overseas court change would mean starting over, finding lawyers in another country, and learning another set of legal procedures and precedents before the facts of the case could be heard. Their lawyers appealed to the Second Circuit Court of Appeals.

In October 1999, nearly three years after the initial filing, litigants argued again about the case's proper location, this time before the Second Circuit Court of Appeals. Eleven months later, a three-judge panel—James Oakes, Pierre Leval, and Rosemary Pooler—agreed with the Ogoni people, overturning Wood's dismissal based upon forum non conveniens. Wood's decision, according to the circuit court, was inadequately justified; the US had an express interest in designating its courts to address human rights violations, and they noted, precedent generally deferred to the plaintiffs' forum choice.[82]

Shell's lawyers appealed to the Supreme Court, but the high court denied certiorari. Having failed to dismantle the US case, the oil company reshaped its narrative, portraying itself as the "victim of an extortion movement that advocated violence and secession." Saro-Wiwa, the company claimed, was a provocateur who had advocated and provoked violence, ultimately forcing Shell out of Nigeria.[83]

The plaintiffs countered Shell's story with their own, and after thirteen years of motions, a trial date was set to hear the facts. Rather than face trial, the litigants settled out of court. On June 8, 2009, Royal Dutch Petroleum agreed to compensate the victims with $15.5 million, which established the Kiisi Trust for education, literacy, and enterprise support, as redress for the injuries the community had suffered.[84] The company never apologized or admitted wrongdoing.

Two wins-by-settlement for EarthRights' clients suggested that redress was possible for those survivors of international human rights abuses. But the lawyers' real hope was for prevention, that the cases would deter recklessness. "I think that through the actual process of bringing the case and getting discovery and public disclosure acts as a deterrent to future bad conduct," said Hoffman. "I think the corporations are scared about being publicly identified as human rights abusers because of the damage to their brand." [85]

The law was young, and the advocates knew it would take many more cases to weave together a protective legal fabric. Although there was no paucity of potential cases, few lawyers could sustain complex human rights cases against such powerful, resourced defendants. And those few could only manage a small case load.[86]

A third iteration of the legal team convened to represent another indigenous group, the Ilaje people, farmers and fishers from the Niger Delta. Chevron's dredging, gas flaring, oil spills, and sea incursion contaminated, salinated, and ruined their drinking water, crops, trees, and fish on which they relied.[87] "The [water] wells are destroyed; the rivers are polluted, villages have been totally decimated because they can't fish, and they have no freshwater. It's not like [they] can pick up and go. . . . People can't really move, so they become internally displaced," explained Stormer.[88]

To find another source of drinking water, the Ilaje people were forced to paddle "round trips of up to ten or twelve hours," added their co-counsel Bert Voorhees. They pleaded with oil company executives, wrote letters, asking for remedies. When executives stopped responding, the Ilaje launched a protest, "taking over an offshore [oil] platform," according to Simons.[89]

Roughly 100 Ilaje people staged a "sit-in on [Chevron's] offshore platform at Parabe," while another group remained onshore, negotiating. In their tentative agreement, protesters would leave the platform the next morning, said Voorhees. Morning arrived, and as boats arrived to collect the protesting Ilaje, Nigerian military forces in Chevron helicopters rained gunfire on them, killing two Ilaje people, injuring two, then detained and tortured another, according to court records, interviews, and press accounts. In May 1999, Larry Bowoto and his fellow Ilaje sued Chevron in US federal and California district courts.[90]

Chevron's lawyers peppered the court with motions to prevent the case from advancing, filing "something like 15 summary judgment motions— unbelievable—and most judges wouldn't have let them," recalled Voorhees. For example, "out of the blue" the company accused the Ilaje of witness-tampering, forcing Voorhees to travel to a region deemed too dangerous to enter by the US State Department. "I had to make an entire trip to question people and prepare declarations and submit them in the court on completely trumped up charges," he said, adding that the region was one where "Chevron lawyers would not go." The barrage of motions "created mountains of work . . . They dragged [us] through every possible fight in order to [for example] get a document."[91]

These tactics shifted attention away from the company's alleged wrong-doing and onto more procedural matters, according to Voorhees. "They want the story to be about the litigation, not how Chevron is killing and maiming people to get oil out of Africa . . . [and] the actual incident in which they did just that," he said.[92]

Each motion delayed the trial, due to response time from the court, recalled co-counsel Cindy Cohn of the Electronic Frontier Foundation. After roughly nine years of these motions, Judge Susan Illston scheduled the trial, based on evidence that "a reasonable jury could consider and determine that we would win," said Cohn. That included "how Chevron's corporate structure really works" to establish "that the parent company could be held responsible for what the subsidiary did here . . . We did a bunch of discovery about how Chevron is an integrated company. And even if you work for the subsidiaries, your loyalty is to the parent company. . . . The way people move up in Chevron's hierarchy is not about the particular subsidiary you're assigned to. It's about being assigned to multiple ones, over time, to make your way up the corporate ladder, and that was a sign that the parent company was really in charge of these decisions."[93] Cohn also tracked and analyzed telephone "calls between the US and Nigeria," which "showed a spike right before the attacks."[94]

The trial opened with a judicial order in which Illston ordered Chevron to take down its sponsored Google and Yahoo links, strategically placed to direct web traffic to the corporation's version of the events.[95] In trial, the military assault on protesters went undisputed, leaving the company's role and liability as the controversy. Stormer's opening statement described the Ilaje's plight: "Watching their communities die" from poverty and pollution, and frustrated by Chevron ignoring their pleas, they "decided to have a peaceful protest," carrying placards to the barge. The company responded by calling "notoriously brutal and vicious" mobile troops, which were "transported, paid, housed, fed and supervised by Chevron," he said.[96]

Known locally as "kill and go," the troops sprayed the Ilaje people with tear gas and opened fire as they were preparing to leave the barge, Stormer said, adding that community leader Larry Bowoto took bullets to the elbow, side, and buttocks and was left bleeding on the platform.[97]

Chevron's counsel, Bob Mittelstaedt, argued the reverse. He described the Ilaje as "invaders . . . sophisticated criminals and sea pirates who executed a commando-style raid where they stormed the oil barge, taking radio stations and heliports to prevent anyone from leaving the platform or communicating with the outside world." In his description, they committed "sea piracy," and an "illegal" hijacking, while the corporation properly notified authorities of the platform takeover. Payments to the military, he characterized as normal business, and the company as having a right to act,[98] even lethally, because of the "ticking time bomb" onshore agreement.[99]

Mittelstaedt called up a Chevron staff member who reported feeling like "a hostage," saying diesel fuel was poured on the deck.[100] The Ilaje denied his account, recalling camaraderie with the oil workers, singing and playing cards and games with them. The armed security staff, they said, expressed neither concern nor hostility.[101]

On the witness stand, Bowoto described paddling to the tugboat holding placards—"Concerned Ilaje Citizens: We want to speak with George Kirkland [Chevron general manager]" and "CIC: enough is enough"[102]— and singing, "Give Peace a Chance" with a lyric variation: "All we are saying is give us our rights / all we are saying is give us our jobs . . ." When they reached the barge, Chevron representatives agreed to talks, and by the fourth day, he said, they reached a tentative agreement.[103]

"Does ransom mean holding someone against their will and asking money for their release?" challenged Mittelstaedt in cross examination. "Boarding a platform and not letting workers go is kidnapping, correct? Calling Chevron and refusing to release workers until you receive money is hostage taking, correct?"[104]

"If you go to the platform in a peaceful protest, this is not hostage-taking. If you go to demand money in exchange for releasing people, this is [hostage-taking]. If you go to the platform in peace, carrying placards, you are not taking hostages," responded Bowoto, adding later, "If we were going for piracy, we would not have met with the governor of Ondo state first. If we were going for piracy, we would not have carried placards in our boats."[105]

Raising the allegation of pouring diesel fuel onto the deck and threatening to light it, Mittelstaedt asked, "Would Mr. Bowoto consider such an act peaceful?"[106]

"If this happened, it would not be peaceful; but this never happened; none of the protesters poured diesel on the barge," Bowoto replied.[107]

For the Ilaje and their counsel, their uphill battle against a powerful corporation was compounded by "language barriers, cultural barriers, thick accents, difficulty understanding" for an American jury, explained Voorhees. "Part of how trials work is to get people to connect to each other. And the minute you begin to tell stories that are embedded in another language and have to be translated, or deeply embedded in another culture, and you have to bring people across that cultural divide, it gets harder and harder, I think, for people to connect. And we knew that this would be an issue at trial."[108]

Translation posed additional challenges. "There are no official translators; there's no certification process for a translator in Ilaje that would be recognized as such in American courts," explained Voorhees. It "became an issue, for example, when, there's one word in Ilaje for any vehicle. It's the word for boat. . . . Someone would say, 'Yes, the police, the militia got flown in on a flying boat.' But a flying boat is a helicopter. It's just the word for vehicle is just always the word for boat. It's a very simple language. Any piece of paper, from a book to a calendar to a three by five note card, the word that you use is simply the word for paper. So, again, you have to translate from context."[109]

Initially, these differences puzzled even the Ilaje's counsel. "People were calling each other 'brother' all the time," recalled Cindy Cohn, co-counsel on the case. "It took me a while to be able to figure out how to ask the right questions to figure out—because this is a family, right, who has a claim? . . . I had to work really hard to figure out who the right people were. Because they're all 'aunties' and 'uncles.'"[110]

Chevron's lawyers seized upon these differences to generate fear, according to Voorhees. "It was all about 'otherness.' . . . The story they [Chevron] wanted to tell was the 'hostage situation' and being afraid," emphasizing "'big, black males,'" and making them seem "scary."[111]

In closing arguments, Stormer argued that Chevron "made up a story and covered it with distractions. They sent in people who were notoriously vicious. Then they said it was to drive them [the Ilaje] onto the platform, the same platform that was supposedly so unsafe and unstable that it posed the original security concerns that made them go in there." Chevron hired "their own private army to go in there and evict people, without any back-up plan other than deadly force," he said. "[Chevron's] Mike Browne himself had the responsibility to report all payments made to military personnel. They had documented all the payments. They knew."[112]

Mittelstaedt repeated his argument that the Ilaje were the guilty ones: "Here's the essence of this case when you step back and think about it: It's a claim by people who held hostages . . . against the victims of that crime. They're saying that the victims of the crime—Chevron Nigeria, representing the barge workers—should not have reported this to the law enforcement authorities, should not have called for a rescue mission, and instead should have paid whatever money they were asked."[113]

After the jury left to deliberate, Judge Illston approached the Ilaje people. "I want to shake hands with everyone," she said. "Not the lawyers, but the real people." She then turned to acknowledge translators and attorneys.[114]

The jury returned in only six hours, which Bowoto's lawyers suspected signaled defeat. "Typically for every week of trial, you're going to get a day or a day and a half of deliberation, and we were like a four-and-a-half-week trial. I knew . . . 'it was too fast. We're dead,'" admitted Voorhees.[115]

The jury sided with Chevron, whose lawyers then filed an instant motion to force the Ilaje people to pay the corporation's legal fees— including "witness per diems, service of subpoenas, court reporters, videotaping, transcription, and photocopying in this county"—and to provide the court with assets.[116]

"Defendants' objection is not well taken. It can reasonably be assumed that plaintiffs do not earn pensions or accrue other significant assets through their work as, for instance, fish sellers in a Nigerian village," responded Illston.[117]

In retrospect, Stormer summarized Chevron's theme as "Black people should not take white people hostage," he said, adding, "To my everlasting discredit, I didn't recognize it as it was happening."[118]

Chevron ostensibly "changed its strategy in the middle of the trial. They got a new lawyer, and they changed to a kind of 'heart of darkness' strategy, that these were dark and dangerous people, that they were holding white people hostage, which they'd done a little of before, but not much. But they really piled it on and changed their strategy. Again, I don't think we understood that it had pivoted as fast as we should have," added Cohn. "The one thing we got back from [the jury] was that they didn't think that we had proven that Chevron controlled the guys who opened fire, and that was something Chevron admitted. . . . They weren't even with us on that really pretty obvious point that we'd already won."[119]

The defeat "took a long time to get over" for the lawyers, admitted Cohn. "We took it harder than the clients, because they didn't expect justice, and we did." In contrast, the Ilaje expressed feeling victorious. "We were sort of like, 'Oh, my God, we are so sorry we lost,'" recalled Redford. "And they were just like, 'Are you kidding? We came to America, and we sat in a courtroom with Chevron, and they had to listen to us, and a judge and a jury. And they couldn't ignore us and flick us away like they have in Nigeria for the past however many years.' They were like, 'This is a victory, we never would have believed that anyone would listen to us.' . . . And that's how they feel, like 'We don't count.' But in the courtroom in the United States, they counted."[120]

Privately, still, the Ilaje expressed disappointment and disbelief, according to Voorhees. "It was inconceivable to them that the lauded American justice system, which would absolutely see through the lies . . . got it wrong," he said. "Because to them, the truth of the story was so obvious, and they believed in the American justice system. . . . I got a call as recently as maybe three years ago from folks trying to find out if it's really true."[121]

Beyond Bowoto

Doe v. Unocal, Wiwa v. Royal Dutch Petroleum, Bowoto v. Chevron, and related corporate human rights cases reveal some of the obstacles to mitigating some of globalization's harms to local people, land, and culture. Through their business deals, multinational corporations were, whether intentional or not, aiding and financing oppressive governments, and benefiting from human rights abuses and environmental destruction.

When victims of repressive governments, without justice available in their own countries, turned to the corporate beneficiaries for redress, mixed court outcomes painted a confusing picture about the potential for remedies from the US courts. Some received compensation from corporations after facing long, drawn-out, vicious legal fights. Others fought for years, only to be dismissed in the end by either jury or judge.

The results contrasted with outcomes from lawsuits against individual torturers or killers in which defendants were less prepared for seasoned litigators in US courts. "When Paul [Hoffman] and others had sued these dictators . . . the defense was never very rigorous. They didn't go out and hire [large firms like] O'Melveny & Myers, or Gibson, Dunn & Crutcher to defend themselves. They sometimes weren't even represented," explained Collingsworth. "Once the corporations got involved, they hired so many giant law firms that are now quite good at poking the right buttons for a conservative panel [of judges] to help them out."[122]

Out-of-court corporate settlements were also inconsistent, ranging from paltry sums to circa $6 billion in what became known as the Holocaust cases.[123] While the terms of many settlements, including *Doe v. Reddy* (2004) and *Xiaoning v. Yahoo!* (2007) remained undisclosed, others became public, including a $20 million settlement award for sweatshop laborers by multinational retailers, including the Gap, Nordstrom, and J. Crew Group.[124]

Trials involving corporate defendants were also unpredictable. For example, cases such as *Bowoto v. Chevron, Licea v. Curacao Drydock*, and *Estate of Rodriguez v. Drummond Co.* each concluded differently. While juries acquitted companies such as Chevron and Drummond of human rights violations in Nigeria and Colombia, respectively, plaintiffs won the *Licea* and *Jama* cases. In *Licea*, a Florida judge ordered one of the world's largest drydock companies to pay its Cuban slaves $80 million.[125]

For most lawyers, high risks and complications deter representation of human rights abuse victims against large corporations. The few willing to try them carefully select cases, knowing that uphill legal battles require investing years of dedicated brain power, creativity, and financial resources to front and sustain long-term litigation against wealthy corporate defenders. In *Bowoto*, for example, Hadsell Stormer's unreimbursed costs reached "almost $3 million, and the time spent on it was a total of 10 years of employee/lawyer time," admitted Stormer.

Human rights lawyers themselves have become targets in some instances, including two cases in which the corporations sued them. An Alabama-based coal company, Drummond, for example, sued Collingsworth after he had filed lawsuits against the company for aiding and abetting atrocities in Colombia. Drummond's countersuit claimed defamation and racketeering, the latter based upon support Collingsworth had provided to Colombian witnesses.[126] "I relocated their families to safe places, so the witnesses could testify without fear that their families would be killed. We modeled our efforts on what the US Department of Justice does in its witness protection program," Collingsworth explained.[127]

These strategies—flooding the opposition and courts with motions and turning the tables on the human rights lawyers—were some of the ways that corporate defenders used their resources to crush the cases. Outnumbered and stretched thin for time and resources, human rights lawyers could easily be crippled should they pursue multiple corporate cases at a time.

Corporate lobby groups have also gained political ground since the 1970s, using their might to shift political winds, which developed into legislation, laws, norms, and judges collectively granting the companies freer rein, greater protections, less responsibility, and creating higher thresholds for those harmed by the corporate activity abroad. Chapters 7 and 8 explore the manifestation of these changes, what they have meant for the future of human rights, and how human rights lawyers have navigated these shifts.

FIVE

Rights and Redress in a "War on Terror"

It's a US paradox: a founding force of the United Nations, a leader in the Nuremberg trials, a country where foreign torture victims found redress also supported brutal dictatorships in its fight against "communism." During the Cold War, the US Central Intelligence Agency (CIA) trained Latin American military leaders in the Debility, Dependency, Dread program, a systematic "attack on the sense of self" that used torture and deprivation of sleep, food, and senses to induce helplessness among captives. In the twenty-first century, the US itself turned to torture, using these methods on its own detainees.[1]

A watershed moment, the September 11, 2001 attacks on the New York City Twin Towers precipitated the country's turn to direct human rights violations, first at home in the roundup and brutal treatment of Arab, South Asian, and Muslim men, then continuing abroad, using torture to extract information from "terror suspects." Three days after the attacks, a CIA division chief began searching for "black sites"—secret detention facilities in foreign lands. Within a week, President George W. Bush authorized the agency to identify and capture people posing a "serious threat" or planning terrorist activities that could harm the US, its people, or property.[2]

Casting wide nets and offering monetary rewards for suspects, the US began hunting for "terrorists" and their "affiliates." With mass distributed flyers offering "wealth and power beyond your dreams . . . millions of dollars,"[3] bounty programs ensnared hundreds of innocent and unaware people, either mistakenly identified as terror suspects or deliberately turned in for revenge or financial reward.[4]

In early 2002, with advice from White House counsel Alberto Gonzales,[5] the Bush administration declared a "new paradigm" within which "none of the provisions of [the] Geneva [Convention] apply to our conflict with Al Qaeda in Afghanistan or elsewhere throughout the world." Paradoxically, Bush affirmed a previous order to treat detainees "humanely."[6] A 50-page memorandum by Jay Bybee, then an assistant attorney general, justified and declared legal interrogation tactics just short of US court-defined torture. Torture, he wrote, only meant acts, such as removing extremities, burning, electrically shocking genitalia, raping, injuring sex organs, forced watching of torture, or threatening torture or death: "Interrogation techniques would have to be similar to these in their extreme nature and in the type of harm caused to violate the law."[7]

Hundreds of men and boys, many falsely identified as terrorists, were rounded up, imprisoned, and abused for months, sometimes years, in many cases causing grave physical, mental, financial, social, and economic injury. With arrests and detention surrounded by secrecy and silence, many simply disappeared. Absent information about identities, locations, and conditions, no lawyer could secure their rights. Heightened fear and anger across the US reduced receptivity about the rights of the accused, even for the innocent.

A small group of lawyers tried first to ascertain the captives' identities and conditions—a cause that, initially, virtually no one would support. In time, however, scores of private, high-powered lawyers from across the bar joined the cause, donating their time and expertise to the detainees who suffered in abysmal conditions. Sixteen years of complex litigation that continues today pitted essentially powerless aliens in jurisdictional black holes against the top US officials. Weaving their way through the court system—advancing from one court to the next and back again—the victims and advocates battled claims of immunity, state secrets, and absence of personal responsibilities for the violations. The few wins paled in comparison to the losses and what they meant for the making and unmaking of rights in the US.

The next three sections summarize some important cases against the US government and its officials, first with those involving abuses on US soil, then the rendition and torture of Maher Arar, and, finally, the detainees of Guantánamo Bay Naval Station Detention Center.

The Beatings in Brooklyn

Just after the September 11 attacks, the Federal Bureau of Investigation (FBI) launched the "massive investigation" known as PENTTBOM. US

Attorney General John Ashcroft directed the FBI to use "'every available law enforcement tool' to arrest persons who 'participated in, or lend support to, terrorist activities.'"[8] By November 2001, law enforcement officials had detained "more than 1,200" people, including 762 foreigners.[9]

As they rounded up men and boys, Steven Watt had just begun a post–master of laws (LLM) internship at Center for Constitutional Rights. "It was two days after the President's military order had been handed down, which was the formal recognition that the President can pick up anyone he deems to be a member of Al Qaeda or an associate of Al Qaeda, [arguing] 'I can do basically whatever I choose to do with them as the commander in chief,'" explained Watt. "That was two days before I arrived."[10]

Overcoming the secrecy, the "real lack of information," required physically going to the jails, Watt said. "People were being secreted away in the middle of the night, that kind of thing. Also, they [the detained] did not have proper documentation, so therefore the law then, as it does now, would allow authorities to pick them up. But they were picking them up on pretextual reasons. They had suspicions they were involved in 9/11."[11]

A Pakistani father of four, Syed Amjad Ali Jaffri, was among those arrested, detained in "unduly harsh conditions" in which corrections officers beat, kicked, and slammed detainees into walls, and eventually released them without charge.[12] Jaffri fainted from the abuses, according to the complaint filed by CCR lawyer Barbara Oshansky, Paul Hoffman, and David Cole.[13]

A lawsuit filed in April 2002, *Turkmen v. Ashcroft*, named Jaffri as one of three plaintiffs[14] but represented a class of post-9/11 Arab, Muslim, and South Asian men detained and abused in Brooklyn's Metropolitan Detention Center and Passaic County Jail against US officials, including Ashcroft and FBI director Robert Mueller. They asked for a jury trial, declaratory relief, "fair, just, reasonable" compensation, and other appropriate remedies.[15]

A year later (April 2003), the Department of Justice's Office of the Inspector General revealed that Jaffri's experience was not unusual: "Almost all of the detainees in one facility were slammed against the walls." The "pattern of abuse" included verbal and physical attacks, causing extreme pain, and "handling them in other rough and inappropriate ways."[16]

The Inspector General's investigation enabled human rights lawyers to discover and name the jail's corrections officers as defendants. It may have also prompted two additional victims—Egyptian citizen Ehab Elmaghraby and Pakistani citizen Jafaid Iqbal—to bring an action in 2004. Officers had kicked, punched, dragged, slammed, and raped Elmaghraby with objects including a flashlight and a pencil, causing bleeding at least once, according to his complaint.[17]

Represented by New York nonprofit Urban Justice Center's Haeyoung Yoon and New York-based prisoners' rights lawyer Alexander Reinert, Elmaghraby and Iqbal sued dozens of US officials for "brutal mistreatment and discrimination"—excessive force, daily strip searches, repeated body cavity searches, prolonged solitary confinement, and "denial of medical treatment . . . adequate nutrition . . . [and] exercise."[18] Their basis for the suit was federal, constitutional, and international law violations, the ATS as jurisdiction for aliens, and a common law known by its case name, *Bivens*,[19] which enabled victims of Fourth Amendment rights[20] violations to recover damages from federal officials.

The officials moved for dismissal, claiming immunity from civil liability and emphasizing heightened security needs arising from the September 11 attacks. But the court proceeded with claims for offenses that "flagrantly violated our Constitution."[21]

One plaintiff, Elmaghraby, accepted the government's offer of $300,000 compensation.[22] While Iqbal and the remaining plaintiffs pressed their civil action, the Department of Justice pursued criminal charges against individual corrections officers, ultimately convicting ten guards for attacking, inflicting pain, falsifying statements, and compromising "the integrity and safety of the detention facility, other inmates, and their fellow employees."[23] The officers "repeatedly struck, kicked and beat the inmate, leaving a pool of blood and clumps of the inmate's dreadlocks on the floor of the cell," then attempted to hide their crime by "tying inmate's bedsheet into a noose and wrapping it around the bars of the cell's window . . . to make it appear that the inmate had tried to hang himself," according to the department's report.[24]

Both district and appellate courts advanced the civil claims. But the executive official defendants, including Ashcroft and Mueller, petitioned the Supreme Court, claiming immunity from civil action and absence of personal involvement. The high court focused on the latter issue, asking, Should executive level officials be held responsible for abuses committed by lower level employees?

Yes, argued Iqbal's lawyer, Reinert, calling Ashcroft the "principal architect" of the policy and Mueller "instrumental" in its execution. They "'designed,' 'approved,' 'condoned,' and 'agreed'" with the discriminatory and abusive policy, he said, citing[25] the Inspector General's investigation: "Direction to make conditions of confinement as harsh as possible" came from the "Attorney General's Office."[26]

No, responded the government's acting solicitor general, Gregory Garre. The abuses and discrimination were "lower level" decisions made with "an ad hoc criteria [*sic*]," he said, adding that Iqbal had failed to demonstrate the executive officials' "personal involvement."[27]

More "liberal" justices, such as David Souter, observed "close involvement of the Attorney General and FBI director," while "conservatives," such as Antonin Scalia, saw none, remarking, "I don't know on what basis any of these allegations against the high-level officials are made."[28] Relying on a 2007 case, *Bell Atlantic v. Twombly*, the majority reversed the circuit courts' decisions to proceed: Iqbal had not shown "plausible entitlement to relief" or "invidious discrimination . . . Purposeful discrimination requires more than intent,"[29] it said before sending the case back to the Second Circuit Court to decide if Iqbal could "amend his deficient complaint."[30]

Iqbal instead accepted the government's settlement offer of a "substantial sum of money."[31] Five plaintiffs in the CCR-filed case settled for $1.26 million divided between them.[32] But CCR lawyers continued with additional plaintiffs and details about Ashcroft's and Mueller's involvement: "Ashcroft told Mueller to vigorously question any male between 18 and 40 from a Middle Eastern country . . . and to tell the INS to round up every immigration violator who fit that profile," said the amended complaint. "Both men were aware that this would result in the arrest of many individuals about whom they had no information to connect to terrorism. Mueller expressed reservations but nevertheless knowingly joined Ashcroft in creating and implementing a policy that targeted innocent Muslims and Arabs."[33]

Back in district court, the government repeated immunity claims as grounds for dismissal. Based on the high court's heightened pleading standards, Judge John Gleason dismissed claims against the executive officials, but allowed the remainder to proceed. The Second Circuit's two-judge panel disagreed. Through staff briefings, media coverage, the Inspector General's report, and concerns raised by other departments, Ashcroft had understood and "affirmatively supported" the conditions and discrimination, it said.[34] Prison officials were told to "take policies to their legal limit."[35] Clearing the plausibility hurdle, the panel reversed.

The defendants appealed, first for an en banc Circuit Court hearing, and upon rejection, to the Supreme Court, which consolidated and renamed related cases *Ziglar v. Abassi*. Based upon separation of powers, the 4–2[36] opinion granted immunity for the executive officials in the conspiracy claims, arguing that "national security" policy "is the prerogative of the Congress and President" with exceptions—incompetence or knowingly violating the law.[37] The case against the remaining defendants was pending at the time of this writing.

Rectifying violations beyond US borders proved more difficult than those occurring stateside. After the September 11 attacks, the CIA intensified its rendition program,[38] rounding up and rendering at least 119 men into overseas black sites. At least 26 were innocent, according to a Senate investigation,[39] and most were never charged with a crime, according to Gallagher.[40] But the Bush administration had argued that their rights ended at US borders, applying neither to the torture victims in either CIA black sites nor to Guantánamo Bay.

Through human rights advocacy networks, information trickled through to human rights lawyers, who began the quest for fair trials and redress for victims of the "war on terror." One of those victims was a Canadian telecommunications engineer, Maher Arar.

Extraordinary Rendition

On September 26, 2002, after a holiday in Tunisia, Arar stopped to change planes at New York's John F. Kennedy Airport. Based on information from Canadian law enforcement falsely identifying Arar as an Al Qaeda affiliate, US officials arrested, interrogated, strip-searched, and detained him, according to court records.[41] A lawyer who had been in the Metropolitan Detention Center "heard about a Canadian of Syrian descent" who "they are thinking of sending . . . to Syria," recalled Watt. "They just called CCR and got me."[42]

Watt began making calls in hopes of stopping the rendition. Human rights lawyer Judith Brown Chomsky "just happened to be up in Montreal," he recalled. They "tracked down [Arar's] brother and wife, who was in Tunisia," to draft a "next friend" habeas corpus petition.[43] They were too late, said Amnesty International in London, which "heard from the Canadian embassy in Damascus."[44]

First interrogated and beaten in Jordan, Arar was then taken to Syria.[45] In daily 18-hour sessions, he was interrogated, whipped, hung, battered, electrically shocked, and threatened with the "spine-breaking 'chair,'" according to court records and news reports.[46] Lawyers in both Canada and the US worked alongside Arar's wife, "trying to figure a way to get him out," recalled Watt. When finally returned to Canada without charges, "a whole network" of human rights advocates traveled to Ottawa to "make sure he had all that he needed to transition back," Watt said.[47]

In preparation for meeting Arar, Watt confided in a colleague, "'I had never met with anyone who had actually been physically tortured. How do I deal with that?' And nobody in the office actually had [either]," he recalled.[48] "I felt totally unprepared. . . . I was just going to listen and see if he wanted to share, or if he wanted to do this another time. And, oh my God, he told me the whole story. It was horrible. . . . I had no training. I didn't really know what to expect. The key thing was to have empathy, and that is what I was there for."[49]

With CCR representation, Arar sued US officials, including Ashcroft, Mueller, Ziglar, the secretary of state for homeland security, Tom Ridge, and a series of lower level personnel, in the US District Court for the Eastern District of New York.[50] Using *Bivens*, constitutional claims, and the Torture Victim Protection Act, Arar asked for declaratory relief and compensation for his suffering.[51] "We thought there was a valid claim under the TVPA because the Syrians committed torture under the color of Syrian law, and the US are responsible because they aided and abetted by handing him over. So we believed the US officials could be sued under the TVPA, under the particular circumstances of that case," explained Watt, adding, "It was only as the case progressed that we found out about the CIA's involvement."[52]

Judge David Trager dismissed Arar's case, rejecting the TVPA's application, and called the constitutionality of torture "unresolved from a doctrinal standpoint."[53] This suggestion that torture may be permissible "contravenes the absolute prohibition on torture under any circumstances under international and federal law," explained Gallagher. "This is the cloud that we have been living under, that the terrorism paradigm has opened the door to lawlessness justifying torture."[54] Although Arar had been "detained at JFK airport and rendered from an airport in New Jersey, Judge Trager also found that Arar could not bring constitutional claims [finding that] . . . he had never been in the United States," she added.[55]

Canada apologized and compensated Arar $10.9 million plus legal fees for its role in his "terrible ordeal." But in the US, the Second Circuit Court, en banc, "had no trouble affirming the district court's conclusions . . . that Arar lacks standing to seek declaratory relief" and that civil damage remedies would need to be "created by Congress."[56] US officials, including Secretary of State Condoleezza Rice, admitted to a congressional committee that the US government mishandled Arar's case.[57] But at "the urging of President Obama's Department of Justice and the defendants, the United States Supreme Court declined to review his case," leaving Arar with no redress from the US government.[58]

Meanwhile, the US dragnet landed approximately 780 men and boys into the Guantánamo Bay detention center, approximately 86 percent from the US bounty program.[59] At least 12 were teenagers at their capture, the youngest, 13, the eldest, 89 years old.[60] After initial reticence, scores of private and NGO lawyers gradually joined the battle to secure habeas corpus rights for Guantánamo's detainees.

Guantánamo Captives: Fewer Rights Than a Cuban Iguana

Civil rights lawyer Clive Stafford Smith queried his network of like-minded attorneys about representing Guantánamo detainees. Like Smith, most of his network had represented people facing the death penalty. But only two lawyers "wanted to have anything to do with" Guantánamo victims, he recalled.[61] One was Michael Ratner, president of CCR, and the other, Minnesota-based civil rights lawyer Joseph Margulies, who had long represented the accused, including men and women on death row.[62]

The absence of information about the detainees' identities made representation impossible. It also called into question the US's principles. "What system do you have where a democratic government locks a bunch of people up and won't tell you who they are?," asked Smith rhetorically in an interview.[63]

Information about two British detainees traveled circuitously to US lawyers: the US government told the British government about Shafir Rasul and Asif Iqbal, who were seized in Afghanistan by a warlord collecting reward money for turning in "terror suspects." The British government notified their families, who retained British attorney Gareth Peirce. She phoned CCR.[64]

While Smith, Margulies, and CCR lawyers were at the forefront of Guantánamo's challenges, the US's affront to human rights eventually impelled scores of private lawyers to take up the cause,[65] loosely establishing a "Guantánamo Bay Bar Association" to help secure fair, legal processes for detainees.[66] The first of the "well-heeled, 'white-shoe' lawyers with America's premier corporate firms"[67] was Thomas Wilner of Shearman & Sterling, a firm representing some of the largest corporations in the US.[68] Through a head-hunter in Washington DC, Wilner met and agreed to represent Kuwaiti families who could not find their children, some of whom had been doing charitable work in other Muslim countries. Wilner sought "to change the government's mind. And I thought, to do that, the court was one way to pressure them," he said.[69]

Habeas corpus petitions filed by the NGO lawyers used the ATS as "an alternative basis for jurisdiction," recalled Watt. Wilner, though, preferred a "normal civil action suit . . . instead of the straight habeas corpus complaint" to petition for "basic due process rights—the right, first of all, to have lawyers; to have contact with families; and for a fair hearing that relied on habeas corpus, the essence of which is a fair hearing before an independent tribunal," he explained. "We did not ask for release. We asked for a fair hearing."[70]

Piece by piece and over time, using lawsuits, diplomatic pressure, and as much media attention as they could garner, Wilner, Margulies, Smith, and CCR lawyers thrust the campaign into the public eye. Wilner tapped former US officials, journalists, and diplomatic contacts in efforts to enlist aid. But each effort butted up against a nervous status quo—resistance from the traditional news media, law professors, congressmembers, and pushback from law firm partners, who feared reputational fallout from Wilner's case. Sometimes, they faced a simple stonewall, such as when Wilner persuaded former national security advisor Tony Lake to pen an opinion article that neither the *New York Times* nor the *Washington Post* would print.[71] At other times, they felt the establishment's wrath. During a network broadcast interview, for example, an interviewer asked Smith "thirteen times if I was a traitor, and I said thirteen times, 'No, this is the American tradition of justice. Personally, I think what is going on in Guantánamo is an anathema, and that we will all live to regret it.'"[72]

Post-interview, Smith received threatening calls on his unlisted number. "Someone managed to track down my home number, more than one person," he recalled. "And in the middle of the night, we got this . . . message on the machine saying, 'You're a traitor and we're coming to get you.' There was a whole bunch of this very, very hostile stuff."[73]

Wilner's growing awareness presented personal quandaries: "I would go to cocktail parties, and people would sit around drinking and laughing, and I'd have the sense—I know this seems crazy—but what were people doing in Nazi Germany, as Hitler was coming up? Were they all laughing and drinking as these things were going on? I knew we had people in a fucking concentration camp, innocent people, and we're sitting and drinking."[74]

On July 30, 2002, the lawyers faced their first legal roadblock. The US District of Columbia District Court dismissed with prejudice their consolidated cases—CCR's *Rasul v. Bush*, representing the Britons and an Australian, and Wilner's *Odah v. USA*, representing Kuwaiti nationals. Judge Colleen Kollar-Kotelly rejected the ATS "or any other jurisdictional bases" except the "writ of habeas corpus," concluding that the court "is without jurisdiction to consider the merits of these two cases . . . No court would have jurisdiction to hear these actions."[75]

On appeal, the DC Circuit Court of Appeals affirmed, deciding that aliens "without property or presence in the United States" had no constitutional rights.[76] The last resort, a Supreme Court review, would be tricky. Working with law professors, the lawyers crafted the petition and recruited former judges, diplomats, "military guys," POWs, and the famous Supreme Court petitioner Fred Korematsu, who had brought suit against the Japanese internment during World War II, to submit amicus briefs.[77] On professor Anthony Amsterdam's advice, they added a petitioner, in case the government released their clients beforehand to moot the case.[78]

In Odah's petition, Wilner added a little-known fact about a legally protected lizard. From *60 Minutes'* producers who had visited Cuba, he learned that in most of Cuba, iguanas could become someone's meal.[79] But on Guantánamo, "anyone, including a government official, who harms an iguana . . . can be prosecuted," Wilner explained. "Here the government was arguing that the detainees down there were not protected by US law. But the iguanas were. I put that in the petition for certiorari."[80] It said, "Human beings held prisoner at Guantánamo are not entitled to the same protection as a Cuban iguana."[81]

The iguanas and amicus briefs "clearly had some impact," recalled Wilner.[82] In November 2003, the Supreme Court agreed to hear the case, which ostensibly prompted the release of British citizens Rasul and Iqbal and other detainees.[83]

The iguanas appeared again during oral arguments just after US solicitor general Theodore B. Olson argued that offshore detainees had no legal rights and that the issue was a "political question," dealing with the "territorial sovereign jurisdiction" of Cuba where US law didn't apply and where US courts had no legitimate business.[84]

How could that be? "We even protect the Cuban iguana" there,[85] noted Justice Souter, reminding of US law on the base.

On June 28, 2004, in a 6–3 opinion, the Supreme Court reversed the lower courts' decisions, finding that federal courts had jurisdiction to hear petitioners' habeas corpus challenges to their detention at Guantánamo.[86] It was a small victory for those trapped in a real-world hell, paving a possible pathway for Guantánamo detainees' freedom through US courts. Soon thereafter, scores of public, nonprofit, and private lawyers with a wide range of specialties joined the quest to free the wrongly detained.

To circumvent federal courts, the Bush administration and Congress created alternative adjudicatory systems within the military and forbade federal courts from hearing actions brought by men deemed "enemy combatants." But the Supreme Court struck down as unconstitutional parts of the statute that attempted to strip detainees from impartial hearings.[87]

Gradually, Guantánamo detainees were being released—approximately 740 at this writing. After months or years of incarceration, many left with physical, psychological, and socioeconomic damage.[88] At least nine died in custody, seven ostensibly by suicide.[89] Others attempted suicide but failed. By its own numbers, in 2003, the Department of Defense reported "350 incidents of self-harm" that included hangings and strangling, according to the Associated Press.[90]

Releases without charges suggested that those detainees were not terrorists after all. For their injuries, their lawyers sought compensation. "It would be very nice if they paid the people released at least as much as they paid the bounty hunters for capturing them," Wilner said in the September 13, 2004 edition of *Legal Times*.[91]

CCR, Smith, private lawyers, law professors, and human rights law school clinics began petitioning the courts for reparations from the US government. But while US courts had, for more than two decades, supported redress for tortured noncitizens, the support evaporated when the defendant was the US government.

Smith and CCR recruited a mainstream Washington, DC-based commercial litigator, Eric Lewis from Baach, Robinson & Lewis, to lead the first damages case.[92] A Ronald Reagan Republican who learned constitutional law from conservative judge Robert Bork, Lewis was representing international banks including the World Bank and Abu Dhabi Commercial Bank. But "when Guantánamo Bay was opened and the US government was torturing people . . . a line had been crossed," Lewis said to journalist David Parnell of *Forbes*. "Guantánamo, indefinite detention, and torture present the signature legal and moral challenges of our era."[93]

Lewis agreed to volunteer his legal skills, calling lawyering "a special profession that . . . imposes a special obligation to give back and to try to do justice," he said. "The return of waterboarding and much worse . . . prisoners dying without ever having been charged" create an "obligation to keep up the pressure in the courts."[94]

Representing the "Tipton Three" (from Tipton, England)—Rasul, Iqbal, Ruhal Ahmed, and a fourth detainee who later radicalized, Jamal Al-Harith—Lewis filed *Rasul v. Rumsfeld* with an aim to preserve "an American ideal—the rule of law," he said.[95] "It is un-American to torture people. It is un-American to hold people indefinitely without access to counsel, courts or family. It is un-American to flout international treaty obligations."[96]

Guantánamo's Damage

Rasul v. Rumsfeld: "Can we be sent back to Guantánamo if we fail?" Lewis's clients asked him before he sued.[97] They feared a return to short-shackling, stress positions, humiliation, and bashing with fists, rifle butts, and kicks, according to their complaint and press accounts.[98] Their ATS-based legal action against US Secretary of Defense Donald Rumsfeld and military leaders asked the courts for $10 million each to compensate for the damage and losses arising from their detention and abuse.[99]

The District Court dismissed all except their Religious Freedom Restoration Act claims, and instead of using the ATS, required the plaintiffs to rely on the Federal Tort Claims Act, in which complainants must exhaust remedies, complete with a written denial directly from the responsible agency, prior to court adjudication.[100] It also applied the Westfall Act, which protects government employees from liability when acting within the scopes of their jobs, even if criminality "incidentally" arose while performing "legitimate employment duties."[101]

On appeal, the DC Circuit Court affirmed in part, calling torture "a foreseeable consequence of the military's detention of suspected enemy combatants."[102] It also struck down Religious Freedom Restoration Act claims by stripping the survivors' "personhood." Aliens were not "persons" with constitutional rights for purposes of the statute, said the court.[103]

On the heels of two Supreme Court decisions—granting Guantánamo detainees habeas corpus rights (*Rasul v. Bush*) and striking down the administration's attempt to circumvent the courts (*Boumediene v. Bush*)—Rasul's lawyers tried again. The high court vacated the circuit court's decision, ordering it to reconsider "in light of *Boumediene v. Bush.*" But the Circuit Court reinstated its "judgment but on a more limited basis . . . We do not believe *Boumediene* changes the outcome in *Rasul I.*"[104] The Supreme Court did not revisit the case.

"It is an awful day for the rule of law and common decency when the Supreme Court lets stand such an inhuman decision," declared Lewis. "Future prospective torturers can now draw comfort from this decision. The lower court found that torture is all in a days' work for the Secretary of Defense and senior generals."[105] In a later *New York Times* opinion piece, Lewis juxtaposed two decisions—one granting personhood to corporations, the other stripping personhood from real human beings, asking, "Who are 'we, the people'?"[106]

While Rasul's case moved between courts, CCR lawyers raised another question, in light of the court's ruling. If detainees were violated after being cleared for release, wouldn't that fall outside of the officials' scope of employment? Representing detainees abused after being scheduled for release, the lawyers sued.

Postclearance Torture

Cleared of charges and scheduled for release, Uzbek and Algerian refugees continued enduring "extreme cruelty"—sprayed with gas and burning chemicals, beaten, humiliated, injected, sleep-deprived, isolated in solitary confinement, and forced into stress positions for long periods of time, they said.[107] *Celikgogus v. Rumsfeld*, filed in 2007 by CCR lawyers, sought to compensate them for their injuries.[108]

An Egyptian-born Kabul University teacher, Sami Abdulaziz Al Laithi, similarly abused after being cleared, left Guantánamo wheelchair-bound.[109] Captured by Pakistanis while fleeing bombs in Afghanistan, Al Laithi landed in Guantánamo Bay, where "they stomped my back . . . threw me on the floor, and they lifted me and slammed me back down," he recalled. "Most prisoners had Americans put their fingers up their anuses, but with me, it was far worse—they shoved some object up my rectum. . . . It was very painful . . . I would prefer to be buried alive than continue to receive the treatment I received. At least I would suffer less and die."[110]

These distinct circumstances made no difference to District Court Chief Judge Royce Lamberth. In his February 1, 2013 ruling for the defendants, he said, "Plaintiffs' constitutional claims fail because they are legally indistinguishable from those addressed in *Rasul II*," in which the court affirmed the defendants' qualified immunity and called the victims' constitutional rights not "clearly established."[111]

On appeal, Al Laithi's lawyers raised the distinctions: "For up to two years" after clearing the plaintiffs of "enemy combatant status," US officials "continued to abuse" them, said Russell Cohen, a corporate litigator and co-counsel with CCR's Shayana Kadidal. Because their behavior was "at odds" with their jobs, it nullified any job-based immunity, he said.[112]

The Circuit Court disagreed. The 2–1 panel opinion affirmed Lamberth's decision, arguing that while "the intelligence rationale has dissipated, the need to maintain an orderly detention environment remained after . . . clearance."[113]

Deaths in Guantánamo

Some men died in detention, among them three who had been cleared of charges awaiting release, according to their attorneys:[114] Yasser Al-Zahrani, 22 years old and detained since he was 17; Salah Ali Abdullah Ahmed Al-Salami, 37; and Mani Shaman Al-Utaybi, 30.[115] Rigor mortis suggested they had been dead for two hours when found.[116] On the heels of a wide-spread hunger strike with which detainees demanded humane conditions and to either face trial or be freed, the men were found hanging in their cells.[117] Guards had responded to the strikes by strapping hunger strikers into "force-feeding chairs . . . wrists, ankles, waist, shoulders" and inserting "a tube of eight or ten millimeters . . . up their noses, down their throats, into their stomach[s]," explained former CCR lawyer Pardiss Kebriaei. "That happened to over forty men."[118]

Details about their June 2006 deaths remain murky. Declared suicide, evidence surfaced that cast some doubt on the official account:[119] a medical escort witnessed a Corpsman tie fabric onto a detainee's wrists, fabric that was "not on the detainees [*sic*] wrists when the Camp 1 guards removed the handcuffs a few minutes earlier," she said.[120] Another witness said rags were stuffed down the victims' throats; their hands and feet were tied together. A guard testified that they had neither the means nor the materials with which to kill themselves. Other soldiers and detainees disputed the official account.[121]

When returned to their families, markings on two bodies suggested violence around the time of their deaths. Reports by medical examiner Patrice Mangin and Al-Salami's father said Salami's body bore bruises, signs of chemical burns, and missing organs around his neck.[122] Al-Zahrani's body bore injuries on his chest and face and a missing larynx, according to his legal complaint.[123]

Hopelessness and despair before their deaths were also evident. The youngest, Al-Zahrani, had lamented, "years . . . inside the cages without wrongdoing or crime," and about "large feeding tubes that tore apart the stomach and noses of those who were on hunger strike because of the inserting by force on the 'chairs of torture' . . . [and] 'leaving them chained for long hours in cloth stained by blood, vomit, urine, and more."[124]

Al-Salami had "lost hope," according to medical reports cited in his family's legal complaint. With chronic intense anxiety, dizziness, crying spells, depression, hallucinations, nightmares, and suicidal ideation, he had lost approximately 50 pounds.[125]

Al Utaybi, scheduled for release the day after his death, was reportedly never told of his imminent release, according to his lawyer, Jeff Davis. After reading thousands of pages of documents, Davis remained convinced that his client had committed suicide. His was "far and away one of the most tragic of all the Guantánamo cases," he said.[126]

A corporate defense lawyer, Vietnam veteran and Republican, Davis came to represent Utaybi upon a call from retired lawyer George Daly. Reading about Guantánamo Bay and its legal and moral issues compelled Daly to reenter the fray, but with shaken faith. Long believing "that we're the world's leader when it comes to human rights, . . . that's no longer who we are," he told journalist Mario Kaiser.[127]

Daly persuaded Davis to volunteer for the cause, then called CCR, which was coordinating Guantánamo detainees' representation. CCR paired the duo with Utaybi, for whom they filed a habeas corpus petition. Like other advocates, they were repeatedly blocked from communicating with their clients by the government.[128]

Al-Zahrani's father learned of his son's death from the news media. Knowing the improbability of redress, he and Al-Salami's father sued as "a way of trying to tell the story and get some kind of acknowledgment that a wrong was committed, even publicly, if not by the courts," explained CCR's Kebriaei.[129] "I, like my colleagues at CCR, want to be able to do more and want to be able to offer more than just saying, 'Yes, we can bring a case, but the chances are extremely slim, and your case may not even get reviewed by a court because of these threshold grounds.' Just having the responsibility to be upfront and sort of realistic about that, but saying that to a grieving family who's gotten nothing from the United States government, or the US public for that matter, is just extremely hard for most of them."[130]

For their sons' deaths, the fathers sued Secretary Rumsfeld, 23 named military personnel, and scores of unnamed military staff. Two years after filing, District Court judge Ellen Segal Huvelle dismissed the case based on the defendants' immunity and lack of jurisdiction.[131] On appeal, the DC Circuit Court affirmed the dismissal. That meant no redress for the families of the dead, when the US or its personnel were defendants. Lawyers had yet another question for the courts: Could detainees receive redress if the violations occurred after their detention was declared illegal? That was Abdul Rassak al Janko's circumstance.[132]

Tortured Confessions and Illegal Detention

As a young man, Janko (also spelled Ginco) traveled to Afghanistan where Taliban forces seized and accused him of being an "American spy."[133] With severe beatings, electrical shocks to his toes and ears, starvation, near drowning, and hanging him from the ceiling, the Taliban extracted his "confession," which they broadcast on Arab national television, after which his family disowned him.[134]

When US forces arrived, Janko offered testimony about the Taliban's human rights abuses. But upon discovering the "confession," the US arrested him for international terrorism. First at Kandahar Air Base, then at Guantánamo Bay, Janko endured years of beatings, solitary confinement, sleep deprivation, humiliation, and threats of forced removal of his fingernails, according to his complaint. US officials broadcast another "confession" through traditional US media. Profoundly traumatized, Janko attempted suicide 17 times.[135]

Four years after federal public defender Stephen Sady filed Janko's habeas corpus petition, DC District Court Judge Richard Leon, a George W. Bush appointee, declared Janko's detention illegal, devoid of common sense, and ordered his release.[136] Another year later, on October 5, 2010, four human rights lawyers—Hoffman, Collingsworth, Chomsky, and Jennifer Green of the University of Minnesota Law School—sued Defense Secretary Rumsfeld, his successor, Robert Gates, and a series of officials and unnamed defendants. Despite his earlier declaration that Janko's detention was illegal, Leon dismissed his complaint, based on jurisdiction. The US legal system was not designed to provide remedy for "inevitable tragedies" during war, he said.[137]

Human rights lawyers were largely "stumped as to what to do," admitted Kebriaei. Although habeas corpus rights were hard fought and won, they "ultimately become a meaningless right." The DC Circuit's standards "have so watered-down real fairness and real protection . . . There are dissenting judges on the DC Circuit who said it's a game that's rigged in the government's favor, so it's sort of impossible for the government to lose."[138] With the apparent futility of bringing redress cases to the DC Circuit, human rights lawyers began looking to other circuits, particularly for Adel Hamad's case.

Adel Hamad

Pakistani officials arrested Sudanese humanitarian aid worker Adel Hamad at his home then turned him over to the US. Detained for more than five years in centers including Bagram and Guantánamo, Hamad's physical and psychological trauma, for which he was hospitalized, was compounded by the death of his three-year-old daughter who needed medical care that his family could not afford without his income.[139] Despite an army major's dissent, which called Hamad's detention "unconscionable," a military panel labeled Hamad an enemy combatant.[140]

In the aftermath of *Rasul v. Bush*, Hamad submitted a hand-written plea for trial and found representation with Oregon-based public defenders Steven Wax and William Teesdale. Wax returned from Guantánamo "angry and upset by what I had seen. What our government was telling us was not true," he told the *Oregonian*'s Julie Sullivan.[141] Fact-finding took Wax and Teesdale to Sudan, Afghanistan, and Pakistan, where they collected 20 sworn video testimonies, posted as "Guantánamo Unclassified" on YouTube, and ultimately secured Hamad's freedom.[142] Before his release, Hamad's captors asked if he would "fight us" once free, he recalled at an event of the Center for the Study of Human Rights in the Americas. "I told them, 'I did not fight you to start with, and I won't fight you in the future. But . . . I will fight you by law. And I will try all my life to get my rights from you.'"[143]

Through Wax, Hamad met human rights lawyer and law professor Gwynne Skinner. In 2010, on Hamad's behalf, she sued Secretary Gates and other US officials thought responsible for Hamad's physical and emotional injuries, lost wages, and damaged reputation.[144] But knowing that cases "probably would not survive if they were filed in Washington, DC," Skinner pursued "a location that made sense and was legitimate legally and that we could get outside of Washington, DC," she explained to Julie Sabatier of *Think Out Loud*. "I had lived in Seattle . . . for many years and knew that [Gates] had a connection to Washington state and owned property there. That allowed us what is called a jurisdictional hook to bring the case [there]."[145]

Hamad's lawyers argued that the *Boumediene* decision invalidated Congress's attempt to circumvent US courts for Guantánamo detainees and submitted a sworn statement from retired US Colonel Lawrence B. Wilkerson that said the Bush administration knew that "the vast majority of Guantánamo detainees were innocent."[146] To the *Willamette Lawyer*, Skinner asked, "Don't these men—who were taken out of their homes, who never had a right to due process, whose families became destitute—have a right to a remedy?"[147]

No, said the court. Though District Court judge Marsha Pechman allowed one claim to proceed, the Ninth Circuit Court of Appeals vacated her decision and ordered the case dismissed. The Military Commissions Act had stripped the court's jurisdiction for nonhabeas "enemy combatant" cases, said the panel.[148]

The Ninth Circuit proved another dead end. Procedural grounds prevented all civil actions for the tortured, abused, wrongfully detained, or killed in "the context of 9/11" from reaching their merits, said Kebriaei. With remedies exhausted in US courts for US-based violations, CCR lawyers Watt, Kebriaei, and Baher Azmy explored alternatives—the Inter-American Commission on Human Rights and to private parties involved in the violations. These are discussed in chapter 7.[149]

SIX

Private Military Profits and the Search for Justice

Human rights lawyer Steven Watt felt "terrible," he said. The human rights lawyers' efforts for "war on terror" victims had "blocked any ATS litigation against US officials . . . [and] I feel responsible for that."[1] Courts had shielded the government and its officials from civil liability, based upon "state secrets," immunity, or the separation of powers doctrine, leaving victims without legal recourse for damage to their lives and livelihoods. But meanwhile, the way war was conducted had changed. Relying increasingly on for-profit corporations[2] raised moral dilemmas but simultaneously suggested an alternative pathway for redress.

Already, indefinite detention, privatization, and torture had left lawyers from across the bar rethinking their roles. Corporate defense lawyer Susan Burke was among them. "The decision by our own country . . . to use torture" catalyzed a shift. After representing corporations, such as IBM and Microsoft, she turned her skills toward trying to "stop the government from using torture," she said. "The election of George Bush and the reelection of George Bush profoundly altered my life. . . . In the past, we had been against [torture]. . . . And now, suddenly, we're like embracing it openly as an acceptable public policy. So that was a sea change, a terrible one from my vantage point. And so it was really that sea change that made me view challenging the torture as my patriotic duty. I have to do this."[3]

Turning first to "friends in the human rights community," then to the University of Pennsylvania Law School, Burke and the law students explored "all sorts of legal mechanisms to try to block the use of torture," she said. That's how she met CCR's president Michael Ratner. "We began a brainstorm, trying to use different tools. [For example], could we seek an injunction?"[4]

Michigan-based insurance and personal injury attorney Shereef Akeel made a similar switch. After September 11, 2001, a Yemeni man asked for representation in a workplace discrimination case. While the Yemeni man's firing, based on national origin, outraged Akeel, the experiences of Haidar Muhsin Saleh most "shocked and bewildered" him, galvanizing his turn to full-time human rights law.[5]

Saleh, the two-time survivor of torture in Iraq's notorious prison, Abu Ghraib—first by Saddam Hussein's regime, second by Americans—walked into Akeel's office detailing gruesome experiences that he "could not believe," Akeel recalled to Amanda Aranowski of the *Michigan Lawyers Weekly*. "It didn't make sense. He was told to tie a rope around his genitals, with other men, and then they push on one man. . . . It was so outrageous, but at the same time, how could someone make something like this up?"[6]

Representing Saleh, Akeel filed a claim under the Foreign Military Claims Act. Then another Iraqi family called. "[They] told me they had five [family] members in Abu Ghraib, one of whom died. He was a 63-year-old man who was stripped naked and made to stand out in the cold at night. They put cold water over him, and he was beaten while his son watched. . . . Three days later, he died," Akeel told Aranowski.[7]

Separately, journalists told Watt, then at CCR, about Saleh, as reports of violations in Abu Ghraib began to surface. The Associated Press and Amnesty International reported beatings, burnings, and humiliation.[8] A leak by military reservist Joe Darby prompted military investigations, revealing "sadistic, blatant and wanton criminal abuses" with electrical shocks, bludgeoning with hard objects, sodomy with broomsticks and chemical lights, and dousing with chemicals.[9] Shocking photos in the *New Yorker*, the *Washington Post*, and on *CBS News* displayed piles of naked people, hooded men connected to electrodes, and Americans smiling while inflicting torture and humiliation.[10]

Watt phoned Akeel, suggesting "essentially a winning formula, where we combine resources, in that CCR[11] provides international law expertise, Susan Burke provides financing, complex litigation expertise, and we provide the clients," recalled Akeel.[12]

With the futility of seeking redress from the US government[13] and the ethical dilemmas of privatizing military duties, the lawyers sued two corporations, CACI International, Inc. and Titan Corporation (later called L-3

Services and Engility), their subsidiaries, and individuals retained to translate, interrogate, and guard at Abu Ghraib. In addition to human rights violation claims, "there is a doctrine that says the government should not delegate inherently governmental functions to . . . for-profit parties," said Burke. "From our perspective, questioning and detaining people, those are inherently governmental functions. So there's a lot of reasons why it made sense to us to pursue these corporations."[14]

Representing more than 200 detention and torture survivors, *Saleh v. Titan* used international, federal, and state law, including the ATS, Racketeer Influence and Corrupt Organizations (RICO), the US Constitution, and common law torts to petition for a permanent injunction, declaratory relief, and compensation. Filed in the US District Court for the Southern District of California, they complained of rape, torture, electrical shocks, abuses to genitals, beatings with hard objects (such as guns), humiliation, being urinated on, and forced watching of a parent tortured to death.[15]

The actions against the private military corporations would "expose . . . what happened in that war, maybe even the 'why' of the war. Is it a war for profit? These contractors are for-profit corporations," explained CCR's Katherine Gallagher. "We see what happens when there isn't appropriate oversight . . . when there is a profit-motive driving things, and . . . what happens when there are fuzzy laws around accountability."[16]

A local Iraqi, retained to help locate, screen, and understand the torture victims' language, served as the initial contact point between the lawyers and their class of clients. "People would hear about her, and . . . go to her. She would then do a preliminary screening to ensure that they had been detained and get the dates of the detention and the locations and the like and do a preliminary interview of what had happened to them," explained Burke.[17]

The dangers in Iraq required meeting survivors, doctors, lawyers, local leaders, human rights activists, and witnesses in a third country. With travel expenses underwritten by Burke's law firm,[18] the lawyers flew to Jordan then had victims "driven across in SUVs," recalled Burke. But "that border was shut down, so then we needed to start flying them out, and we met in Istanbul. We did this maybe ten to twelve times. And we would interview groups one by one. . . . It was sobering to directly interview the people on the receiving end of American brutality."[19]

The fact-finding led to a dire realization: "It was not just Abu Ghraib that was involved, but more than 23 detention centers," said Akeel. "There were [also] more than 2,000 photos that had not yet been disclosed."[20]

Hazy divisions of responsibility and hidden identities complicated fact-finding and adjudication. "Sometimes the translators actually did the beating, and in one instance the interpreter raped an individual," explained Akeel to *Michigan Lawyers*. "They would take off their jackets and name tags, so you wouldn't know who it was, and then they would put hoods over the detainees' heads."[21]

Conflicts about the case arose with some of Burke's law partners at Montgomery, McCracken, Walker & Rhoads, prompting her resignation from the firm. Although "the management committee had approved [taking Saleh's case]," opposition among others generated "tension and a lot of strife within the firm. And I felt really bad because they had been a collegial partnership. And then suddenly I bring forward this issue that creates a lot of consternation. So really to avoid tearing that firm apart, I left and I started my own law firm," recalled Burke.[22]

As the first part of what Burke described as "your typical scorched earth litigation," defendants filed a four-pronged response, which as "complex litigation in this country, that is the way it is done," she explained. "Essentially, you [plaintiffs' counsel] have to survive a series of efforts to dismiss you based on various procedural arguments. Then you have to fight about discovery, and you have to move to compel to get the evidence out from the other side. It's just the way that litigation is conducted."[23]

The defense lawyers won forum changes, first to Virginia on the basis of convenience for witnesses, then to Washington, DC, for RICO jurisdiction. They fought using the ATS for claims arising during wartime, called the case a nonjusticiable political question, and the charges "abject falsity." The survivors, they said, were willing to "make up facts, attaching the caveat that such allegations are 'upon information and belief.'"[24]

Beyond the courtroom, the lawyers invited creative artists, including Daniel Heyman, photographer Chris Bartlett, author Nick Flynn, and a playwright, to attend interviews and use their art to convey the survivors' experiences. "We viewed the legal documents as telling the story to the court, but does that really tell the story to the public?" Burke recalled. "We basically told the victims, 'We're here to hear your story and respect the story and bring the story out both in the courts and the public domain, if that's something you're comfortable with.'"[25]

With photos and "some of their words," Bartlett used photography to "restore their dignity," remarked Gallagher. "This photographer has traveled around the United States with his photos, bringing Iraqis' words and faces into communities in Kansas and Iowa and all over, which is pretty amazing."[26]

The unconventional approach prompted the departure of one member of their legal team, ostensibly because it would waive the attorney-client privilege over some interactions between lawyers and their clients, which protects clients' confidentiality, a privilege that Burke thought unnecessary in this case. "Privilege is very important when you are a defense attorney, and you're dealing with somebody's culpability and their wrongdoing. You definitely want to shield that. You want to have frank discussions about that, and you don't want that made public. But here, if you think about it, we were doing something slightly different. We were helping people who had been injured . . . to obtain compensation," she explained.[27]

In 2007, about three years after the initial filing, Judge James Robinson of the District Court for the District of Columbia dismissed claims against Titan/L-3, based upon the company's integration with military units. His logic: "Their duties under the direct command and exclusive operational control of military personnel" meant that they functioned "as soldiers in all but name." CACI, however, "retained significant authority" and could thus be held accountable.[28]

Burke, Akeel, and Gallagher appealed the Titan dismissal, continued the action against CACI, and filed two additional lawsuits, bifurcating the defendants, actions, and courts.[29] "We basically separated out the defendants and opened a second wave of lawsuits with another whole group of victims in Maryland," explained Burke.[30]

Despite similar facts, law, and representation, these three cases against private military corporations—*Saleh*, *Al-Quraishi v. Adel Nakhla*, and *Al Shimari v. CACI*—took markedly different turns. The first, *Saleh* died on appeal. On the eighth anniversary of the 9/11 attacks, two judges, Brett Kavanaugh (now a Supreme Court justice) and Laurence Silberman, voted to dismiss the case, opining that the contractors' integration with the military barred the litigation and that the ATS applied only to state, not private, actors, which shielded corporations.[31] The decision reversed the survivors' district court advance against CACI and solidified their loss against Titan/L-3. "I don't think that date, obviously, was coincidental," remarked Gallagher.[32]

Rejected for an en banc hearing of the entire circuit, the lawyers petitioned the Supreme Court, supported by amicus briefs from law professors, retired military officers, and rights organizations. "Horrific images . . . have left a deep stain on this nation's honor," said the law professors. "The DC Circuit attempted to shield Titan from liability" using a "new federal common law immunity defense that has no basis in any federal statute or Supreme Court decision."[33] Retired military officers added, "Persons engaging in shocking behavior that the US military does not itself tolerate for its own members have broad impunity from accountability."[34]

In its Supreme Court-invited brief, the US solicitor general suggested delaying adjudication to allow the issue to "percolate."[35] The Court denied certiorari. "It was early in the first Obama administration, and we were very disappointed," explained Burke. "We were stuck with the loss. . . . That original group of victims, they did not recover anything. . . . It was really depressing."[36]

Al Quraishi v. Adel Nakhla: The second case, the Maryland-filed *Al Quraishi v. Adel Nakhla,* reached an opposite end. Representing 72 Iraqi survivors, the lawyers sued L-3, its subsidiaries, and Adel Nakhla individually for holding "Al-Quraishi down while a co-conspirator poured feces on him," for piling "naked prisoners . . . on top of each other," and for forcibly holding down "a fourteen-year old boy as his co-conspirator raped the boy by placing a toothbrush in his anus," according to their complaint.[37]

The case survived a series of defense motions to change venues and dismiss, based on claims of immunity, challenges to ATS use, and the plaintiffs' standing.[38] "A defendant can only claim immunity under the laws of war if its actions comport with the laws of war," said Judge Peter Jo Messite. The ATS applied to "actions . . . deemed so repulsive to mankind, or so disconnected from prosecuting and winning a war, that they are universally condemned," and US courts were traditionally "open to nonresident aliens."[39]

A reversal by a Fourth Circuit Court of Appeals panel was reversed again by the entire circuit, which remanded the case to the district court for trial,[40] prompting settlement talks and another unorthodox idea by the survivors' lawyers. "We had the defense counsel from the other side fly with us to the Middle East to meet the victims," recalled Burke. "When you meet these folks that have endured this torture, it's very compelling. I mean, you talk to them through translators, obviously, but I thought that any kind of issues [such as accusations of exaggeration] would just disappear if the defense counsel was given direct access to the victims. And certainly, on our side, we had nothing to hide. We knew these people; we trusted them, and in addition to their testimony, we had various corroborating evidence."[41]

In light of *Saleh's* loss, the lawyers were "pleased [to] . . . get the victims some amount of compensation," said Burke, who negotiated the settlement as the final conclusion of her efforts against torture.[42] The settlement, reportedly $5.28 million, was divided among the 71 victims.[43]

Al-Quraishi's four-year litigation settled relatively quickly compared to its companion case, *Al Shimari v. CACI,* which remains unresolved as of this writing.

Al Shimari v. CACI: On June 30, 2008, four Iraqi torture survivors sued CACI, L-3, their subsidiaries, and interrogator Timothy Dugan, who was identified by a US soldier as a torturer, for electric shocks, taser shots to the head, mock executions, beatings that broke bones, harmed genitals, and damaged vision, or for forced watching of rape, according to their complaint.[44] Originally filed in Ohio, the case moved to the Eastern District of Virginia, after which the survivors' lawyers motioned to dismiss claims against L-3 and Dugan. Depending on the judge—or at one point, the same judge—the courts reached opposite conclusions. For example, early in the case, district court judge Gerald Bruce Lee denied the defendants' motions to dismiss, except for the ATS claims, which he dismissed, then reinstated. That decision was reversed on appeal by a Fourth Circuit Court of Appeals panel, and reversed again by the entire circuit (along with *Al Quraishi*).

A court-invited government brief disputed the contractor's "freedom from trial giving rise to an interlocutory appeal as of right . . . There should be no federal preemption" when "a contractor has committed torture," it said. "The totality of the federal interests . . . does not require that state-law tort suits against contractors be preempted."[45]

Returned to district court, CACI's motions successfully struck the common law claims, then the ATS claims after the *Kiobel v. Royal Dutch Petroleum* decision, which limited ATS applicability in extraterritorial cases (*Kiobel* is discussed in chapters 7 and 8). Reduced to practically nothing, Lee dismissed the case and ordered the four torture victims to pay CACI's legal costs. The Fourth Circuit Court reversed again.

Back in district court, CACI argued that "the military exercised complete control" over its conduct. Lee dismissed again, this time on the "political question" doctrine. In another reversal, the circuit opined, "Conduct by CACI employees that was unlawful when committed is justiciable, irrespective of whether that conduct occurred under the control of the military."[46]

Lee then self-recused. His replacement, Judge Leonie Brinkema, ordered video-link depositions and encouraged the parties to settle. "You've been up to the Fourth Circuit now three times or maybe four times, and each time, it's come back," she said to the defense lawyers. "This is not a pleasant topic, and, you know, it's obviously costing CACI resources and distraction. . . . It would not be unwise to just give some serious thought at this point because there's a lot of litigation ahead of you. There's constant expense. There's [*sic*] still public relations issues."[47]

CACI's lawyers instead motioned to dismiss again, arguing, "We are never going to find out who, if anyone, was . . . on the scene with these plaintiffs, because the United States has a monopoly on that information."[48]

"I'm sorry, but CACI had to have had supervisors on the scene," Brinkema said.[49]

"The government's records identify who the lead interrogator for Mr. Al Shimari was, and it was an employee of CACI," added the survivors' co-counsel Robert LoBue. "We have testimony from the MPs who were ultimately court-martialed that they took their orders from CACI. . . . And we have testimony from our own witnesses."[50]

Again urging settlement, Brinkema assured "the defense . . . we're not dismissing this complaint. It's going to go forward . . . so you have really two options . . . carving out some discovery issues . . . [or] see what you can work out."[51]

CACI instead sued the US government in a third-party complaint, which Brinkema later dismissed.[52] Drawing from military investigations, documents, and corroborated testimony, Brinkema detailed CACI's duties: assisting, supervising, coordinating, and monitoring "all aspects of interrogation activities." Its employees, "the de facto supervisors . . . expressly ordered [military police] to take specific actions to 'soften up,' 'rough up' or 'humiliate' detainees, 'allegedly in preparation for their interrogations.' The MPs at the site believed that they were obligated to follow these orders,"[53] she wrote. "Even after the prisoner abuse became public, and the military conducted multiple investigations, CACI failed to discipline its employees, whom the military determined were involved in the abuse. Instead, CACI . . . cleared its employees . . . refused to remove Johnson from the contract . . . despite the government's request . . . and promoted Stefanowicz . . . to site lead."[54]

CACI again motioned to dismiss, based on a fresh ATS-related Supreme Court decision, *Jesner v. Arab Bank*, which ruled that aliens could not use the ATS to sue foreign corporations in US courts.

Jesner "doesn't even apply to this case . . . That's mixing apples with grapefruit. . . . It's not even close to this case," said Brinkema, again urging a settlement. "My marching orders are to resolve this case."[55]

CACI's lawyers appealed again. Dismissed by the Fourth Circuit, they requested an en banc hearing, which was denied. They petitioned the Supreme Court, which on January 27, 2020, invited the US solicitor general to file a brief. At this writing, the case is unresolved.

In private military corporation–related cases, heightened war-zone dangers constrain collective political action that is sometimes useful in other cases, making "tap[ping] into a movement . . . nearly impossible," said Gallagher. "They [the survivor plaintiffs] are living in a very unsafe place . . . [so] they do not want their profile raised. And being known as plaintiffs in cases against powerful companies might put a target on them."[56]

Neither can they rely on state law claims used in other human rights cases. State laws are preempted when "there is a uniquely federal interest," such as national security, or when laws conflict, she added. "We spent years litigating whether or not our state law claims were viable or whether they implicated the Government Contractor Defense or something about preemption. That was hell. We lost that in the DC circuit."[57]

Meanwhile, Watt left CCR for the ACLU where his search for "a big project" toward ending US-inflicted torture and rendition led him to German citizen Khaled El-Masri (sometimes spelled Khalid Al-Masri), an extraordinary rendition victim.[58] During his holiday in Macedonia, El-Masri was abducted without explanation, then detained, beaten, stripped naked, sodomized, interrogated, and injected with foreign substances, according to his legal complaint and press accounts.[59] On the 37th day of his hunger strike, hooded men forced a feeding tube through his nose into his stomach.[60] Although the CIA and its director, George Tenet, "quickly concluded El-Masri was not a terrorist," the agency continued to detain him "despite the diminishing rationale," according to the agency's inspector general, which called his "prolonged detention . . . unjustified."[61] Upon the order of National Security Advisor Condoleezza Rice, the agency released El-Masri without charge, leaving him in a deserted region of Albania.[62]

Besieged with stigma, ostracization by neighbors, accusations of "terror" by German newspapers, and without rehabilitation, El-Masri's return home was hardly a respite. Watt flew to meet him, asking, in essence, "'What would you like me to do? . . . What can I do to help you?'" Watt recalled. El-Masri wanted an apology, an admission of the wrongs perpetrated on him.[63]

Knowing that action against government officials would "flounder . . . if the government steps in, which it will," Watt and his colleague Ben Wizner decided to "do it nonetheless with a view to changing discourse, with a view to trying to get legislation that would address the state secrets privilege in a way that would be favorable to future lawsuits, but most importantly, for the individuals [who] were impacted."[64]

Fresh information about private and quasi-private companies, "the little planes," changed their legal strategy "to go after extraordinary rendition, to get accountability for men who had been subjected to torture," recalled Watt. Through plane spotters, journalists, and human rights activists, the human rights lawyers pieced together an alternative path for redress.

The Plane-Spotter Revelation

The plane-spotters' (airplane enthusiasts) regular hobby—photographing airplanes— revealed connections between quasi-private airplane companies and CIA renditions: Aero Contractors LTD's identification and flight paths matched El-Masri's rendition route—from Palma de Mallorca to Skopje, Macedonia, then to Baghdad and Kabul.[65]

US-based journalists at the *Washington Post* and the *New York Times* then discovered complicated company structures, "invented" directors and officers, and post office box company addresses, suggesting "front companies" were obfuscating CIA activities. The *Washington Post*'s Dana Priest found 325 names "registered to five post office boxes" and with "no previous addresses, no past or current telephone numbers, no business or corporate records," suggesting a large "roster of false identities."[66] From public records and news and web searches, Priest compiled and reported information about additional renditions, with dates, airplane companies, and tail numbers.[67] The *New York Times* journalists, Scott Shane, Stephen Grey, and Margot Williams, detailed the CIA's 26-plane fleet and seven "shell corporations that appear to have no employees and no function apart from owning the aircraft." The company, Aero Contractors, ostensibly owned the shell-operated plane used to rendition El-Masri.[68]

With no explicit immunity granted to nongovernmental entities, Watt thought, "This is how we get around the sovereignty issue. . . . Go after the corporations that own and operate the aircraft."[69]

Representing El-Masri, on December 6, 2005, Watt, his ACLU colleagues (Ann Beeson, Ben Wizner, Melissa Goodman, Rebecca Glenberg), and Paul Hoffman sued CIA director George Tenet and three companies ostensibly involved in El-Masri's rendition—Premier Executive Transport Services, Keeler and Tate Management, and Aero Contractors Limited. On May 12, 2006, Judge Thomas Ellis of the US District Court for the Eastern District of Virginia agreed with the government, dismissing the case, based on the risks of revealing "state secrets."[70]

The Fourth Circuit Court of Appeals upheld the dismissal, and the Supreme Court declined certiorari. El-Masri's case had reached its end in US courts. His lawyers filed cases in the Interamerican Commission of Human Rights and the European Court of Human Rights, the latter of which ordered Macedonia to pay El-Masri $78,000 for its role in the violations.[71]

The small bit of redress, arriving nearly a decade after his ordeal, ostensibly came too late. "A broken man," according to McClatchy staff writer

Matthew Schofield's report, El-Masri was "broke, unkempt, paranoid, and completely alone." He had "abandoned his home," was "no longer part of the lives of his wife or children; friends can't find him; his attorneys can't find him." His mental instability, marked by bouts of rage-filled violence, landed him back in jail.[72]

The message from the courts appeared to imply that these front companies were off limits. So human rights lawyers looked elsewhere for their clients' redress. "We didn't want to file another case against the front companies because it would have been gotten rid of really quickly," acknowledged Watt. "We were looking for another way to advance these issues, trying to avoid state secrets implications."[73] The necessary information came through another set of journalists from Italy, Sweden, and the US, each uncovering pieces of key data for other rendition victims' cases.

The Private Military Contractors of Rendition

Jane Meyer's 2006 article in the *New Yorker*, "The CIA's Travel Agent," revealed a Boeing subsidiary, Jeppesen International Trip Planning, that "managed flight plans, clearance to fly over other countries, hotel reservations, and ground-crew arrangements" for the CIA's extraordinary rendition program.[74] A completely private company could potentially be held liable in a redress case, circumventing immunity and state secrets defenses, Watt thought.[75]

Steve Shapiro, then ACLU legal director, connected Watt to Italian journalist Claudio Gatti of *Il Sole 24 Ore*. Researching the fates of Italian rendition survivors, Gatti used public records to develop a database. It implicated Jeppesen in the rendition of Watt's clients, Ahmed Agiza and Mohamed el-Zery (sometimes spelled Alzery or Al-Zery). Gatti's December 24, 2001 entry corresponded with the day they "were rendered to Sweden and then from Sweden to Egypt," Watt recalled. Though "[Gatti] had the record, and he said it was a Jeppesen flight," Watt needed verification.[76]

On Gatti's suggestion, Watt pursued records from the Swedish civil aviation authorities, initially turning to a Swedish journalist, asking if Jeppesen was involved in his clients' renditions. "He goes, 'oh, absolutely they were,'" and provided the "evidentiary information" for the complaint.[77]

In May 2007, a team of human rights lawyers—Watt, his ACLU colleagues, Hoffman, Clive Stafford Smith and Zachary Katznelson of UK-based NGO Reprieve, and Yale University's human rights clinic's Hope Metcalf—sued Jeppesen in its home state, California, on behalf of five rendition survivors. *Mohamed et al. v. Jeppesen Dataplan, Inc.* complained of Jeppesen's facilitating "more than 70 secret rendition flights" in which the survivors were "unlawfully apprehended, transported, imprisoned, interrogated, and in some instances, tortured."[78]

The Bush administration intervened, motioning for dismissal, again arguing to protect "state secrets." Judge James Ware of the District Court for the Northern District of California agreed, dismissing the case with prejudice "on the ground that the very subject matter of the case is a state secret," its divulgence potentially harming national security.[79]

By the time the case reached the Ninth Circuit Court of Appeals, Barack Obama had ascended to the presidency. By executive order, the new president had denounced and banned torture, and ordered closure of CIA detention facilities and Guantánamo Bay.[80] But in court the new administration maintained the previous government's position. "The opening words from the presiding judge [to government lawyers] were . . . 'Do you have anything to tell us about a changed government position, perhaps on the state's secrets?' And he says, 'no,' and their position on state secrets was even more encompassing than their predecessor's," Watt recalled.[81]

The Ninth Circuit panel nonetheless sided with the rendition victims, remanding the case to the district court for trial. The matter "is not a state secret because it is not predicated on the existence of a secret agreement between plaintiffs and the Executive, and recognizing that our limited inquiry under Federal Rule of Civil Procedure 12(b)(6) precludes prospective consideration of hypothetical evidence, we reverse and remand," it said.[82] But in an en banc review by the entire circuit, the Obama administration prevailed. Seeking to strike "the difficult balance . . . between fundamental principles of our liberty, including justice, transparency, accountability and national security," the circuit reversed the panel's decision.[83] "We narrowly lost that 6–5," admitted Watt.[84] Denied certiorari by the Supreme Court, the survivors had no further recourse in the US.

Another set of for-profit corporations, including Aegis, Triple Canopy, and Blackwater USA (also called Xe, Academi, and Constellis after it acquired Triple Canopy) were implicated in the unprovoked killing of civilians. Blackwater faced civil and criminal charges for its violations.

Blackwater/Xe/Academi

US taxpayers paid Blackwater approximately $1.6 billion for security in Iraq, according to a 2007 House Committee on Oversight and Government Reform staff memorandum.[85] But government reports suggest the company instigated violence. For example, between 2005 and October 2007, the company was involved in "at least 195 'escalation of force' incidents in Iraq." Blackwater personnel "fired the first shots" in "over 80% of shooting incidents" despite authority to "engage in only defensive use of force."[86] The unprovoked shootings violated private security contractor rules, according to both FBI and Iraq government investigations.[87]

In separate incidents, Blackwater staff reportedly shot dead the bodyguard for Iraq's vice president, a member of the country's Interior Ministry, and 17 civilians, including a nine-year-old child, the latter in a busy section of Iraq called Nisour Square, according to investigations, court records, and press accounts.[88]

"I believe we operated appropriately," said Blackwater CEO Erik Prince to the House committee, adding later, "Accidents happen. . . . People make mistakes; they do stupid things sometimes. . . . Based on everything we know, the Blackwater team acted appropriately while operating in a very complex war zone."[89]

The following year, federal agents raided the company, seized 22 weapons,[90] and later indicted three high-level Blackwater officials for firearms violations, including stockpiling automatic weapons, "straw purchases," and hiding a firearms gift to King Abdullah of Jordan, according to press reports.[91] Separately, four Blackwater guards were convicted for the Nisour Square massacre.[92]

Represented by CCR, Burke, and Akeel, massacre survivors sued Blackwater and Prince for war crimes, assault, battery, wrongful death, and negligence, according to their complaint. Using the ATS, they filed actions in the District Court of the District of Columbia, then moved the case to the Eastern District Court of Virginia.[93] Consolidated with three other actions, the cumulative case, *In re: Xe Services*, represented 64 plaintiffs—45 Iraqi nationals and the estates of 19 who perished.[94]

In addition to the standard corporate defenses, Blackwater's counsel sought to silence the survivors[95] and to invoke the Westfall Act, a statute enabling the government to stand as defendant in place of its employees. Judge T. S. Ellis III denied the motion to enjoin "extrajudicial statements" while the government opposed using Westfall in the case. "Defendants have not shown that they are entitled to demand substitution for the United States as the party defendant in these actions," wrote Assistant US Attorney General Tony West. "Defendants have not come even close to carrying the burden of the current record."[96]

In 2010, the parties settled the case for an undisclosed sum, reportedly

$100,000 per death and between $20,000 and $30,000 per injury, according to the *Los Angeles Times*. While Blackwater was reportedly pleased with the outcome,[97] some plaintiffs complained of pressure to accept less than they desired.[98] Later in the year, Blackwater agreed to fines of approximately $42 million for "hundreds of violations" related to illegal weapons exports, according to the *New York Times*.[99]

Long after the redress case settled, an anonymous Wikipedia post appeared,[100] alleging that Burke had been "sanctioned by a federal judge, Judge Urbina, who handled the criminal [Blackwater] case, who I have never appeared before," recalled Burke. After having the post removed, it reappeared.[101] So Burke sued to reveal the author, claiming defamation, winning in district court. On appeal, her "public figure"[102] status heightened the legal threshold, requiring proof of malice—a difficult task, given anonymity. The reversal meant paying "$400,000 to this rightwing nonprofit [the Center for Individual Rights] that stepped in and represented this anonymous person" under an anti-SLAPP-suit provision, she complained.[103]

Through civil actions against private corporations, some "war on terror" victims were winning bits of redress. But victims of CIA rendition and torture remained un-redressed; their failures left "a bad legacy of bad case law," according to Hoffman, who insisted, "It's not that we like losing cases. It has been suggested to me that I have that wish."[104]

In 2014, years after El-Masri's and Mohamed's cases failed, a Senate Select Committee on Intelligence study shifted the public debate and influenced "judicial discourse," said Watt. The 6,700-page Senate committee report condemned torture, revealed names, and detailed the CIA's interrogations of 119 known detainees. Slammed against walls, hooded, dragged, beaten, and waterboarded to the point of convulsions and vomiting, one detainee became "completely unresponsive with bubbles rising through his open full mouth," said the report. Sleep deprivation for up to 100 hours in standing or forced stress positions with hands shackled above their heads drove five or more men into hallucinations, but the tactics continued. One man, Gul Rahman, died while short-shackled, sleep-deprived, and isolated in extreme cold and darkness with constant loud noise. Others suffered a "series of near drownings," were placed in ice water, or subjected to "rectal rehydration," according to the report.[105] "Existing US law and treaty obligations should have prevented . . . indefinite detention," the "brutal interrogation techniques," and what amounted to "cruel, inhuman and degrading" techniques, said the committee chair, Senator Dianne Feinstein.[106]

The report identified two psychologists who "devised . . . and played a central role in the operation, assessment and management." They "personally conducted interrogations . . . formed a company specifically for the purpose of conducting work with the CIA," after which "the CIA outsourced virtually all aspects of the program," the report said. By their 2009 contract termination, James Elmer Mitchell and John "Bruce" Jessen had reportedly received $81 million of their $180 million contract.[107]

Details of previously secret tactics, an official public rebuke of torture, and newly revealed names of victims and the two psychologists made way for another case of redress: the first successful civil action for CIA torture victims, Suleiman Salim and Mohamed Ahmed Ben Soud, and the family of Rahman, who died dehydrated, hungry, half naked, and restrained to a concrete floor in extreme cold.[108]

Salim v. Mitchell

Watt had known about "Salim for many years," both through his client El-Masri and through a UK-based human rights lawyer, Clara Usiskin. Incarcerated in the "same prison," El-Masri and Salim had spoken "though the wall" and "hatched a business plan," Watt said. "When Khaled was going through a really rough time . . . Suleiman was happy to . . . write a note to him saying, 'I am thinking of you; you will get through this.'"[109]

Seized in 2003 by Kenyan security forces, Salim was renditioned to COBALT, an Afghanistan-based "black site" where he was sodomized, bludgeoned, starved, sleep-deprived, wrapped in ice water, stuffed into a small box, kicked, hung, near drowned, injected with a substance, disoriented with a spinning device, and humiliated, according to his complaint. Eventually transferred to Bagram Air Force Base, Salim endured another four years of detention before being released in 2008 when the US Department of Defense admitted he posed no threat. A newlywed at the time of capture, Salim searched for but never found his wife.[110] Suffering similar treatment, Ben Soud survived, while Rahman died from "hypothermia," according to CIA and coroner's reports.[111]

The Senate report prompted Usiskin to phone Watt, drawing his attention to Salim's name. "I said, 'Do you think he would be interested in being a plaintiff?' And she thought so," recalled Watt. The three met by phone before Watt traveled to Dubai to meet Salim in person. He then met with Ben Soud in Istanbul, because he "couldn't get into Libya."[112]

Both wanted an apology, "an acknowledgement of wrongdoing," said Watt. "They don't care about money; they want acknowledgment."[113]

As a step toward that end, Watt sent each a copy of the Senate report, which "was really moving" for them, he said. Watt and his colleagues would pursue the apology through the "formal legal process, in which you would have an acknowledgment [that] what was done to you was wrong."[114]

In separate calls, Watt and Shapiro phoned Hoffman to discuss a potential case, initially thinking "it might end the same way all the other cases ended," in defeat, admitted Hoffman. But the Senate report suggested a pivot, "a way to . . . actually succeed."[115] Its publicly available documents diminished the need to protect state secrets[116] while the rebuke built a "credible argument," they thought.[117]

The psychologists' respective bases in Washington State and Florida presented a forum decision. Florida offered a more sympathetic jury pool but a less sympathetic circuit, said Hoffman. Spokane, Washington featured "a terrible jury pool but a great circuit" (the Ninth) for human rights.[118] On October 13, 2015, representing Salim, Ben Soud, and Rahman's family, the advocates sued the psychologists in Spokane, "not such a great idea, [but] we thought we'd have a better chance in the Ninth Circuit," Hoffman explained.[119] Their claims included "torture . . . non-consensual experimentation" and "war crimes."[120]

To preempt government intervention, the ACLU appealed to Attorney General Loretta Lynch, arguing, "This case is different. The plaintiffs' allegations are based on officially acknowledged, detailed, public information from official government reports . . . and Defendant Mitchell's own public admissions," thus revealing no state secrets.[121] Ostensibly persuaded, the Department of Justice attended official proceedings, including depositions, to protect undisclosed classified and privileged information, without claiming state secrets nor seeking to protect the defendants.[122]

While the Department of Justice's stand-down ostensibly helped the plaintiffs' case, perhaps "the most important [factor] was that we got assigned to Judge [Justin] Quackenbush," said Hoffman. The 88-year-old judge "only has to answer to his God, and he did not like torture. He had been a naval officer and had been taught that torture was a bad thing. . . . We were lucky [that] we got a judge who wanted [the case] to see the light of day."[123]

Watt agreed. Unlike younger judges who might "get intimidated" by arguments that "the whole security apparatus of this country will come down on your head if you allow this case to go forward," the seasoned judge was "no nonsense . . . a law and order person."[124]

In an early signal, Quackenbush referred to the interrogation tactics as "'torture,'" recalled Watt. When the defense lawyer challenged that, Quackenbush retorted, "'Come on, putting somebody inside a small box for thirty minutes in the dark? That is torture, sorry,'" according to Watt.[125]

The defense's motions to dismiss included arguments that the case "does not belong in this court," that "foreign citizens—improperly bring this action," and that private contractors and agents of the government were "entitled to derivative sovereign immunity." The plaintiffs, they said, were properly detained "enemy combatants,"[126] the Senate report partisan. Denying the motions, Quackenbush refused to allow the case to "become a political trial."[127]

Neither was Quackenbush a pushover for the plaintiffs, challenging their lawyers to furnish evidence that the psychologists had personally supervised or tortured the victims. Aside from evidence about one defendant's role in Rahman's death, ACLU litigator Dror Ladin struggled to show the personal involvement in Salim's or Ben Soud's torture.[128]

The defendants' counsel sought secret documents and testimony from high-level CIA officials, including Gina Haspel (later CIA director), and Directorate of Operations James Cotsana, which the government fought. Without those pieces, his clients were "hamstrung . . . from explaining that they—at all times—acted specifically at the Government's direction," protested defense lawyer Brian Paszamant of Blank Rome.[129]

They also demanded Salim and Ben Soud undergo "highly invasive endoscope and rectal examination"[130] and appear for local depositions. "I got a call from a defense lawyer . . . and he says, 'Would you like to do [depositions] in New York or Philadelphia?,'" recalled Watt. "And I said, 'Well, we have to get visas.' And he went, 'You mean you haven't applied for visas yet?' I had, but I am not telling him [yet]."[131]

Watt had twice tried and failed to gain his clients legal entry into the US, an outcome that the defense lawyers used as another dismissal effort. "They said [to the court], 'We can't depose these guys. We [therefore] want them dismissed from the lawsuit because we have a right to deposition,'" recalled Watt.[132]

In light of "all reasonable efforts" made by the survivors and their counsel, Quackenbush suggested the litigants choose a "mutually agreeable alternative location . . . outside of the United States in a locale where Salim and Ben Soud may perhaps have better success obtaining entry," he said, adding, "The Grand Cayman Islands allow visitors from Tanzania to enter the country without a visa."[133]

Salim, a Tanzanian, had more options than Ben Soud, a Libyan citizen. "They could get into St Vincent or Dominica, and Dominica was slightly closer," explained Watt. But getting both survivors to Dominica, "the only place where we could do it,"[134] was mired by securitization. "Suleiman couldn't get into Dominica because . . . they had to be ticketed [for the entire route] from one country [to the other], because if they stopped, they would have needed a transit visa, and they couldn't get transit visas. So Watt purchased Salim's ticket from Zanzibar to Dominica, but security blocked Salim in Dar es Salaam. Watt bought another ticket, this time routing Salim through Amman and Abu Dhabi. But security again prevented Salim's boarding.[135]

In court, Salim's lawyers pleaded for an alternative venue, eventually settling on South Africa. Watt "pick[ed] him up in Zanzibar, and we flew down together," he recalled. "We went through the airport rapidly because he is dealing with officials, which is very hard for him. He just wanted to get through, and he wanted to make sure he got to South Africa. And of course, I am the foreigner. . . . We eventually got through. [At one point] I lost him, but then he turns up. And I said, 'Where were you?' And he had been in the prayer room."[136]

After Salim's deposition and requisite medical examinations, Hoffman and Watt flew again to Dominica for Ben Soud, who "had to fly from Libya to Dominica twice, and it was horrible. I remember the second time I went to pick him up from the airport in Dominica. . . . He is a nice, affable guy, but he had been traveling for 24 hours, and he had been through immigration, and it is just hell. He doesn't speak English, but he goes, 'Oh it is so hard.'"[137]

Depositions of Mitchell, Jessen, and CIA officials, including Jose Rodriguez, director of the Counter-Terrorism Center, revealed greater details of their roles. Under oath, Rodriguez acknowledged that he had retained the psychologists to interrogate then suspected Al Qaeda leader, Abu Zubaydah (whose alleged leadership is ostensibly unfounded) to "tell us about the pending attacks on the US."[138] Eighty-three episodes of waterboarding left Abu Zubaydah "completely unresponsive, with bubbles rising through his open, full mouth," according to the Senate report. The psychologists defended their actions as "soldiers doing what we were instructed to do," and facing pressure from the CIA to continue "distressing" innocent men, even when they wanted to stop, they said.[139]

In an odd defense, the psychologists' lawyer drew from the Nuremberg exoneration of a technician who helped develop poison gas used to kill Jews. Drawing a parallel, they argued the psychologists only designed the techniques or drafted "guidelines" and "didn't know they were going to be applied at CIA black-site prisons."[140] When "the defendants wanted to stop waterboarding (Abu) Zubaydah, they had to obtain (headquarter's) approval to do so—which was denied," they said.[141]

Unpersuaded, Quackenbush advanced toward trial. The "factual record would support a finding [that] defendants had a role in the design of the program, trained interrogators for the program, and exercised some discretion in the application of the program," he said[142] before urging the litigants to settle:[143] "I speak for the families of the decedent and the plaintiffs. . . . It is in their best interests, and in the government's best interest, to sit down and seriously discuss a resolution to this case."[144]

Watt prepared his clients, "asking these horrible questions over and over again," he recalled.[145] The defendants soon made a "serious settlement offer," added Hoffman. [146]

In long Skype conversations, the plaintiffs expressed "mixed feelings" about their options, particularly "about the media circus, because they wanted to live their lives. One of them wanted the case to be over. Every day it went on was a hurt for him. The other two were feeling less that way," recalled Hoffman. Obaidullah, Rahman family's representative, needed to consult with the rest of his family. "He may have wanted to go to trial, but it is easier for them because they don't have to testify."[147]

The survivors also inquired about the ACLU's preference. While "the lawyers preferred to try the case [particularly for] a better impact . . . it is almost always the case that it's better for the clients to settle," said Hoffman.[148]

In the end, an undisclosed settlement provided "resources that will change their lives . . . And they got a public acknowledgment [although it] was not the greatest," said Hoffman.[149] In their statement, the defendants offered no apology, denied responsibility, consent, knowledge of the violations, and avoided the term "torture": "It is regrettable that Mr. Rahman, Mr. Salim and Mr. Ben Soud suffered the abuse," said the psychologists. "Neither Dr. Mitchell nor I knew about, condoned, participated in, or sanctioned the unauthorized actions that formed the basis for this lawsuit. We served our country at a time when freedom and safety hung in the balance. The actions that we actually participated in were legal and authorized and protected our country from another vicious attack."[150]

Apologies did come but not from the psychologists. Donating their time and service for Mohamed's interviews, the court reporter and videographer "apologized to him on behalf of the US government," recalled Hoffman.[151] The process and closure ostensibly supported the survivors' recovery, particularly for Salim, the more debilitated of the survivors.[152] It may also have advanced the cause by "educating people about US torture," added Hoffman. "Our clients were pretty eloquent about what happened to them and why it was wrong."[153] In their statement, they said, "We brought this case seeking accountability and to help ensure that no one else has to endure torture and abuse, and we feel that we have achieved our goals."[154]

SEVEN

The New Impunity

A $15.5 million compensation settlement in the battle against Royal Dutch Petroleum wouldn't bring back loved ones, restore their indigenous lands, or alleviate the angst from their traumas. But the funds would create programs to help the Wiwas and their fellow plaintiffs rebuild parts of their broken lives. Their win perhaps gave Esther Kiobel hope for her own and fellow survivors' case. Her husband, honorable commissioner and doctor Barinem Kiobel had suffered a fate similar to that of Ken Saro-Wiwa. On May 22, 1994, as one of the "Ogoni 9," Barinem was arrested, tortured, imprisoned, and food-deprived, according to court pleadings. When Esther brought him food, guards seized, stripped, and beat her with a high-tension wire before imprisoning her, her complaint said.[1] A year later, Barinem was hanged.[2] Her coplaintiffs and their families suffered from beatings, whippings, chemicals, and harsh incarcerations.[3] Kiobel fled with her seven children to nearby Benin Republic, then to the US, where she received asylum status. On May 14, 2004, she sued the oil corporation for its role in her husband's death, human rights abuses in Ogoniland, and the destruction of their homeland.[4]

Judge Kimba Wood, who had adjudicated the related *Wiwa v. Royal Dutch Petroleum*, permitted three charges to advance—aiding and abetting torture, crimes against humanity, and arbitrary detention—and dismissed the rest. She then certified her order for interlocutory appeal to the Second Circuit Court of Appeals, which considered a different question: Could aliens sue corporations using the Alien Tort Statute?[5]

In a two-judge decision, the Second Circuit lamented, "Once again we consider a case brought under the Alien Tort Statute" and complained about the "abundance of litigation" under the ATS. Sidestepping the merits of the case, they opined that by its silence, the ATS excluded corporate liability cases because corporate liability, they said, was grounded in domestic law, while the ATS granted jurisdiction based on international law. Recognizing corporate liability in human rights cases, they argued, would create a new norm of "customary international law."[6]

The decision suggested two legal standards for corporate human rights violations: they could be held accountable for human rights violations within US borders but not for violations abroad. An already limited legal toolbox for overseas victims of corporate-connected human rights abuses grew narrower in the Second Circuit's jurisdiction.

On appeal, the US Supreme Court held two sets of oral arguments. The February 28, 2012 hearing on corporate liability divided justices along ideological lines. Fearing greater numbers of lawsuits against corporations, "conservative" justices argued that international law did not apply to corporations, as it did to individuals or states. "Under international law, it is critically pertinent who's undertaking the conduct," said Chief Justice John Roberts. "If an individual private group seizes a ship, it's piracy. If the navy does it, it's not. Governmental torture violates international norms. Private conduct does not."[7]

"Liberal" justices could not justify what seemed like a new impunity. International law applied to all entities, whether or not they were specified, they said. "Do you think in the 18th century, if they'd brought Pirates, Incorporated, and we get all their gold, and Blackbeard gets up and he says, 'oh, it isn't me; it's the corporation,' do you think that they would have then said: 'Oh, I see, it's a corporation. Good-bye. Go home?'" asked Justice Stephen Breyer.[8]

Added Justice Elena Kagan: "It's as if somebody came and said, you know, this—this norm of international law does not apply to Norwegians . . . [because] There's no case about Norwegian . . . it doesn't specifically say 'Norwegians.' But, of course, it applies to Norwegians because it prevents everybody from committing a certain kind of act."[9]

The US deputy solicitor general, Edwin Kneedler, agreed with Kagan, adding three points: the ATS specifies only the plaintiff's alien status, remaining silent about defendants; international law prohibits human rights violations, leaving enforcement to individual nations; no independent prohibition exists in either international or domestic law against suing corporations. Kneedler concluded by providing historical evidence supporting the recognition of corporate liability under the ATS.[10]

The second theme—distinguishing civil from criminal law—also divided the justices. Conservative justices agreed with the oil companies' counsel, Kathleen Sullivan, who argued that corporations were intentionally excluded from International Criminal Court rules and that no customary international law holds corporations liable for human rights offenses.[11]

But criminal law did not apply to the case, argued Hoffman, Kiobel's counsel. Kiobel's case was grounded in civil law, a "more expansive" body than criminal law.[12]

It was the third theme—extraterritoriality—that set a new and difficult precedent for atrocity survivors. The "curve ball," hurled by Justice Anthony Kennedy, came soon after Hoffman's opening statement. Ostensibly drawing from defense-side amicus briefs, Kennedy asserted, "No other nation in the world permits its court to exercise universal civil jurisdiction over alleged extraterritorial human rights abuses to which the nation has no connection."[13]

Not true, said Hoffman. From its inception, the US and other countries, including the UK and the Netherlands, imposed both civil and criminal remedies for corporate human rights violations, he said.[14]

Justice Samuel Alito challenged the court's jurisdiction. "There's no particular connection between the events here and the United States." The ATS's intent, he said, was to "prevent international tension . . . Do you really think the first Congress wanted victims of the French Revolution to be able to sue . . . French defendants in the courts of the United States?"[15]

Yes, Hoffman replied. The statute was "an expression of the Nation's commitment to international law" and to avoid "giving . . . safe haven to torturers and others," he said. "The Founders . . . believed that [the ATS] would be extraterritorial," a premise decided in the precedent-setting *Sosa v. Alvarez-Machain*.[16]

In rearguments held the following October, Justice Scalia established his position: "I believe strongly in the presumption against extraterritorial application," he said. "Why does this case belong in the courts of the United States when it has nothing to do with the United States other than the fact that a subsidiary of the defendant has a big operation here?"[17]

To the oil company's counsel, Justice Kennedy asked, "Is there any way in which we can use the principle of extraterritoriality to rule in your favor?"[18]

"We think there is," she replied. "We think the principle of extraterritoriality is . . . essentially a democracy-forcing device to send these questions back to Congress."[19]

Liberal justices sought legal nuances about how the case fits with precedents, such as *Filártiga*, *Marcos*, and *Sosa*, asking was Royal Dutch Petroleum asking the court to overturn precedents?

Perhaps the reversal from the US solicitor general's office helped persuade the court. Initially favoring Kiobel, this time Solicitor General Donald Verrilli argued for the defendant, making three distinctions between the current case and precedent: an indirect violation—aiding and abetting—differed from direct violations such as torture; the defendant—a corporation—not an individual; potential friction "with foreign governments . . . In subjecting a foreign sovereign's acts to scrutiny in the United States . . . the risk of reciprocal exposure to American companies would also exist."[20]

Corporate cases deserved additional consideration, such as the "strength of the interests of the United States, the foreign relations interests of the United States . . . to avoid undermining the credibility [of the US]," added Verrilli. "The views of the State Department do deserve deference."[21]

While Justice Sonia Sotomayor had "trouble with this," she ultimately signed on to the decision favoring Royal Dutch Petroleum. So did Justice Elena Kagan, who had noted, "We gave a stamp of approval to Filártiga" and quoted from its decision: "'For purposes of civil liability, the torturer has become like the pirate and slave trader before him, an enemy of all mankind.'"[22]

In ruling for Royal Dutch Petroleum, the Supreme Court reduced the ATS's jurisdiction to cases that "touch and concern" the US with "sufficient force" to outweigh a "presumption against extraterritoriality." The new legal boundary, loosely following the country's physical border, would "protect against . . . unintended clashes between our laws and those of other nations, which could result in international discord" and against "unwarranted judicial interference in the conduct of foreign policy."[23]

For Kiobel and survivors like her, another door to justice had closed. "There are going to be very few ATS cases against anybody because all of the Filártiga type of cases were extraterritorial. Nobody's going to bring [them] under the ATS," predicted Hoffman. "Realistically, why would you spend enormous time and money and everything on a case that has low chances?"[24]

Collingsworth agreed, admitting his own reticence. "For a small human rights organization like mine, the ducks have to be pretty much in a row now for us to say, 'Yeah, we'll go out on that limb,'" he said.[25]

Together with the TVPA case, *Mohamed v. Palestinian Authority*, which limited the TVPA's application to "natural persons," thus excluding corporations or other entities, the *Kiobel* decision dealt a crushing blow to human rights advocates' hopes to expand the statute's reach. "[We] really were salivating over how much we could do with this statute, and instead, now we're hunkered down to try to hang on to just a couple of claims and prove that there's enough connection to the US to survive," admitted Terrence Collingsworth, who blames the development on the presidency. "We were changing the law in a positive way until [George W.] Bush was elected and really had a huge impact on the Supreme Court and the Courts of Appeals. So, like it or not, we're now changing the law in a negative way."[26]

The decisions' effects created a legal void for redress, according to human rights lawyer Agnieszka Fryszman. "They can't get jurisdiction over these companies in their own country, right? There's no jurisdiction [for example] in Nepal over [the private contractor] KBR. There's no jurisdiction in Jordan over KBR, right? The only place you can bring suit is here [in the US], which is why that extraterritoriality jurisprudence is so frustrating and so one-sided. Like, you can't sue them here. You can't sue them there. Is that it? There's no place in the world where you can bring them to justice? That surely can't be right," she said.[27]

It isn't right, according to international law, which mandates remedies for human rights abuses.[28] In 2011, the United Nations adopted its Guiding Principles on Business and Human Rights, which calls upon corporations to prevent and remedy human rights violations and upon states to protect and redress. It also recognized the "need for greater access to effective remedy."[29]

But neither law nor principle is meaningful without the will and structures to enforce them. In the US, the legal landscape "looks pretty bleak," remarked Cindy Cohn of the Electronic Frontier Foundation. "Judges across the board are getting trickier and trickier about standing, jurisdiction, and all of these procedural hurdles to justice. . . . I think it's going to cheapen and darken the judiciary, which was kind of a shining star of fairness."[30]

The decisions portended a shift in the role human rights lawyers see for themselves. "It would break my heart if we were not able . . . to give the world, as a society that has a well-functioning judicial system, the ability for people to use that system, when the companies, the people who they're trying to get justice from, are legitimately in the jurisdiction of the United States," Cohn added. "I get that we can't decide all the world's problems, but [for] a pretty good chunk of human rights problems, there is enough of a link to the United States that our courts ought to be able to decide them."[31]

Some lawyers, including Morton Sklar, EarthRights's general counsel

Marco Simons, and Judith Brown Chomsky, remain unfazed. "There are virtually no cases that you could file under the Alien Tort Statute that you can't file without it," said Simons. "It has been a feature of Anglo-American law since the 18th century that if the defendant is present in the court's jurisdiction, you can sue that defendant for wrongs that they have committed anywhere in the world. . . . That has been a feature of the common law. We don't need a statute to let us do that."[32]

Overreliance on the ATS and common law has long been criticized by Sklar. "You have to go beyond that and find some new ground . . . find new approaches that will do the same thing," he argued, suggesting, for example, using terrorism laws and electronic communication laws to pursue government violators.[33] But even in ATS cases, Sklar emphasized ways to demonstrate local involvement, such in his case, *Wang Xiaoning v. Yahoo!* His group "point[ed] to involvement by the US headquarters of Yahoo! so as to overcome the argument of the Yahoo! lawyers that only the Chinese affiliate (Yahoo! China, later Alibaba) could be held responsible," he recalled. "The involvement, and basis for holding Yahoo! USA responsible, was that the General Counsel of Yahoo! here in California . . . was actually the official who decided that the Internet user information on the Chinese dissidents should be revealed to security officials in China. So the decision to provide this user information came from US headquarters, directly involving the US company. Congress found that he . . . lied about this in his testimony to them, and this added to the pressures for Yahoo! to settle the case."[34]

Alternative strategies are under way, according to Chomsky: "We're just changing techniques. I think as long as US corporations are involved in human rights violations, and as long as the US is a haven for . . . perpetrators of human rights violations, we will still be finding ways to bring them to justice, even though it may not be the ATS," she said, stressing the importance of corporate lawsuits for human rights. "The wrongdoers in individual cases, other people will take their place, and you haven't advanced human rights in any significant way. Whereas if corporations can be convinced that they can't do that, it has a much greater effect. It affects other corporations and of course, the [defendant] corporation. Shell in Nigeria is more powerful than Nigeria. Its income is more than the GDP of Nigeria."[35]

In *Doe v. ExxonMobil*, common law provided the discovery leverage to advance the case with the ATS. Representing survivors of torture and massacres in Aceh, Indonesia against one of the world's largest corporations, lawyers have been litigating for approximately 19 years at this writing.

Doe v. Exxon

Caught between a separatist movement and an oppressive government, residents of Aceh lived amid violence, oppression, poverty, and the effects of the oil and gas industry, which generated approximately $1 billion in Indonesia's annual revenue.[36] There, in the noisy, smoky "petro-city" Lhok Seumawe sits an infamous building known by local residents as a rape, torture, and execution center, where victims suffered electric shocks, bludgeoning, genital mutilation, and immersions in fetid water, according to the survivors' complaint and human rights reports. Indonesian soldiers who had raped, tortured, and burned down homes found security jobs with Mobil Oil, continuing the torture and torching homes while on the corporation's payroll, according to scholarship.[37] Mobil's equipment dug mass graves; its facilities served as torture sites; its money paid soldiers' salaries.[38]

In 2001, 11 survivors (later 15) sued then-merged ExxonMobil in the District Court of the District of Columbia, complaining of assault, battery, wrongful death, arbitrary arrest, detention, false imprisonment, intentional infliction of emotional distress, and negligence. Through its subsidiaries and "agents," ExxonMobil "acted with the intent to cause injury and actually did cause injury, damage, loss and harm," they claimed.[39]

Denying its role in "alleged human rights abuses by security forces in Aceh," the corporation motioned to dismiss using standard corporate defenses: jurisdiction, ATS and TVPA-application, nonjusticiability, statutes of limitations, and forum non conveniens.[40] A year later, on Judge Louis Oberdorfer's invitation, the US State Department submitted a brief, advising against adjudication, based upon risking "potentially serious adverse impact on significant interests of the United States . . . including against international terrorism." An attached Indonesian ambassador's submission asserted that Indonesia "cannot accept the extra-territorial jurisdiction of a United States court over an allegation against an Indonesian government institution eq [*sic*] the Indonesian military."[41]

Ostensibly striking a balance between judicial independence and deference to the government, three years later Oberdorfer dismissed federal claims—the ATS, the TVPA, and Violence Against Women Act—but advanced the case based on state common law[42] with "enough evidence under DC state law to prove battery, assault and negligent supervision," recalled Doe's co-counsel Fryszman.[43] The decision enabled discovery but under tight restrictions to prevent "interfering in Indonesian affairs" or "intrusion into Indonesian sovereignty." Any discovery in Indonesia would require the country's authorization.[44]

ExxonMobil appealed, seeking to dismiss Doe's remaining common law claims, calling them nonjusticiable political questions.[45] But the circuit court disagreed: "Exxon has not established that the political question doctrine confers a 'right not to stand trial,'" said the two-judge circuit court panel. "It would create a bizarre anomaly to immunize corporations from liability for the conduct of their agents in lawsuits brought for 'shockingly egregious violations of universally recognized principles of international law.' . . . The law of the United States has been uniform since its founding that corporations can be held liable for the torts committed by their agents. This is confirmed in international practice, both in treaties and in legal systems throughout the world."[46]

Asserting that the decision "threatens to unleash a flood of litigation in US courts for actions lacking any salient connection to the United States" that "vastly expanded" the ATS, and affected the US's foreign policy interests, ExxonMobil's counsel, O'Melveny & Myers's Sri Srinivasan (now chief judge in the Court of Appeals, District of Columbia Circuit), petitioned for an en banc, then a Supreme Court review.[47] The Supreme Court denied certiorari.[48]

Back in the district court, a more conservative Judge Royce Lamberth replaced the retiring Oberdorfer and dismissed the case, opining that nonresident aliens had no standing.[49] The circuit court panel reversed his decision, opining that aliens' standing and "aiding and abetting" were "well-established" in the ATS.[50] But in agreement with Exxon, the panel decided, "Indonesian law ought to apply."[51] The lone dissenter, Judge Brett Kavanaugh (now a Supreme Court Justice), argued that corporations were excluded from corporate liability and that the case could harm US-Indonesian relations,[52] arguments that would reappear in future corporate defenses. The survivors' lawyers had "to do it all over again under Indonesian law," recalled Fryszman, who remained untroubled. "Negligence laws are the same everywhere. There's really no difference between DC and [Indonesia] because it's [Indonesia's law] based on the Dutch law."[53]

Publicly, Exxon's counsel Patrick McGinn said, "the plaintiff's claims are without merit . . . ExxonMobil has worked for generations to improve the quality of life in Aceh through employment of local workers, provision of health services, and extensive community investment. . . . The company strongly condemns human rights violations in any form."[54] Yet, in court, ExxonMobil's primary strategy was avoiding the case's merits,[55] according to Fryszman. "Exxon is barraging us with crazy motions because they have the money to file them," she said. That included motions to dismiss based on the survivors' visa restrictions.[56] "[They] tried to get our case dismissed on the grounds that our clients couldn't get visas to come to the United

States, which could hardly be a surprise, given that they are indigent villagers from an area of restive Muslim insurgencies. There's just no chance of them getting a visa either before or after the Muslim ban."[57]

The company also accused the survivors' co-counsel Collingsworth of impropriety,[58] again turning attention away from the case's facts and draining time from Doe's counsel to respond.[59] Its key lever, however, came in 2013. After *Kiobel*, the appellate court vacated its ruling and remanded the case to Lamberth. By this time, however, evidence had revealed the local connection: ExxonMobil "made all the decisions in the United States," recalled Fryszman.[60] That evidence took "twelve years of [discovery] . . . under state law . . . I don't know that I would've gotten over that hurdle [without them]. . . . How would I have known that they made all those decisions in the United States? I only knew that because we had all that discovery on those other [state] claims."[61]

Despite Lamberth's previous dismissal, the foreign policy implications, the country's changing ideology, a powerful defendant, and the new *Kiobel* standard, Lamberth granted the Acehnese survivors a trial, though with fewer claims and one less defendant (Exxon Mobil of Indonesia). The company's local "planning and authorizing the location of deployments . . . placed military security in proximity and in contact with local community" and ordered supplies "used to violate international law," ultimately passing the "touch and concern" test created by the *Kiobel* precedent.[62]

With the ATS claims returned, "we were actually better off legally," said Fryszman. "We had the Alien Tort Statute claims [again], but we were going under Indonesian law. So that's a case that's now under three different bodies of law, first DC state tort law and now Indonesian law."[63]

To "put an end to the pain," plaintiffs requested a 2018 trial date, said Fryszman. "Until we get a trial date, all we're going to do is spend all our time answering progressively more crazy motions."[64] After 19 years of litigation, the Acehnese survivors were still awaiting trial as of this writing.

Kiobel also affected Colombian survivors of paramilitary torture and massacres. After the ruling, the Eleventh Circuit Court of Appeals ended the survivors' redress case against a US corporation, Chiquita Brands International. But human rights lawyers continued their pursuit of redress in part by naming the individual executives who made the deadly decisions.

Deadly Bananas

In Colombia, the lengthiest armed conflict in the Western Hemisphere[65] took more than 220,000 lives, of which 80 percent were civilian,[66] and displaced more than 4.5 million people. Thousands were abducted, tortured, or disappeared.[67] Known for quartering people with chainsaws, cutting off tongues and testicles, and pouring battery acid down people's throats, the paramilitary organization Autodefensas Unidas Campesinas (AUC) admitted to killing more than 50,000 civilians, many by torture.[68] Their prime targets in Colombia's banana-growing regions were union members, according to *Colombia Reports*.[69] In 2001, the US officially designated the AUC a "foreign terrorist organization," making it a crime to do business with its members.[70]

A local labor union leader, John Doe 9[71] had supported his family by working at Chiquita's Colombian banana plantation. In July 1997, Doe 9's motorcycle ride was forcibly stopped by the AUC. Its members tortured, decapitated, and dismembered him, a crime for which a member has confessed, according to his survivors' legal complaint.[72] John Doe 10, an independent banana cooperative leader, was abducted and found dead with six bullet wounds. Four fellow coop members suffered similar fates.[73] In another incident, paramilitary members appeared at a banana farm, located their victim, "cut off his head with a machete, dumped the weapon, then calmly . . . drove off without saying a word," recalled a witness to Sibylla Brodzinsky of the *Christian Science Monitor*.[74]

Through illicit drug trade money and corporate funding, the AUC's power grew. One of its funders, Chiquita had channeled $1.7 million to the paramilitary group through "various intermediaries," including the company's Colombian subsidiary, Banadex, and government-licensed "neighborhood watch" groups known as Convivirs. Marked "security services," the payments ostensibly helped suppress union organizing, social protest, or restiveness on banana plantations.[75]

In 1998, two *Cincinnati Enquirer* journalists, Mike Gallagher and Cameron McWhirter, published an exposé on Chiquita, detailing cocaine smuggling, bribery, brute force, decimated villages, deadly substances, and murder on the corporation's plantation. Chiquita secured a public apology and Gallagher's dismissal from the newspaper. But two government investigations followed. The first, by the Securities and Exchange Commission, uncovered Chiquita's funding of the AUC and two violent guerrilla groups—Fuerzas Armadas Revolucionarias de Colombia (FARC) and the Ejército de Liberación Nacional. The second, by the FBI and the Department of Justice,[76] revealed that high-ranking Chiquita executives and officers had approved six years of AUC funding, against legal advice and for which the corporation "never received any actual security services."[77] In 2007, the corporation pled guilty and paid a $25 million fine.[78]

Chiquita's confession answered long-held questions about sources of AUC's financial support but did little to assuage the survivors' suffering and did nothing to help rebuild devastated lives. Turning to US courts and lawyers, scores of survivors sued Chiquita in Washington, DC, New Jersey, Florida, and New York for the company's role in the violent deaths of their loved ones.[79] Drawing from a 2003 Organization of the American States report, one complaint detailed "3,400 AK-47 rifles and 4 million rounds of ammunition in a Banadex-controlled dock . . . destined for the AUC," a basketball court transformed into a "court of execution . . . a rampage of torture, rape and killing" that included a "six-year-old girl" and an elderly woman. Some were "shot after being tortured; others were stabbed or beaten to death, and several more were strangled," said the complaint.[80] The Chiquita-AUC "conspiracy . . . included the political, military and economic control of the Republic of Colombia and specifically of the banana growing regions."[81]

Chiquita denied its role in the atrocities and peppered the courts with motions, first to move the cases to Washington, DC, then to dismiss the cases on procedural grounds. Judge Kenneth Marra of the Southern District Court of Florida denied the forum transfer.[82] On February 20, 2008, a multidistrict judicial panel consolidated the actions under Marra's courtroom. Collectively, *In Re: Chiquita* represented thousands of survivors.[83]

Additional lawsuits followed, including by US survivors, who sued for Chiquita's support of the FARC, which abducted, held for ransom, and killed five US missionaries, according to media reports and court records.[84] Another group of Colombian survivors sued after witnessing weapons crates emblazoned with the corporation's name being unloaded by AUC members, they said.[85] Company shareholders also sued for breached duties by Chiquita's terror funding.[86]

Chiquita reiterated its defenses, claiming the company fell victim to extortionists, denying its role, and warned the court against setting "a dangerous and unprecedented form of activist lawmaking, far beyond anything permitted by the limited common law authority of federal courts."[87] Its lawyers, including Eric Holder (later US attorney general), argued that the ATS didn't apply to charges of funding terrorism and accused the victims of attempting to "invent a common law remedy for their expansive and unprecedented claims."[88]

To Chiquita's motions, "655 victims of murder and torture . . . family members of the trade unionists, banana workers, political organizers, activists and others killed by the AUC, with Chiquita's support" integrated official investigation findings into their complaint: "'Chiquita's money helped buy weapons and ammunition used to kill innocent victims,'" through which "the AUC became an agent of Chiquita." Through "pacification of the banana-growing regions," Chiquita operated "in an environment in which labor and community opposition to the company was suppressed and competition destroyed. Chiquita was able to seize land from peasants; eliminate or dominate labor union organizers . . . and acquire and maintain monopolistic control over banana commerce," they said.[89]

Following four years of procedural motions, emerging facts, and amended complaints, Judge Marra granted the victims a trial. His 95-page opinion and order maintained the ATS and TVPA claims of torture and extrajudicial killing, crimes against humanity, and war crimes, but dismissed (then later restored) common law claims of wrongful death.[90] But the *Kiobel* and *Mohamed* decisions provided Chiquita with leverage. The company's counsel petitioned for interlocutory appeal to the Eleventh Circuit Court of Appeals, calling the torts extraterritorial based on the "site of the conduct." Characterizing the case as violence "by Colombians against Colombians in Colombia," they argued the case belonged in Colombia and that "there is nothing to suggest that plaintiffs can't bring similar claims in Colombia."[91]

In court, Hoffman responded: a US-based corporation making US-based decisions to pay the terror groups "touched and concerned" the US, he said. "I can't say it any other way: It was mass murder. . . . How could that not touch and concern the United States?"[92]

In a 2–1 decision, the panel agreed with Chiquita, dismissed the ATS and TVPA claims, and opined that the case lacked "sufficient force to displace the presumption against extraterritorial application . . . Our ultimate disposition is not dependent on specificity of fact."[93]

In her dissent, Judge Beverly Martin pointed to the US connection: "Chiquita's corporate officers reviewed, approved and concealed payments and weapons transfers to Colombian terrorist organizations . . . with the purpose that the terrorists would use them to commit extrajudicial killings and other war crimes," she wrote.[94] When violations are "committed within the territory of the United States," the *Kiobel* standard is no "impediment to providing a remedy to civilians harmed by a decades-long campaign of terror,"[95] adding, in "international law . . . every State has the sovereign authority to regulate the conduct of its own citizens, regardless of whether that conduct occurs inside or outside of the State's territory." Further, Martin said, the decision would "disarm innocents against American corporations that engage in human rights violations abroad. I understand the ATS to have been deliberately crafted to avoid this regrettable result."[96]

The survivors sought en banc and Supreme Court reviews. Both were denied.

CCR's Katherine Gallagher considered the majority decision "perverse, which is not a word I throw out often," she said. "This is a US company that the US government prosecuted criminally for its complicity in terrorism by working with the AUC. How in the world can that company's actions not touch and concern [the US] when even the Department of Justice investigated and prosecuted?"[97]

Meanwhile, George Washington University's National Security Archives had obtained and published thousands of pages of the Chiquita Papers, revealing details about payments, history, and motivations. While "the names . . . are redacted [from reports], . . . with 48,000 pages, there are a lot of things that aren't redacted" because censors "miss things, especially on hand-written documents. And there are the factual proffer(s) . . . that also listed ten individuals . . . the people involved in the payments," explained Michael Evans, director of the National Security Archives' Colombia project. "It was kind of like unravelling a mystery."[98]

That evidence provided the survivors' lawyers a means to name Chiquita's decision-makers as defendants (the accused, their positions, and the allegations are presented in table 1), enabling redress claims to potentially advance via the TVPA. And the documents suggested connections to the atrocities: "payments to the Seventeenth Brigade, payments to a particular battalion, payments to the Convivir that is attached to the Seventeenth Brigade . . . just a few weeks before the Mapiripán massacre. And we know that people from that Convivir were involved in that massacre. And we also know that the paramilitaries came from the airport controlled by the Seventeenth Brigade. And now, the guy from the Seventeenth Brigade, who is already in prison for a different murder, is going to be charged," explained Evans. These provide a "snapshot of one company among many companies but also a very important one that controlled a lot of land and a big piece of the economy of one particular part of Colombia where the paramilitaries happened to be very strong."[99]

Unique access to information provided the survivors a means to continue pursuing redress. "We were able to name those corporate officers individually . . . because there's all that evidence from the guilty plea and from the FOIA [Freedom of Information Act] requests that were made public by the National Archive. And if you didn't have all that evidence already, like, so, I don't know what kind of playing field that leaves for people who don't have the advantage of all that discovery and all that evidence," explained Fryszman.[100]

Similar accusations have dogged other transnational corporations operating in Colombia, including Drummond, Coca Cola, Odebrecht, other fruit companies, and the Swiss corporation Nestle. But these cases "suffer from a lack of good documentation," according to Evans.[101]

Chiquita's lawyers again motioned to dismiss the entire case, citing the statute of limitations and the survivors' need to exhaust Colombian remedies, which Marra denied. "Plaintiffs admit that they have not exhausted

TABLE 1. Allegations against Chiquita Executives

Named	Position	Allegation	Additional Allegations
William Tsacalis	Former controller and CAO, Chiquita	Approvals for payments through convivir and routing through "income distribution" to Banadex.	
Charles Keiser	Former manager of Chiquita Colombian operations	Meetings with AUC leaders, brokering agreement to pay through convivirs and a personal account	
Cyrus Freidheim (Individual A)	Chairman of the board	Approving payments, procedures that disguised, against counsel advice	"Just let them sue us."
Roderick Hills (deceased) (Individual B)	Former director and president of Chiquita Audit Committee	Reporting AUC's "FTO" status, approving AUC payments	Warning DOJ about mass exodus of US companies from Colombia
Robert Olson (Individual C)	Former vice president and general counsel	Approving procedures that disguise AUC payments	"Just let them sue us." Told outside counsel law didn't require payments to stop.
Robert Kistinger (Individual D)	Former president and COO of Chiquita Fresh	Approving payments to FARC and convivirs	Including after FTO designation
Ferdinand Aguirre	CEO from January 2004 and chairman of board since May 2004	On "60 Minutes" said Chiquita hid AUC payments well	
Steven Warshaw	Held various positions, e.g., CEO, CFO, COO	Approval of AUC payments	
Keith Lindner	President and COO until 1997, vice chair until 2002	Worked with Freidheim re AUC	

available remedies in Colombia but allege facts suggesting such redress would be futile because of the ongoing risk of violent retaliation," he wrote.[102] Marra advanced the common law and TVPA claims against all but two named executives but using Colombian law.[103]

Six American families settled with Chiquita.[104] But in September 2019, Marra granted the individual defendants' joint motion for summary judgment, based upon the survivors' inability to prove causation related to "extrajudicial killings," defined as a "'deliberated' act, i.e. 'undertaken with studied consideration and purpose' that is linked to a state actor." They needed to show "that the AUC was responsible for the murder of each decedent," said Marra, who concluded that the evidence—Colombian government records, deposition testimony and affidavits describing the deaths, matching the geography, patterns and killing methods to those other AUC killings—"were not admissible evidence supporting their core theory."[105]

In March 2020, representing hundreds of Colombian survivors, EarthRights brought another lawsuit against Chiquita in the United States District Court for the District of New Jersey, claiming that Chiquita "funded, armed, and otherwise supported" the terror groups that tortured, mutilated, or executed their loved ones.[106] The case is pending as of this writing.

Criminal charges against Chiquita followed in Colombia. Prosecutors charged 13 former executives with terrorism support, using death squads to increase profits in "para-economics," and crimes against humanity, according to media reports.[107] The payments were "for an illegal armed group whose methods include murder," said Colombian prosecutor Mario Iguaran in 2006 to the *Christian Science Monitor* about the indictment of the Chiquita executives.[108]

Colombian human rights organizations working with Harvard University's International Human Rights Law Clinic also submitted an "Article 15 Communication" to the International Criminal Court (Article 15 of the Rome Statute established the court). They identified 14 Chiquita executives and employees who were "overseeing, authorizing and/or making repeated payments" to terror groups, said the submission, which included remarks from the US prosecutor: "What made [Chiquita's] conduct so morally repugnant is that the company went forward month after month, year after year, to pay the same terrorists. . . . Chiquita was paying money to buy the bullets that killed innocent Colombians off of those farms."[109]

With unique evidentiary leverage and resilient, strategic lawyering, the human rights teams for both *Doe v. Chiquita* and *Doe v. Exxon* prevented early defeats arising from expanding legal hurdles. The Supreme Court established "a kind of standard [that] I don't know if plaintiffs can meet," explained Fryszman.[110] But years after the initial filing, they continue to seek a trial for their clients.

A few additional cases advanced the cause despite the *Kiobel* ruling. In the Ninth Circuit, for example, *Doe v. Nestle* affirmed corporate liability under the ATS and applied the statute to aiding and abetting slavery, but the Supreme Court decided in favor of the corporations.[111] For Kiobel herself—with US-based remedies exhausted—she took her case abroad, finally getting a day in court in the Netherlands as part of a new cross-border collaboration, discussed in the next chapter.

EIGHT

The Globalization of Justice

The US's new potential rights revolution had faltered, arising in part from a counterrevolution that was transforming the polity and courts to reverse hard-won gains in civil and human rights.[1] For victims abroad with hopes pinned on the US justice system, the shift cut from two ends. New legal impositions and thresholds limited access to US courts while the US's domestic civil rights crisis divided the attention of overextended lawyers. The consequence, whether inadvertent or intentional, protected the already strong from legal challenges, despite sometimes deadly transgressions.

The battleground is shifting. Inspired by early ATS cases, advocates have converged across borders, sharing ideas and information, according to Judith Brown Chomsky and Katherine Gallagher. "There is now a movement . . . a universal justice movement. It is not just the United States. In fact, at this point, it's advancing more outside of the United States," said Chomsky.[2] The ATS "helped set up a framework" for "human rights discourse and . . . norms," added Gallagher.[3]

ATS pioneer Peter Weiss took another leading role. Seeking to remedy the US failure to hold its top officials accountable for torture, he looked overseas, using universal jurisdiction,[4] which argues that courts anywhere can prosecute the most heinous international crimes, such as torture, genocide, and terrorism.[5] European countries such as Belgium and Spain had previously investigated cases for violations in Argentina, Chile, Guatemala, Haiti, Rwanda, Congo, Algeria, and Afghanistan[6] before restricting their universal jurisdiction statutes. Still, "there was an ideal law in Germany, which would apply to [US Secretary of Defense, Donald] Rumsfeld, even about matters that had no direct connection [to Germany]," Weiss said, calling it "one of the best universal jurisdiction laws."[7]

For his German counterpart, Weiss tapped Berlin-based attorney Wolfgang Kaleck. Long steeped in civil and human rights, Kaleck had a large network and understood both the US and European legal systems.[8]

"The first time we brought the case against Rumsfeld and . . . others, the German prosecutor" declined the case, based on "the principle of complementarity. Some sergeant [received] a six-year sentence, so the German prosecutor said, 'Oh, look, this guy was convicted in the United States for torture. . . . Why shouldn't Rumsfeld also be convicted in the United States?' Complementarity. It's a ridiculous position," Weiss said.[9]

Improbability of success sealed the fate of the second case.[10] But the Weiss-Kaleck collaboration continued, spawning a new NGO, the European Centre for Constitutional and Human Rights (ECCHR). The Berlin-based organization developed into a "large network" of lawyers and survivors of violations, according to Andreas Schüller, ECCHR's director of international crimes and accountability. "It's difficult for law firms to do these cases and also to assess political impact. So the CCR with Wolfgang Kaleck and some other individuals like Lotte Leicht of Human Rights Watch . . . thought it would be better to have not only single lawyers but also litigation organizations [to work on] transnational litigation."[11]

In "legal solidarity," ECCHR, long-standing and newer human rights organizations created "a solidarity network" in which advocates "seeking the same . . . democratic standards and values [and] also social standards worldwide" collaborate on strategy, case development, and jurisdictional decisions, for example, "Do we go the civil way? Do we go the criminal law way? Do we go to Germany or [another] jurisdiction—and how to build the cases in terms of evidence . . . how to frame them [for] the public?" explained Schüller.[12]

Connected by "the understanding that you're basically on the same side—of views, of ideas, that the victim or affected persons in Colombia or India is not different to the affected person of mining in Germany but probably more powerless to challenge that"—they work on "the other side of globalization . . . the people side . . . [for] social standards, human rights, social rights, as a counterpart to [corporate] globalization," said Schüller. "I think we see each other closer to some lawyers in India, Philippines or Colombia than to the next law firm in Berlin . . . like a team on one side of the struggle."[13]

"Part of a larger system," a global virtual team coordinates legal actions, amicus briefs, case intervention, fact-finding, and moral support. Gallagher, for example, files ATS cases in the US "but I'm also involved in cases under universal jurisdiction in foreign courts, and I'm looking at the ICC, so you look at whatever lever one can pull," she said.[14] For example, as legal representative for two torture survivors detained at Guantánamo, Gallagher argued part of an appeal that led to led to the ICC investigation related to the war in Afghanistan, an ICC state party.[15] "[That] includes the investigation of U.S. actors for their role in war crimes and crimes against humanity in Afghanistan as well as CIA 'black sites' in Romania, Lithuania and Poland," she added.[16] Afghanistan has requested a deferral of the investigation.[17]

Even when not directly collaborating, "you need support," added UK-based Martyn Day. "People within the same world will understand the pressures, so there's a communality, a comradeship."[18]

Together, human rights legal organizations, such as TRIAL International, REDRESS, International Federation for Human Rights,[19] ECCHR, and FIBGAR (Baltasar Garzon International Foundation), reported a 106 percent increase in universal jurisdiction or related cases in 2017: 127 accused in 14 countries, including 55 charges for torture, 12 for genocide, 46 for crimes against humanity, and 91 for war crimes, with 13 convictions and 119 pending cases as of 2018.[20]

Atrocity survivors have also found justice through other state or interstate courts. For example, rejected by US courts based upon "state secrets," two of Khaled El-Masri's lawyers—Open Society Institute's James Goldston and Darian Pavli[21]—pursued redress through the European Court of Human Rights, which found for El-Masri and ordered Macedonia to compensate him $78,000 for its role in his rendition and torture. His lawyers also filed with the Inter-American Commission for Human Rights. Growing numbers of cases there and at the European Court of Human Rights and a recently established African Court on Human and Peoples' Rights suggest this avenue for redress may be expanding.[22]

Simultaneously, a growing "global movement for corporate accountability" tries cases in either the corporations' or survivors' home countries, explained Gallagher. "While [the US] may be putting up barricades . . . there is a silver lining if countries are now holding their own corporations accountable for what they do outside their borders."[23]

The UK is one country where lawyers are taking local action against their own governments and corporations for human rights violations. In the lead is Martyn Day, senior partner at Leigh Day, working to secure redress for survivors abroad suffering from violations involving the British government or UK-based multinational corporations.

A Day in Court

By 2015, Leigh Day had 10 teams working in the "dark, inhospitable corners of the world where miners, oil and mineral companies and governments can often get away with what they could not if they were working in Britain," Day told *Guardian* reporter John Vidal.[24] A contrast from his early days working essentially alone, his team has "about 80 people" and "about seven partners doing this sort of stuff," he said.[25]

Day turned to human rights after briefly working as a personal injury lawyer. "One of the nicest cases I ever did was getting some old lady about £3,000 when she had fallen and damaged her wrist and was in a bit of a state," he said. "But it wasn't massively stimulating. I wanted to find work I could put my heart and soul into."[26]

The NGO Greenpeace and Day's prisoner of war uncle prompted the shift. "I got active around prisoners of war from the Japanese who wanted me to help them," recalled Day. "My uncle, by chance, who was one of them . . . asked if we would help."[27]

Day realized then "There was more to life than ordinary injuries"; his lawyering could have broad influence, "the whole rationale" for shifting his practice: "We don't want to be wasting our time with cases that don't really have some sort of social or political impact . . . [such as] making sure that multinationals were more worried about the power of local people, and were more sympathetic to their concerns," he said.[28] For example, British entities should treat people abroad "the same way as they would people in Birmingham," he argued.[29]

"Successful cases" could advance the cause, even those settling with confidentiality agreements in opposition to campaigners' desires, he thought. "Often the NGO would much prefer it to go to trial so you got big coverage. . . . But often the clients just want to get it resolved . . . they want to get on with their lives, and the settlement means that they can do that."[30]

By 2015, Day had won approximately £150 million for some of the world's poorest who suffered disproportionally from the actions of some of the richest.[31] That included cases against transnational oil and mining companies and the British military, the latter of which left local Kenyans wounded, dismembered, or incapacitated by munitions left in the pastures.[32] In 2002, while in Kenya for that case, Day "got a knock on my door at the Stanley Hotel in the middle of Nairobi, and it was a couple of Black guys. And they said, 'We're from the Mau Mau. Could you help?' Well, to be frank, I didn't know anything about that," he recalled.[33]

Initial research made him skeptical. "[It] basically, was saying . . . [they]

are dodgy bastards who actually killed and mangled a lot of white people.' So I was saying to them, 'Well, look, what on earth are you about? Looks like you were the dodgy ones,'" recalled Day. But a deeper look, with research from historians Caroline Elkins and David Anderson, led him to realize he had it wrong: "Tens if not hundreds of thousands were put behind bars, treated like dirt, and tortured."[34]

Politically, legally, and pragmatically troubled from the start, the case had little probability of success, given huge expenses, a statute of limitations, and political unpopularity. "My partners thought that I was nuts," Day recalled. And progressive Queen's Counsel also declined participation. "We went to a very senior guy called Sidney Kentridge, who had actually been Steve Biko's QC [Queen's Counsel] back in his trial, back in the 1980s. And he's a very well-known leftie barrister and he said, 'No, well you haven't got a chance in hell. No, thank you.'"[35]

Despite slim chances of success, high costs, and a powerful government defendant, the "ancillary issues" compelled Day, he said. "There was the politics. I really felt, once I'd gotten into the case, gotten to know the people, I felt determined [that] we were going to do it. . . . I felt in my heart of hearts that this was a terrible wrong that we had done as Britain to these people. And it was right and just that we should put our resources and efforts into it, even though the risks were very high."[36]

Eventually, Day recruited Queen's Counsel Keir Starmer and drew a sympathetic judge, "who loved the case. And that is such a big thing," remarked Day. "With a judge who's actually interested in your case, you've got a long way along the line, especially something like this with [time] limitation, where it's down to the judge's discretion."[37]

After decades of silence, Mau Mau elders testified in court, describing years of detentions, mostly shackled, with beatings, torture, castration, and torched homes. Women detailed rape, some with bottles of hot water. "[They] took our land. They killed our people, and they burnt down our houses," said Wambugu Wa Nyingi.[38]

For its defense, the British government didn't deny the abuses, and instead relied on the time limitations and law of state succession, the latter of which blamed the Kenyan colonial administration, rather than the British government.[39] The time limitation was "the much bigger issue," said Day. "Obviously, 50 years is a very long time when the limitation period was normally three years or six years. So we were asking for the judge's discretion to say that that could still be a fair trial despite all this time. And our main argument was that there was lots of documentary evidence to show what happened. And the court, by going through all the records, would be able to get a good feel on what happened, and that there were still some few people still alive who could give some color to what was being said in the documents."[40]

While "out there in Nairobi," Day got the call: Judge "McCombe decided in our favor. . . . When we told the clients, they were absolutely singing and shouting. It was fantastic."[41]

The four-year case compensated 5,228 Kenyans with £19.9 million, a memorial to the victims in Nairobi, and an acknowledgment of the "torture and ill-treatment at the hands of the colonial administration."[42] But if Day's win signaled hope for other Mau Mau sufferers, their hopes were dashed. In 2018, another judge (Peter Stewart), dismissed a group case brought by 40,000 Kenyans for abuses during a similar time period. Filed by UK firm Tandem Law and Kenyan lawyer Cecil Miller, the large group case faced the Foreign and Commonwealth Office's denial of the plaintiff's account and the time barrier.[43] However, a case of British colonial abuses in Cyprus settled for £1 million. Representing 33 Greek Cypriot members of independence group Eoka, British lawyer Howard Shelley settled the case. But without official apologies, the veterans, then in their 80s, expressed disappointment. "What are we going to do with the money at our age? What we want is an apology," said Thassos Sophocleous to *the Guardian*. "If the Germans can say sorry, the English should say sorry too."[44]

With no ATS-equivalent in the UK, Day uses common law, suing British entities as a "matter of right," he explained. "If . . . we can show to the court that they are not actually properly behaving, then we say that they've been negligent, or in breach of their duties. . . . When [they] are listed in the London Stock Exchange, that puts a lot of pressure on the parent company to show that it is controlling its subsidiaries in a good manner. . . . We use that then. And that's why they get pissed off with us. We obviously use that to say, 'Well, look, here is Unilever or Shell or whatever saying, 'We're good corporate citizens. We make sure that our subsidiaries are behaving in a proper, decent manner in this way and that way and blah-de-blah-de-blah.' And we say, 'Well look, they haven't. And you are making these statements that you are taking responsibility. . . . You can't say this is what you are doing, and not do it.'"[45]

While the courts often apply the local law from the site of the violation, most "tend to be Commonwealth jurisdictional countries where common law applies. So Zambia, Zimbabwe, Nigeria, Sierra Leone, most of them are based on English law, so actually, the difference is pretty marginal," Day explained.[46] Day sued Vedanta Resources for environmental destruction in Zambia, Unilever for deadly violence on its Kenyan plantation, and African Mining for complicity in rape, assault, false imprisonment, and wrongful death in Sierra Leone. In the latter case, *Kadie Kalma & others and African Minerals Limited et al.*, families forced from their homes to make way for the Tonkolili Iron Ore mine began protesting the bulldozing of homes, crops, and farms. Security forces responded with gunfire, assault, and rape, according to NGO and news reports.[47] Already traumatized by war, survivors worried about losing "all we have worked for, for a second time," according to a Sierra Leone Human Rights Commission report.[48] A British judge, Mark Turner, took testimony in Sierra Leone but decided the corporation was neither complicit nor liable for police-instigated violence.[49]

With investigations each costing between "£30 and £40 thousand," losing the case set Day back. Another case "cost us about 15 million" and "about eight years," Day admitted. But neither has detracted from his optimism. And on balance, the firm's human rights arm remains financially successful. With others in the 450-lawyer firm pursuing more lucrative cases, Day can "take on bigger risks and bigger companies."[50]

His pursuits, however, make "big enemies. They don't like us much. But I would say in many, many court hearings, the barrister for the defendant will get up and slag us off," he said. "But very rarely have we actually seen the courts really be influenced by that."[51] Day has faced other controversies as well. The Law Society of Kenya accused Day of taking disproportionate fees from his Mau Mau clients.[52] And the UK's al-Sweady inquiry found some of Day's Iraqi clients' claims false,[53] which landed him before the UK's Solicitors Disciplinary Tribunal. Neither body found against Day; he was acquitted by the tribunal after a seven-week hearing. The Solicitors Regulatory Authority appealed, charging him for "unbalanced and sensationalist" language at a press conference.[54] "Obviously, we've been taken on by our own regulator in light of the Iraqi stuff," Day said, but he relished the challenges: "People thought I was weird when I said at the tribunal that I quite enjoyed it. But I did, because pitching somebody against you for four and a half days, cross-examining you, puts you on your toes, doesn't it? I'm not saying it wasn't tough. It was tough. But there's also the pleasure to be had from it."[55]

Day's chief disappointment is the field's underdevelopment. "We're not seeing other firms out there, certainly in this country, and even for the rest of the world. I mean we rarely bump into lawyers who are doing similar sort of work. There's maybe two or three law firms in the whole of the rest of Europe that I'm aware of doing this sort of work—hardly any," he said.[56]

A few Canadian lawyers, however, have begun pressing international human rights cases despite structural obstacles, such as high risks and costs, which escalate in systems of "loser-pays" all litigation costs, according to human rights lawyer Matt Eisenbrandt. "Even if you lose a motion on a preliminary issue, you have to pay the other side's expenses," a difficult proposition, "assuming your clients are either indigent or have very limited resources," he said. "Civil damages awards in Canada are [also] much smaller than in the United States," making it harder for "lawyers and law firms that might be able to even get involved."[57] But survivors of human rights abuses from Congo, Guatemala, and Eritrea have found Canadian representation in actions against Canadian corporations associated with their violations. The cases developed upon a strategy shift by Canadian NGOs.

The Canadian Turn

In 2000, Center for Justice and Accountability (CJA) cofounder Gerald Gray moved his ideas over the northern border. With Canada's leadership in establishing the International Criminal Court (ICC) and its Crimes against Humanity and War Crimes Act,[58] the country appeared ideal for advancing criminal prosecutions against human rights violators.[59] Toward this end, with Canadian human rights organizations, Gray cofounded the Canadian Centre for International Justice (CCIJ), where Eisenbrandt, former CJA legal director, moved.[60]

It didn't go exactly as planned. "The [Conservative] government [of Prime Minister Stephen Harper] seemed to pretty clearly deemphasize universal jurisdiction. And there were comments by different ministers that Canada wasn't going to be the police force for the world, [making it] pretty clear there wasn't a lot of interest," recalled Eisenbrandt. "Canada did two criminal prosecutions with one guilty verdict and one acquittal . . . involving Rwanda. . . . Since that time, there haven't been any criminal prosecutions. . . . So I think that what was envisioned to be sort of the main thrust of CCIJ's work . . . hasn't necessarily played out that way."[61]

Despite prosecutorial reticence with others' transgressions, Canada acknowledged and redressed some of its own. In contrast with its southern neighbor, which refused Maher Arar a day in court, for example, Canada investigated, apologized, and compensated Arar with more than $10 million for falsely identifying him as a terrorist, which had landed him in a Syrian torture chamber.[62] Its Royal Canadian Mounted Police has since charged Syrian colonel George Salloum for Arar's torture and issued a warrant and Interpol notice for his arrest.[63]

Paradoxically, the country's mining industry—the largest in the world—is linked to human rights violations abroad, according to NGOs Mining Watch and Amnesty International. But large Canadian law firms "are almost always going to have mining companies or oil companies or whoever as clients," explained Eisenbrandt. "They know they aren't going to have the business interest in pursuing a plaintiff-side case if it upsets some of their extractive sector clients."[64]

A Canadian court's rejection of a 1997 case against gold producer Cambior Inc. potentially discouraged others, particularly after the court ordered the impoverished Guyanese victims to pay Cambior's legal costs. Another case, 12 years later, against Mesa Mining, faced a similar fate.[65] But, more recently, Canadian courts have ostensibly taken more seriously redressing survivors of human rights violations connected to Canadian corporations.

In 2004, the Congolese military tortured, raped, and executed between 70 and 100 civilians in the town of Kilwa, ostensibly with Canada-based Anvil Mining's vehicles, drivers, and logistical support. After Congo's failure to prosecute the violators, Congolese survivors, through the Canadian Association Against Impunity (CAAI), sued Anvil in Quebec for complicity. Represented by Trudel & Johnston, the case survived a forum non conveniens claim,[66] but, on appeal, the higher court dismissed the case for lack of jurisdiction, although it expressed regrets that "citizens have so much difficulty obtaining justice . . . sympathy that must be felt for the victims and the admiration that the NGOs' involvement within the CAAI inspires." It did not award costs.[67]

Two groups of injured Guatemalans followed, suing mining companies HudBay Resources and Tahoe Resources in Canada, using common law claims such as negligence, which is "standard and very well-accepted in Canadian courts," explained Eisenbrandt. In Guatemala, indigenous Mayans had already suffered mass violence and widespread massacres before the mining ordeals began. During the 36-year Guatemalan Civil War, more than 160,000 Mayans lost their lives, amounting to approximately 83 percent of the conflict's casualties. Amid the violence, the military government had granted a 40-year lease to Canadian mining company Inco on land that contained indigenous homes and farmlands.[68] In a "reign of terror" that killed between 3,000 and 6,000 indigenous people, security personnel forced the Mayans off their traditional lands.[69]

The project's suspension prompted the Mayans return.[70] After the project changed hands from Inco to Sky Resources (later HMI Nickel, then HudBay), armed forces again evicted the Mayans with gunfire and by burning down their homes, according to reports, press accounts, and claims.[71] Security forces reportedly gang-raped 11 women. A local school-teacher and community leader, Adolfo Ich Chamán, was seized, dragged, bludgeoned, hacked by machetes, then shot dead, according to his widow's claim.[72] An altercation on a soccer field left 21-year-old German Chub paraplegic, with one working lung, unable to work, dependent on his parents, and bereft after his wife left him and took their son.[73] These claims became the basis of three negligence lawsuits filed in 2010 and 2011 by Canadian lawyers Murray Klippenstein and Cory Wanless against HudBay Minerals, for authorizing "reckless and provocative deployment of heavily-armed security personnel" with a history of "unreasonable violence" in an already violent region.[74]

HudBay denied these accounts, and instead accused protesters of stealing weapons and attacking property,[75] then sought dismissal based on forum non conveniens, jurisdiction, and claims of no "duty of care" over subsidiaries, or control over "unforeseeable" events.[76] On January 21, 2020, the Superior Court of Justice found "sufficient particulars of Skye's alleged negligence for the forced evictions, the violence and the harm suffered by the Plaintiffs including the alleged sexual assaults." The case remained unresolved at this writing.[77]

Another Guatemalan indigenous community, the Xinca, protested Tahoe Resources' Escobal Silver Mine during its construction, fearing contaminated food and water. Security forces opened fire on the protesters while they fled. Seven people took bullets to their faces, backs, feet, or legs, according to claims.[78] "It's with bullets that they learn," said security supervisor Alberto Rotondo, who ordered the attack, then told staff to break equipment, clean the guns and area to claim the Xinca "entered and attacked us."[79]

On behalf of the injured protesters, Canadian attorney Joe Fiorante of Camp, Fiorante, Matthews, Mogerman sued Canada-registered Tahoe Resources in British Columbia, claiming negligence and battery. Tahoe denied responsibility, claiming Rotondo had "violated the company's rules" and orders, then argued to move the case to Guatemala.[80]

Four factors led Justice Laura Gerow to agree with Tahoe: its US base, the location of events and plaintiffs, Guatemala's pending criminal case against Rotondo, and the principle of comity.[81] "The public interest requires that Canadian courts proceed extremely cautiously in finding that a foreign court is incapable of providing justice to its own citizens. To hold otherwise is to ignore the principle of comity and risk that other jurisdictions will treat the Canadian judicial system with similar disregard," she said. "The plaintiffs are already seeking compensation for their injuries in

Guatemala . . . both the alleged battery and the alleged breaches of duty on the part of Tahoe occurred in Guatemala and perhaps Nevada."[82]

On appeal, the survivors and Amnesty International as intervenor raised concerns about Guatemala's discovery constraints, its substandard rule-of-law, corruption, the country's deposed and repressed judges, and the statute of limitations. By this time, Rotondo had escaped to Peru, causing a suspension in the Guatemalan proceedings.[83]

In a unanimous reversal, the appellate court agreed with the survivors, casting "doubt on whether the appellants will be able to pursue a civil suit against Tahoe in Guatemala," it said.[84] The Supreme Court of Canada declined to hear Tahoe's appeal.[85] Escobal protester Angel Estuardo Quevedo has since been killed; Guatemala's Constitutional Court suspended Tahoe's mining license, pending environmental reviews,[86] after which the corporation cut 250 jobs. In July 2019, Tahoe's acquiring company, Pan American Silver, apologized to the protestors as part of a settlement agreement, stating "the shooting on April 27, 2013, infringed the human rights of the protestors. . . . Pan American, on behalf of Tahoe, apologizes to the victims and to the community." Its president and CEO added, "We sincerely hope that this resolution provides some measure of closure." The attorney for the plaintiffs called the result "a very important precedent" that "confirms that Canadian courts are the appropriate forum for human rights claims arising from the activities of Canadian mining companies."[87]

Known for widespread human rights violations, Eritrea used forced labor for its mining operations, including in the multimillion-dollar Bisha Mine, which was 60 percent owned by Canada-based Nevsun Resources.[88] Workers lived and worked long hours in extreme heat, with malnutrition, confinement to bed-less, electricity-less work camps, and punishments, including beatings and being bound under the hot sun for hours. Three survivors, Gize Yebeyo Araya, Kesete Tekle Fshazion, and Mihretab Yemane Tekle, fled both the Bisha Mine and their country.[89]

In 2013, representing Bisha Mine survivors, Fiorante sued Nevsun in the British Columbia Supreme Court, claiming the company "facilitated, aided, abetted, contributed to, and became an accomplice" to the violations.[90] Alongside common law claims of negligence, battery, unlawful confinement, conversion, and conspiracy, Fiorante's team incorporated international law claims—forced labor, slavery, torture, and cruel, inhuman, or degrading treatment.[91] "If crimes against humanity were committed, and a company is complicit in that, you can . . . fit that under the guise of negligence, but . . . crimes against humanity [is] much more specific to what they are," explained Eisenbrandt, who added, "according to the Supreme

Court of Canada, international law is directly implemented into Canadian law," making a Canadian ATS-equivalent unnecessary. However, "those claims make the case more complex," he admitted.[92]

Documents suggested that "executives at the highest level" knew about the forced labor,[93] which Nevsun denied. Calling the Bisha company "an employer of choice," offering "well-paying, intrinsically-rewarding jobs for local people," Nevsun's VP of corporate social responsibility Todd Romaine called Nevsun "a force for good."[94] For its legal defense, Nevsun's lawyers argued to move proceedings to Eritrea, warned against adjudicating foreign states' acts, and claimed that international law could not apply to the case.[95]

Persuaded by the plaintiffs' "allegations of the most serious nature," the very "real consequences" that refugees would face in Eritrea, and widespread knowledge about Eritrea's human rights violations, the BC Supreme Court rejected Nevsun's motions.[96] After the decision was affirmed by a unanimous BC Court of Appeals,[97] Nevsun appealed to Canada's Supreme Court, which took arguments in January 2019, and ruled that the company can be sued in Canada. In 2020, the corporation settled with the survivors for an undisclosed amount.[98]

In Europe, human rights lawyers also took action against their own transnational corporations for claims of complicity in war crimes, crimes against humanity, pillaging, money laundering, torture, and terrorism.[99] In Switzerland, for example, TRIAL International found evidence that Swiss refinery Argor-Haraeus was dealing in illegal Congolese gold, which experts argued was fueling a deadly conflict. "We found that the public records were enough to incriminate them" for "pillaging . . . within an armed conflict," which could mean complicity in "a war crime," said Benedict De Moerloose, TRIAL's head of international investigations and litigation.[100] The gold "was coming through Uganda—where they don't produce any gold . . . And there was a war . . . in the DRC."[101]

De Moerloose filed a criminal complaint with the Swiss prosecutor against the company for pillaging and money laundering, prompting an investigation. But even though no indictments ensued,[102] De Moerloose considers the action successful. "The fact that the premises of Argor were searched, the fact that we heard that the refiners . . . felt that they were not untouchable anymore, that was a victory. It was also a victory to have a decision where the fact that the looted gold actually had come to Switzerland, four tons in two years directly coming from bloody conflicts, and that was written down in the decisions, and that nobody can contest it now," he said. "It was important to see also that this could have been a crime of pillage committed by the Swiss if the intention was clearly defined, so this is something that you can use in terms of case law."[103]

Then the case and surrounding campaigns ostensibly helped shape policy, persuading, for example, US president "Obama to change the law on conflict minerals and to apply very strict regulations with the companies' activities in the DRC," he said, adding, "I think that Trump wants to get rid of this."[104]

In France, the NGO Sherpa and the ECCHR, along with 11 former employees of French corporation LaFarge, filed a complaint against the cement company for financing terror, aiding and abetting crimes against humanity, deliberately endangering people, and exploiting its labor. LaFarge had contracted with the Islamic State (IS) and required employees to work under life-threatening conditions, which included crossing IS checkpoints. The company later paid IS after the group abducted nine LaFarge employees. The legal action named the corporation, its past and present CEOs,[105] and its Syrian subsidiary.[106] The Coordination of Christians of the East followed with another complaint. Police searches of Lafarge premises in Paris and Brussels led to indictments of six former corporate executives, with charges for financing terrorism and complicity in crimes against humanity.[107] A later merged LaFargeHolcim admitted "significant errors in judgment" and "unacceptable" measures in its operations.[108] In 2019, a French court upheld preliminary criminal charges against the company for financing IS and endangering employees' lives but rejected crimes against humanity charges. The case was pending as of this writing.[109]

In 2011 and 2012, NGOs International Federation for Human Rights and the League for the Rights of Man filed complaints in the Paris Tribunal against French corporations Qosmos and Amesys for supplying software technology used by Syria and Libya, respectively, to track and torture opponents. "In selling this (surveillance) material, you cannot ignore its end use," said the International Federation for Human Rights' honorary president, Patrick Baudouin. "It's equivalent to a weapon because it's a tool of repression to arrest and torture."[110] Through the action, lawyers hoped to reveal the "large-scale communications surveillance system" used "to harm the Syrian people," added the honorary president of the League for the Rights of Man, Michel Tubiana. Qosmos denied the claims and filed a defamation suit against the human rights organizations but was declared an "assisted witness," a broad term that can precede indictments. The case had not resolved at the time of this writing. Another French company, Exxelia Technologies, faces a complaint for complicity in war crimes for selling products used by Israel that aided the killing of three Palestinian children. No further information was available at the time of this writing.[111]

The Netherlands have convicted at least two corporate executives: Guus Kouwenhoven, for aiding and abetting war crimes in Liberia by importing, storing, and distributing weapons through his timber companies, and Frans van Anraat, for supplying chemical weapons components to Saddam Hussein, which "enabled, if not facilitated, the execution of a large number of bombings of defenseless civilians."[112]

Colombia, Brazil, and Argentina are among Latin American countries taking action against multinational corporations implicated in human rights violations. A Colombian prosecutor has reportedly charged 200 multinational companies, including Chiquita, Dole Food Company, Del Monte, Coca Cola, and Argos, with crimes against humanity for materially supporting or benefitting from the AUC paramilitary's widespread violence and terror.[113] In Brazil, former Volkswagen employees sued their employer for allowing torture and detention in its factory.[114] In Argentina, executives from corporations, including Ford and Mercedes-Benz, were indicted for aiding military abductions or torture.[115]

New laws are also enabling legal actions. For example, Argentina's National Congress passed legislation allowing NGOs to act as private prosecutors for egregious human rights abuses. And several "countries that may not [have] previously had a crimes-against-humanity statute or a war crimes statute—as they're putting those [policies] in—they are now providing for corporate liability, corporate criminal liability [in them]. France, the Netherlands, Switzerland, they have either adopted new laws or had more cases that have been proceeding," explained Gallagher.[116]

Cross-border efforts include the development of global standards for corporations, trade agreements, and "a possible treaty . . . for transnational corporations," which has been promoted through the Economic, Social and Cultural Rights Network, Gallagher added.[117] And cross-border collaborations on individual cases are working to surmount political obstacles. For example, after Royal Dutch Petroleum (Shell) defeated Esther Kiobel in both Nigeria and the US, the justice system in the company's home country, the Netherlands, granted Kiobel a trial for which her lawyers in both the US and the Netherlands collaborated to surmount the legal obstacles. Shell also faced criminal charges in the Netherlands, and a civil action in the UK.[118] Day settled the latter action on behalf of 15,600 Ogoni people for £55 million, according to press reports.[119]

Truth across Borders

Kiobel's 17-year legal battle in the US produced no redress; her case helped close the US courtroom doors for other survivors. But she took her case to The Hague, where she and Dutch lawyer Channa Samkalden were initially blocked from obtaining evidence. "They couldn't get any of the discovery from the Kiobel case here [the US] . . . or from our Wiwa case . . . because [what was filed] was all under seal," recalled EarthRights cofounder Katie Redford. As the US-based cases drew to their conclusions, a "confidentiality order [had] prevented us from using the materials outside the US litigation and . . . required us to return or destroy most of the materials," added the NGO's general counsel, Marco Simons.

Using the Foreign Legal Assistance statute, which authorizes "interested parties" to provide evidence to foreign legal proceedings, EarthRights filed "a discovery action against Cravath [Swaine & Moore], the lawyers for Shell, in this country [the US] to get all of their documents from her original case," explained Redford.[120] But while unable to obtain the material through the FLA action, a "separate court action . . . led to Shell agreeing that the documents could be used," added Simons.[121]

For survivors in Peru, Nigeria, India, and Tanzania, who are taking action against transnational corporations in their own countries, EarthRights similarly does "the discovery action, and then they litigate it there with all the extra evidence that they are able to get from the United States," explained Redford.[122] "We've gotten documents; we've gotten discovery; we've gotten to depose people from Newmont mining that the Peruvian prosecutors could never have gotten jurisdiction. . . . It turned out they had video footage of shooting protesters at their mine. . . . And we got it in this simple discovery request, which is now a game-changer for this case."[123]

Building legal networks and legal/leadership programs in Asia and the Amazon, EarthRights and their partners share information, ideas, and "help them get funding . . . technical legal support and build power through the power of convening," explained Redford.[124] EarthRights has also intervened in Canadian cases.[125]

Similarly, human rights lawyers and NGOs use cross-country strategies for cases against governments and officials, the pressing challenges for Almudena Bernabeu. "For me, the violence [that] comes from the structure of the state [is] . . . graver and more serious, because you have the whole state . . . helping . . . to do exactly the opposite of what you're supposed to do," she explained. "I'm not saying that [groups like] the FARC crimes are not important. I'm not saying that some of them didn't even amount to the gravity of an international crime. All I'm saying is that it cannot be a crime committed under the Rome Statute, [and] that the same crimes committed by the state are more serious to me. . . . It has armed forces, and it has a budget. It has everything. And it has the structure to keep the [citizens] healthy, not to kill them or to torture them."[126]

With British barrister Toby Cadman, Bernabeu, the 12-year CJA veteran, created a transnational NGO, Guernica 37, primarily to hold officials to account. Combining respective legal experiences in the US, the UK, and Spain, the team seeks "the [best] country" for prosecution, whether in "the United States, Spain, Belgium," Bernabeu said. "It is transnational. . . . You can open three fronts at the same time, so [for example] the Syrian cases in Germany and in Spain are different cases, but we're working together."[127]

Syria, for example, had escaped prosecution: it never ratified the Rome Statute, and Bashar al-Assad's allies had blocked action from the UN Security Council.[128] But the combined actions of civil society and human rights advocates using universal jurisdiction created a foothold to the rungs of justice. The legal developments following the life-risking actions of a Syrian regime photographer, Caesar, demonstrates this confluence.

European Collaborations for Justice in Syria

An official Syrian government photographer, Caesar,[129] had long-captured images of crimes, suicides, house fires, and traffic accidents for evidentiary purposes. During the uprising, his assignment switched to photographing corpses, mostly of demonstrators, who bore marks of torture. "Some had their eyes gouged out, their teeth broken, you could see traces of lashes with those cables you use to start cars. There were wounds full of pus, as if they'd been left untreated for a long time," he told Garance le Caisne of the *Guardian*.[130] The bodies became numbers, their deaths attributed to natural causes—usually heart or respiratory failure, he explained.[131]

Caesar secretly digitized the photos, copied them to flash drives,[132] tucked them into his shoes and belt, and smuggled them past "four or five" army checkpoints into the hands of a trusted friend, who duplicated the files and sent them out of Syria. Their hope: "The dead people's families would know that their loved ones had passed away. People had to know what was going on in the prisons and detention centers," he said. Hoping for official action, they showed the photos to the European Union, the US Congress, and the UN Human Rights Council. But with no action arising from those entities, their hopes were dashed.[133]

What Caesar didn't know was that Syrian refugee communities had begun using his photos in an arduous process of finding the deceased's relatives across Europe in hopes of using universal jurisdiction in legal actions. "It was a very creative effort. The Syrian community in exile started picking some of the photos of those people . . . the bodies [that] were more recognizable [and] less gruesome. . . . They started putting them on social media, Facebook, Twitter . . . and they started creating these Excel sheets to identify them," recalled Bernabeu. "They thought, if we find people with nationalities of the countries that may have lost people . . . a French citizen or a Spanish citizen or a German citizen [as] the victims, you can trigger universal jurisdiction of those countries. So these guys were actually trying to find people with those nationalities."[134]

While initially "quite skeptical" about the strategy, the images "devastated" Bernabeu. "The condition of the bodies—horrible. . . . Not even the Holocaust produced this collection of victims, numbered, identified."[135] She offered to represent in Spanish courts anyone of Spanish descent or "with a dual nationality" for Spanish jurisdiction. Time lapsed; no one contacted her.[136]

At a CJA event, Stephen Rapp, former US ambassador-at-large for war crimes issues, handed Bernabeu the phone number of Spaniard-Syrian citizen, Amal Hag Hamdo Anfalis. Among Caesar's photographs, Anfalis's nephew had identified his father (Anfalis's brother), Abdulmuemen Alhaj Hamdo, marked by beatings, burnings, and starvation.[137] On Anfalis's behalf, Bernabeu filed a universal jurisdiction criminal complaint in Spain against nine Syrian officials. "It was easy to establish . . . the chain of command from the prison to the government, following the line of intelligence services. So we decided that those would be the defendants," explained Bernabeu.[138]

Two developments hampered the case. Spain, the country that previously used universal jurisdiction to charge heads of state, including Chilean military dictator Augusto Pinochet for war crimes, had dramatically diminished its universal jurisdiction law. "[Spain] closed the war crimes universal jurisdiction component," leaving "state terrorism" as a cause of action, explained Schüller.[139]

Cases also required "direct" victimization of a Spaniard. Identifying Anfalis as a "victim" under the Spanish Statute of Victims and in European and international law, Judge Eloy Velasco accepted the case. The Spanish state prosecutor disagreed, arguing she was an indirect victim. "It's kind of customary that the prosecutors always oppose these cases," said Bernabeu. "They [have] become like bulldogs who protect 'integrity,' they say, of the Spanish courts. And the reasons why they deny it or they oppose it, they cannot [legitimately] argue, depending on the case."[140]

The appellate panel's majority sided with the prosecutor, citing 2014 legal reforms intended to prevent diplomatic conflicts. "The [new] law is so awful. It used to be that the law in Spain back in the days of [prosecuting] Pinochet . . . said international crimes are within Spanish jurisdiction, regardless of the Spanish nationality," said Bernabeu.[141]

Despite the failed prosecution, "it's an important case" that can "potentially be used in the German case[s]," said Schüller.[142] Germany's robust universal jurisdiction laws empower its federal public prosecutor to investigate any international crimes and to take evidence before filing cases.[143] The refuge for hundreds of thousands of fleeing Syrians[144] who provided troves of evidence through first-hand accounts, Germany enabled structural investigations into the war as early as 2011. "By 2012, we represented some victims and witnesses [as] they . . . gave statements to the federal prosecutor here, the federal police, and the war crimes unit," recalled Schüller. "We needed to start somewhere, and you never know where it leads you. But if you talk about war crimes, it can easily be then a ten, twenty-year perspective certainly, and we wanted to get started somewhere as early as possible."[145]

The mass refugee influx "expanded the scope" of ECCHR's strategy. "We got two Syrian lawyers into ECCHR for three months internships," showed them "how we work," and learned from them, said Schüller. "[We] developed a network from there of . . . prominent lawyers also living in Berlin and in Syria. There is a network here also of Syrians, which is unprecedented . . . all these victims and witnesses here, also really good experienced journalists and lawyers and civil society people who had to leave their country."[146]

Syrian civil society amassed more evidence. Working with defectors, rebels, and Western advisers, Syrian lawyers, students, and journalists risked their lives, seizing, cataloguing, and analyzing forensic data, including orders, chains of commands, and technical analysis about each attack,[147] records that were integrated into cases filed in Europe, the US, and into the UN High Commissioner for Human Rights' reports.[148] Facebook posts added to the evidence.

In May 2016, Germany began war crimes trials, first for Syrian jihadists accused of kidnapping and torture.[149] The next year, nine Syrian torture survivors, the ECCHR, and Syrian lawyers Anwar al-Bunni and Mazen Darwish[150] submitted complaints in Germany against six high-level Syrian officials. Prosecutors took testimony about daily electric shocks, whippings, and bludgeoning with cables and nail-studded posts, then began matching metadata from Caesar's photographs to the Syrian detention centers.[151]

Two years later, the German prosecutor issued an international arrest warrant for Jamil Hassan, the head of Syria's Air Force Intelligence Directorate, for torture, crimes against humanity, and war crimes.[152] It convicted and sentenced Syrian opposition group members for charges including membership in terrorist organizations, posing in pictures with severed heads, mutilating an enemy soldier's body, and attacking humanitarian or peacekeeping personnel. In early 2019, German officials charged Syrians Anwar Raslan and Eyad al-Gharib, who had served in Syria's secret service, with complicity in and aiding and abetting crimes against humanity. Raslan's accusations include electrocution, bludgeoning and stuffing victims into vehicle tires. Their trial began in April 2020 after they had been arrested in Germany.[153]

In Austria, the ECCHR collaborated with 16 Syrians and the Center for the Enforcement of Human Rights International to file complaints against 24 Syrian officials for torture and crimes against humanity.[154] In 2017 Austrian prosecutors convicted a member of the Farouq Brigade for murdering 20 unarmed injured Syrian soldiers in Homs. Overturned by the Austrian Supreme Court, the case was returned for retrial.[155] The case was pending as of this writing.

In France, the International Federation of Human Rights and the Human Rights League joined with French citizen Obeida Dabbagh to lodge a complaint for the deaths of his brother and nephew. After arresting second-year university student Patrick Dabbagh at his home, Syrian guards arrested Patrick's father for "failing" to raise his son correctly, according to the International Federation of Human Rights. Patrick died shortly after his arrest, his father nearly four years later, according to death certificates and media accounts.[156] The French war crimes unit opened the case, took testimony from witnesses, and issued arrest warrants for three high-level members of the Assad regime—Jamil Hassan; Ali Mamlouk, director of the Syrian Intelligence Agency; and his deputy, Abdel Salam.

French prosecutors opened additional preliminary investigations related to Caesar's photographs and the bombing of the Baba Media Center in Homs, which killed American journalist Marie Colvin and French photojournalist Remi Ochlik.[157] The French law firm Vigo also filed an action with evidentiary support from CJA and the US case, according to Beth Van Schaack.[158] "A vehicle" toward exposing attacks on civilians, catalyzing "future prosecutions," and understanding how "these systemic atrocities happened," *Colvin v. Syrian Arab Republic* won a judgment worth more than $300 million for Colvin's family, said lead lawyer Scott Gilmore.[159] "Marie was killed hours after reporting that the Syrian government was committing widespread attacks against civilians."[160] The French case was ongoing as of this writing.[161]

Sweden opened cases against at least 14 suspects of war crimes and convicted two lower-level Syrians—from the Free Syrian Army and the Assad regime.[162] Nine torture victims working with five legal NGOs filed complaints against four high-level members of the Assad regime.[163] The Netherlands identified some 30 war crimes suspects at this writing,[164] while the Dutch-based Syria Legal Network is bringing cases.[165] Several countries are collaborating through the European Genocide Network.[166]

Three countries brought charges against Assad's uncle, Rifaat al-Assad, former commander of the Defense Brigades, which massacred thousands of people in the 1980s. In Switzerland, al-Assad may face charges of war crimes with evidence supplied by TRIAL, while in Spain and France, he faces embezzlement charges.[167]

In addition to the Syria cases, advocates have taken action against a wide swath of suspected violators, including CIA agents in Italy for participating in extraordinary rendition, some of whom were convicted in absentia.[168] The cross-border efforts are "building a kind of transnational legal profession," said Gilmore. "We'll have co-counsel from US law firms who might also be working with lawyers in-country where the abuse occurred, who are assisting with the investigation or . . . with local legal issues."[169]

Advocates in the countries of violation "are way readier, and they have been craving this kind of work," added Bernabeu.[170] Her ideas influenced expansion at other NGOs. Where historically, "we [CJA] would have said, 'Oh well, that person's not here, so we can't do anything,' and now it would be, 'Well, what country do they travel to? Where else might they go? And do we have colleagues in that country who can help?,'" explained Kathy Roberts, CJA's former legal director. Working globally, Roberts represents US-based civil parties at tribunals, helping build portfolios to present "to law enforcement in other countries" where the accused may travel, simultaneously focusing "on the country where the crimes were committed . . . That is the future. That is where these trials should happen if they can," she said. Like EarthRights, CJA has begun providing "technical support to prosecutors and victims' attorneys and investigators" and helps "preserve evidence . . . build capacity [and] support the victims for future possible accountability measures."[171]

Together, these efforts are "making the world a little smaller."[172]

NINE

Retrauma and Resilience

The Dynamics of Clients and Counsel

Suleiman Salim, the Tanzanian torture and rendition survivor, had twice tried to get to his pretrial deposition in Dominica for his lawsuit against the two psychologists who evidently designed and helped implement the CIA's interrogation program.[1] But officials, first in Tanzania and later in Abu Dhabi, refused to let Salim board the plane. Unable to reach Dominica, the court moved his deposition to South Africa (discussed in chapter 6). There in Johannesburg, in March 2007, Steven Watt saw it happening, Salim's retraumatization.

James T. Smith, lawyer for the psychologist defendants John Bruce Jessen and James Mitchell, peppered Salim with questions, beginning with basics: name, place of birth, jobs. In the second hour, Smith pressed Salim about his travel complications: Why wasn't he permitted into the United States? Did he try to obtain a visa? Was he ever interviewed for a visa? What about Dominica where the deposition was originally planned? "Did you ever attempt to travel to the nation of Dominica? . . . Were you able to get to Dominica?"

"No," Salim replied through his translator.

"Can you tell me why?"

"I tried twice," he said. "The first time, I went to Dar es Salaam. They told me that I can't go because, first of all, I will pass through many countries that doesn't [*sic*] give Tanzania—any Tanzanian any visa. I tried the second time. I got up to Abu Dhabi. The people in Abu Dhabi told me that

I cannot proceed to Dominica because I'll pass through so many countries in transit."

Smith asked twice more: Why was he refused passage to Dominica?

Salim explained again: The flight route required him to transfer through countries for which, as a Tanzanian, he had no visa.

"Did they tell you why you couldn't pass through those countries?" Smith asked.

Paul Hoffman, Salim's co-counsel, objected. "I'll object to that on the grounds this now has been asked four times, and I'll instruct you [Salim] not to answer it. Move on. He's just given you the answer. You may not like it, but that's the answer," said Hoffman. "Don't badger the witness."

"Maybe you should tell the witness to answer the question," Smith argued.

"Why don't you just stop it? Don't badger the witness."

"I'm not badgering," Smith protested.

"He's trying to do it. Yeah, you are," Hoffman said.

"Can I ask you a question?" asked Salim.

"You want to ask me a question?" remarked Smith.

It was a plea, not a question, but Salim's command of English was imperfect: "Don't be so harsh on me, like the other people that asked me question [*sic*]. Just be—go slow and I'll answer the questions."

Salim tried again:[2] "I got to Abu Dhabi. They asked me where I was going. I told them I was going to Dominica. They asked me where is the visa for France—Dominica. I said there's no—there's no visa. I showed them the paper showing that, as a Tanzanian, I don't need a visa to go to Dominica. They refused. You can't go—they said you can't go to—you can't go to Dominica because you pass through many transits."

For another hour, Salim responded under oath to questions about his history. Then Smith turned to Salim's kidnapping, rendition, and detention in CIA black sites—asking Salim to remember and recount his harrowing experiences.

"I was just kidnapped on the road," said Salim. "I was driving. People came and put—drew a gun and point it at me. I came out and they took me. . . . I was beaten. They beat me a lot."[3]

"And you were beaten to the point where you needed to be taken to the hospital?"

"Yes."

Smith wanted details of injuries, events, the people who abducted and pummeled Salim to the point of hospitalization, the degree of pain Salim had suffered, and his time in Afghanistan. Salim cooperated, describing details as he remembered, and responding to documents. In the third hour,

Smith moved to Salim's detention at the CIA's "black sites," the first of which Salim referred to as "Darkness."

"How many times do you think you were interrogated during the period of time that you were held at the facility that you call 'Darkness'?" asked Smith.

"I cannot recall how many times, but it was almost for two months. . . . All the days that I was in there, they interrogated me."

"Okay. And can you describe for me what would happen during these interrogations?"

"Objection, but you can answer," interjected Hoffman.

Smith rephrased, asking for descriptions.

"I remember being put in a box. I remember being hanged," said Salim demonstrating with his hands. "I remember being naked and a big light. They put a light on my face. I remember being put on the ground in a plastic bag and water is being poured on me. And there was a plastic jug, plastic water jug being put—they were knocking my rectal area with it. I remember being put on a table and, then, I was tied around while being taken around. I remember there were two boxes, they were—there's one that was being put on the ground, and there was one that was also standing position. I remember being tied on the wall, handcuffed to the wall. I couldn't go up or come down. I also remember being handcuffed and naked in the room with not any clothes on. I remember being put on something like a hospital bed, my—my hands tied to both sides of bed. They put something like an injection on me and I lost my conscious. I remember, also, them putting a cloth around—tying a cloth around my neck and, then, they were punching me on the wall, punching."

More details, Smith requested. Where did each torture technique occur? For what duration? What types of injuries did Salim suffer?

"Dizziness," Salim said.

"Okay. And did you suffer any long-term injuries as a result of that dizziness?"

"I still have dizziness."

"And what is the basis for you to believe that your dizziness, presently, is as a result of being spun on that table?"

"Because they had tortured me a lot; I was very weak, and I had no strength. I could not—I didn't have any strength. I did not eat anything. And ever since that happened, I've been experiencing the dizziness."

Smith pushed further. How many times was he forced into each box? How long was he locked in the boxes? How many times was he spun on the table?

Salim described the duration, the frequency, the beatings. "At times, they would put me there, then they'd go and beat me, and then they'd come and put me there and sometimes they just leave me there."

"Who beat you? Was it an American? Was it a CIA agent? How many times were you beaten?"

His abuser was American, the beatings ongoing: "Ever since I was there, it was totally . . ." Salim froze.

"Are you with me?" Smith asked, then pressed again for more details.

"I already told you," said Salim.

"I don't think you did."

"I told you that they tied a cloth on my neck and they were punching me," Salim said. "They were putting me down and kicking me."

"Where did they punch you . . . where did they kick you?"

Salim pointed to his stomach. "Tummy . . . The kicking was more on the lower abdomen."

What about the hanging? Where did it occur? For how long? "Can you describe for me how you were hanged?"

Salim submitted, gesturing with his hands. "There was like a pipe up there, then I was handcuffed, and then it was tied there and I was standing."

What happened during the hanging? What injuries did he suffer? What permanent damage? How was he tied to the wall? Where was the wall? "Was it painful?" Smith asked.

"It's painful."

"Can you describe for me the pain?"

"I can't describe how painful it was."

"Do you presently experience the pain?"

"Yes."

"Can you describe for me the pain that you feel presently?"

Salim snapped: "Maybe I need to tie you here so that—for one hour so you can feel the pain if you want to know the pain." His forehead dropped, face to the table; he sobbed quietly, under his breath. His past was present; he had flashed back to relive the torture.

"Can we take a break?" asked Hoffman.

Knowing Salim's vulnerabilities, Watt had prepared ahead of time, retaining a trauma therapist, who shared techniques he could use if Salim slipped into flashback. "'There's actually two Suleimans [Salim],'" Watt recalled her saying. "'There's Suleiman who is in the room, and there is a Suleiman who is actually in that flashback situation. He's in the manacles. He feels himself physically in there,' [She said]. 'What you have to do, don't hold Suleiman who is in the room, speak to him, because you can speak to him. He'll be there. He'll speak to you,' [She said]. 'And get Suleiman who is here in the room with you. He has to go into the Darkness, and he has to . . . bring [the] other Suleiman out.'"[4]

Watt turned to his client, "I said, 'Suleiman, you're in the room, Suleiman?' And he said, 'Yes.' [I said], 'And other Suleiman, he is Suleiman in the Darkness?' And he said, 'yes.' And I said, 'Can you bring him in? Can you bring him back to here?' Oh my God, and he did it. . . . He did it in the [deposition] room. . . . And there's the whole fucking room full of people. Paul [Hoffman] is there, which was great. And there's the defendant's lawyer, sitting there on his fucking phone."[5]

Watt and Hoffman whisked Salim out of the deposition room. "I remember he grabbed my hand, and it was ice cold, and he just held on," Watt recalled. "And I said, 'Suleiman, you don't have to go back in there. This is the end, if you choose. This is you. You're controlling this deposition. He is not your interrogator.' And he went back in there, and he did it. And he was fucking great."[6]

The Trouble with Trauma

Trauma symptoms can go dormant then resurface, triggered by any number of sounds, incidents, or scenarios that return survivors to relive agonizing events, as Salim did. Published photos of Abu Ghraib torture victims sent other torture survivors such as Neris Gonzalez—some 25 years later—into flashbacks, she told Oscar Avila of the *Chicago Tribune*.

And for still other survivors, they evoked panic attacks, heart palpitations, body tremors, crying fits, nightmares, pain resurgence, and suicidal ideation—requiring "emotional triage" from torture counselors. "One of the most terrible effects of torture is that it never ends. It's with you all your life," explained psychologist Mario Gonzalez to Avila. One cannot "take a pill to erase all that from your mind."[7]

Gray agreed, adding, "It's easy to be retraumatized. God knows I've seen it with people who have gone through political torture directly. And it's very hard to throw off the symptoms. I just had contact with someone I saw years ago who's taken cases against torturers back in her own country now. And she's successful. . . . But her symptoms have risen in the course of doing this, [although] not ruinously as they were at the level when she first came to me."[8]

Rife with triggers, litigation carries intrinsic risks and inevitable distress that often reopen and compound original wounds. Uniformed personnel, depositions, and hostile cross-examinations can evoke recollections of torture as if they were reoccurring, sending survivors into dissociation and flashbacks. Legal proceedings—confrontations, boundary and privacy violations, prolonged proceedings, resource burnout, delayed resolution, disruptions to lives, the rise and fall of hope, unexpected interruptions, rescheduling, and postponements—can themselves traumatize, make avoidance-type coping strategies impossible and trigger insomnia, bouts of shame, or major depression.[9] In essence, the "very severe, legalistic, adversarial, rude culture" of litigation can clash with survivors' needs and cultures," explained Almudena Bernabeu.[10] And "it means they spend their next three or four years caught up with litigation rather than getting on with life," added Day.[11]

In the field's early development, neither clinicians nor lawyers were prepared. "We didn't know about retraumatization in the courtroom in the very beginning. This whole work around torture treatment is very new. It's from about 1984. . . . By the time I did know about it and was referring lawyers to torture treatment clinicians, there was some reluctance, some lack of understanding about the need," explained Gray. "But that's been overcome long since."[12]

An early proponent of litigation as a recovery tool, Gray remained cautious about potential harms, warning, "You don't have a right to push them [survivors]. It could be disastrous for them."[13]

Awareness has since grown of litigation's possible negative effects on survivors. "It's an incredibly stressful process, so we don't want to underestimate the risk of retraumatization," acknowledged Beth Van Schaack. Long trials and intense preparation put "plaintiffs under so much pressure. . . . [It's] really incredibly hard."[14]

UK-based human rights lawyer Martyn Day agreed, calling these the "downsides" to what he believes otherwise "is massive empowerment to the clients . . . It's tough, especially true, like with the Iraqis [I represented]. For them, the emotions were really high, and it was pretty tough getting them to go back through giving evidence about just what had happened."[15]

Understanding these dynamics is critically "important for lawyers as well as any other people working with survivors of human rights abuses," explained Beth Stephens. "Lives have been upended. Even if it's not at that level of problem, you know, they may have lost the breadwinner. They may have lost a child," experiences that can erect barriers to legal processes or working with lawyers at all.[16]

With potential troubles better understood, NGOs' attorneys have integrated health professionals into the legal process. The ACLU, CJA, CCR, and TRIAL International have incorporated psychological support to assist survivor clients through interviews, testimony, medical exams, lending support for regulating emotions, minimizing pain, and strengthening self-esteem and self-trust. This therapeutic accompaniment can allay some negative effects and help repair damage from the original trauma and any arising from litigation.[17] "They are reliving this experience in a way that none of us, as just lawyers representing them, can imagine," so CJA "connects clients [and] others, who contact us, to local treatment providers," which sometimes attend trial, explained former CJA executive director Dixon Osburn.[18] Historically, the organization extended referrals to the affected community, seeking to support "the health of the entire community, and not just . . . on this one client," added Van Schaack, CJA's former executive director. "They do a lot of outreach work."[19]

During the Guantánamo Bay trials, Watt involved trauma psychologist Kate Porterfield to guide and prepare the volunteer lawyers with little experience with trauma. "You need to give lawyers some skills to deal with torture survivors and . . . PTSD symptomology," to help them understand their clients' behavior, and "what they have gone through," said Watt. "Why are they avoiding this?' Because they have got severe PTSD. . . . The key thing is to have empathy."[20]

Lawyers "need to add up the trauma that these people have gone through. And then when they come . . . for such an emotional moment, they really need to be taken good care of," added TRIAL International's Benedict De Moerloose. Survivors can feel "revictimized . . . [and] angry" when "not being taken good care of by the authorities. . . . The Swiss are not doing very great work in this respect."[21]

Effects vary, depending on survivors' personalities, training, and psychosocial and spiritual resources. While Watt's black site clients suffered from similar torture, the survivor with supportive family, military training, and religious faith better managed "his PTSD" whereas "that episode just really destroyed" the other, he said. "Because Mohamed has a family around him. He was also a freedom fighter against the Khadafi regime. He was a soldier, and it is shown that if you are a soldier, you can manage traumatic events in a way that nonsoldiers can't. . . . I asked him how he gets through. He was much more deeply in his Muslim faith, and when he was in the [facility referred to as] Darkness, he would pray, and there would be a routine within that, which was one big traumatic event, like a yearlong episode that he spent in that prison."[22]

Those risks also raise dilemmas for lawyers. "Over the years that I have done this representation, I have always wondered if I am doing more harm than good from a psychological and broader perspective. Am I creating expectations? Am I managing expectations properly?," asked Watt, who ultimately believes that, overall, litigation has benefited his clients.[23]

These concerns, however, add pressure to win, as losing could result in "double trauma," acknowledged Hoffman. "[As] human rights lawyers, if you lose, you're causing a lot of problems for the people you are representing . . . [to] go through all this and . . . then lose. [But] if you win, it's helpful."[24]

In addition to client-based risks, human rights lawyers face their own physical, psychological, and occupational risks, including brushes with traumatic events and secondary trauma. But for the core human rights lawyers, the benefits outweigh these risks.

Physical Risks

"This is not a profession for the faint of heart," admitted Terrence Collingsworth. Caught in conflict zones in Colombia and Indonesia, he recalled "very, very harrowing experiences" during fact-finding.[25] In Aceh, he was "caught in a battle," and to evade getting shot in the crossfire, "We pulled off the road behind some bushes and just tried to lay low in the car," he recalled. "But those are things that happen to anyone who is going to be in a war zone."[26]

The fundamental job requirements mean, "You get off your bottom, and you go out to some dodgy area like Nigeria or Sierra Leone or Ivory Coast or God knows where, and you face those sort of risks," said Day who recalled going "to Sierra Leone . . . to see where the clients lived. . . . We're very used to it. It's what we do . . . but for a lot of people, it's quite daunting, scary. You know, you go to Nigeria, and it's a bloody difficult place to understand it all. But I think we've got enough experience to kind of know when . . . as with everybody, you kind of learn to live with the risks. You kind of get used to it. I don't to get too blasé, and we do take risk seriously. . . . I've been arrested and God knows what."[27]

Day's arrest followed a local member of parliament demanding a payout of the legal settlement Day had negotiated for clients. "I said, 'Look, you haven't been a client.' And he said, 'Well, you see how our system works: I'm the local MP, and I'm entitled to a share of the money.' And I said, 'Sorry that's not the way our system works.' And so he got me arrested," Day recalled. "After three days in prison, we managed to get enough pressure on to have me released. . . . But those are the kind of pressures of the job, really."[28]

In another close call in Nigeria, armed guards whisked Day out of a large community meeting when "things were getting hot. They said, 'Look, we have to get out of here.' And I said, 'Just five minutes.' And they said, 'No! Now!' So we jumped in the vans, and we got out of there," Day recalled.[29]

Interviewees recounted remote, underdeveloped, or lawless regions, where brown water flowed from taps, violence simmered, and strategically placed cash was the only way to secure safe exit. The EarthRights team conducted fact-finding "along the Thai/Burma border for the Unocal case," in "the Niger Delta for *Bowoto v. Chevron* and *Wiwa v. Shell*," and "in rather dicey parts of Colombia for the *Doe v. Chiquita* case," and "took a deposition about a year ago in a Colombian maximum security prison," explained Marco Simons.[30] For *Bowoto*, Bert Voorhees entered regions designated as "no-go" by the US State Department. "I was in the bush . . . out in areas from Lagos to Ondo State, up in Benin City, down to Sapele, with armed police or military sometimes stopping the car and demanding bribes as often as every mile or so. [We were] unable to travel at night for fear of bandits, one group of which we avoided one evening by stopping along the side of the road for an hour or two, watching victims of the robbers straggling back down the road toward us, stripped of their belongings and clothing," he recalled. "Or I'd be in some taxi, driving like mad against traffic on the wrong side of the highway, with craters the size of a bus on the other side of the road, and I would look down between my feet and there would be a hole the size of my backpack through the floor."[31]

Their local counterparts face much worse. "I always have a partner in the country where I'm working . . . those people . . . they're facing danger. They also get ostracized and blacklisted," Collingsworth explained. "I have a local lawyer in Colombia who's been working with me on this Drummond litigation, and he has received death threats. His wife has received death threats. He's had two assassination attempts against him. . . . [They] suffered all kinds of other reprisals."[32]

Gallagher agreed about these real "concerns, not only for my clients but the person we have working on the ground in Iraq who's assisting us in these cases. He's who I worry about, on every level. He's been working with us for all these years supporting 338 torture survivors, being the frontline cell phone number that they have."[33]

Another occupational hazard is trauma transference from survivor to lawyer, counselor, or friend—known as secondary or vicarious trauma—and a range of difficult emotions.[34]

Trauma Transference and Recovery

"I can still feel it now," said Watt about his experiences with Salim's "very severe" flashbacks. "I got a bit of PTSD from that—secondary trauma."[35]

As Watt described Salim's ordeal: "Even with that knowledge and understanding [of PTSD], when I met Salim," he stopped abruptly, choking up and leaving his thoughts incomplete. "He affects me the most. . . . I have done talks on this, and I'll pull out the pictures to show a crowd of people I don't know, and I'm like, uh, it's really hard," he said.[36]

Salim's co-counsel, Paul Hoffman, expressed profound anger at the defense lawyers on Salim's behalf. "I almost got into a fist fight when they purposely put [Salim] into a flashback in the deposition. It was one of the only times I almost got into a fist fight," he admitted to law students at the University of California, Irvine. The "defendants' [lawyers] were trying to retraumatize [him] . . . After putting him into a flashback, [defense counsel] said, 'I'm just doing my job.' I said, 'You could try to be a human being.'"[37]

Horrifying stories inevitably affect the advocates, according to Susan Burke, co-counsel for Abu Ghraib torture victims. "All [of us] suffered to some level or another the vicarious trauma that you get from hearing the stories."[38]

"Emotionally difficult" work requires hearing "the horrors that many plaintiffs have been through, and reliving that and dealing with the human interaction and the fact that they are often scared people, the products and the consequences of having suffered in these ways, and then having agreed to go public with the struggle for justice, which is not an easy role either," added Stephens.[39] "I've spent a lot of the last six months doing investigation on the Bolivia cases talking to witnesses. . . . We were interviewing people about things that happened in 2003, and people were in tears in most of our interviews at one point or another about what they saw."[40]

High exposure to direct or indirect trauma may account for human rights advocates' higher rates of mental health issues—anxiety, depression, and nightmares in "alarming proportions": 19.4 percent have PTSD, 18 percent subthreshold PTSD, 14.7 percent depression, and 19 percent burnout with few seeking counseling or workplace support, according to one study. "I've seen it with colleagues who have suffered from years of work with people who have gone through such terrible things," added Stephens. "Because my work has tended to be more on the papers, I don't think I personally have experienced that."[41]

The realizations have prompted training and preparation for human rights workers to manage work-related chronic stress and trauma or step-ping away from "direct contact . . . I got secondary trauma doing the work for a quarter of a century," said Gray, CJA's cofounder. To alleviate "PTSD symptoms," he shifted "from doing therapy to administrative positions to even board work."[42]

The opposite—the intangible rewards—are also abundant: human rights advocates draw strength, pride, joy, "vicarious resilience," inspira-tion, liberation, and their own self-recovery and psychological healing from working with survivors while simultaneously gaining a sense of pur-pose and challenges that suit their personalities.[43]

Recovery, Resilience, Reward

The work transforms the worker.[44] Service providers are often inspired and awed by their clients' courage and resilience.[45] "Most people [survivors] who I've worked with are just amazing, and I wonder how they're capable of doing this," said Stephens.[46]

For psychologist Mario Gonzalez, it was cotransformative. By help-ing survivors "liberate themselves . . . in turn somehow, I have liberated myself by assisting them along their journey to personal freedom," he said to Sarah Conway of *Chicago Magazine*.[47]

Salim's case helped Hoffman "get over my own grief . . . after my wife died," he said to law students, adding, "These kind of cases—they give something to the lawyers. You get something back in human rights work. It's hard to put your finger on [it]. It makes law practice worth being a lawyer. I'll never look back and think I wasted my time for doing inter-rogatories. This is important work and affects people's lives and affects you in ways that are really profound."[48]

Drawn to the field through personal experiences, emotions, and iden-tity, human rights service providers tend to have "a connection" to sur-vivors, explained Gray. "It may be partly self-healing [or] identification with the victims. And that was true in my case too. . . . I was raised by immigrants and refugees for the first six years of life. So my identification is principally with them and not with people like those members of my [birth] family who are from a wealthy background."[49]

These types of personal connections to human rights injustices such as the Holocaust, pogroms, or abject poverty shape ideas, worldviews, ethics, and forge bonds—into what Cindy Cohn called "a pretty tight posse"—

among the advocates and between advocates and survivors. "Probably every one of us who [does] this work either had an experience of injustice ourselves or at some formative point of our lives, we met people [who had]," explained Katie Redford. It's part of what enables human rights lawyers to "get through it . . . We've met the clients, and we feel bound and connected to them. . . . It's personal. It's in your heart, and that's the difference."[50] Gallagher agreed: "It took me a while to see it as crystal clearly as I do now—what's motivating people in this work is love . . . humanity. You're fighting for something absolutely at the core."[51]

Described as "important," "dream jobs,"[52] "about love,"[53] "privilege,"[54] "heart's work," "important," and "God's work,"[55] this work gives purpose, meaning, while aligning their personal, professional, and political lives. "It's about acting for people [who] we believe deserve our time and attention," according to Martyn Day, who added, "It's a very important part of society."[56]

Kathy Roberts feels "incredibly lucky" to "have real impact for people who I think are left out of the power structure."[57] Agnieszka Fryszman agreed, noting redress's impact: with "money for the Nepali woman, they bought houses, started scholarship funds, sent their kids to school, and established a weaving cooperative."[58] And through the process, "you become more than just a lawyer to survivors of human rights violations. You become like a best friend and a confidante. It is very privileged; I feel very privileged," added Watt.[59]

In contrast with "soul-crushing work . . . [on] the corporate side," human rights lawyers are compelled by a "big, big" emotional pull,[60] said Day. They work on cases they "believe in," representing clients they "agree with," not simply "people who hire you,"[61] according to Stephens and Cohn. "When I occasionally run across a young lawyer who . . . ends up on the defense side of one of these cases, personally, that's not something I would have ever let happen to me," said Beth Stephens.[62] "The rainmakers, maybe they don't care, but the junior assistants, that's not what they wanted to do," added Cohn. "We [witnessed] a number of people who left the Chevron team a little chagrined about what they were doing."[63]

Simultaneously, "overcoming risk, adversity, and danger" in complicated David-versus-Goliath battles fulfills a need for intense intellectual challenge and calls up their peak performance, acknowledged Dan Stormer.[64] Day agreed, crediting the cases for making "life fun . . . interesting" and "exciting," he said. "I like to feel I'm alive, you know. It's tough, but I wouldn't do it if I wasn't enjoying it . . . [and] you get under the skin of society."[65]

Together, these are the making of "momentous" experiences, acknowledged Day, whose victory for the Mau Mau was "one of the most exciting legal moments in my life,"[66] while Richardson's *Doe v. Unocal* win was "one of the highlights of my entire legal career."[67] For Cohn, "It's a good day when we can take a human rights abuser, a corporate human rights abuser, and give them a bad day because that's so rare."[68]

TEN

The Making, Unmaking, and Remaking of a Rights Revolution

"Rights are not gifts," as Charles Epp noted.[1] These ideas become realities when societies decide that they should.[2] Through intergenerational persuasion, creative strategies, and relentless pursuits, US-based rights advocates constructed a foundation for civil rights,[3] then sought to extend those rights to others still falling "below the law"—the unprotected and unredressed beyond US borders where rights ignored can mean death and worse.[4]

Just as rights are "made," they can be "unmade," a reality understood by human rights lawyers. Many came from the cohort who together fought and won civil rights for African Americans, women, workers, the LGBT community, prisoners, or the criminally accused.[5] As greater numbers of lawyers joined the cause to solidify civil rights, a small group from that pool turned their attention toward realizing rights for those abroad who were egregiously harmed without recourse or remedy in their home countries.[6] From Center for Constitutional Rights, specifically founded to advance civil rights,[7] came refugee-turned-attorney Peter Weiss and Rhonda Copelon, who spearheaded the first US-based universal jurisdiction case. With an obscure but deftly-maneuvered Alien Tort Statute, their long-shot win was a stretch and an inspiration—precisely what they were after—stretching the law to include the downtrodden abroad and to persuade others to take up the human rights cause.[8]

The next generation, a small, dedicated crew of advocates, expanded Alien Tort Statute protections through new divisions in existing organizations, new organizations, laws, law clinics, and by attracting additional law-yers to the cause, usually on a part-time or pro bono basis. Against a tide of legal, political, and practical obstacles, they used civil litigation as their tool to mitigate damage, inch toward fulfilling a vision of a just world, and as an expression of their own humanity and politics.[9] Supported either by pro-bono traditions, contingency fees, charitable contributions, or alterna-tive sources of income, these advocates and their clients persuaded judges, built a growing body of case law to pave a rights-based future, and inspired Congress to pass new legislation for the cause.

They challenged military leaders, heads of state, transnational corpora-tions, and states implicated in human rights abuses. But pitting grand ide-als against entrenched state power, corporate wealth, and military might came with consequences. Larger obstacles mounted; cases consumed years of time, energy, and brainpower, frequently applied mostly toward resolv-ing their adversaries' procedural motions made to delay and dismiss the actions before the cases' substance could be heard.

Simultaneously, an ideological backlash was building. Divisive media, political leaders, and their supporters spread contemptuous language that expressed no compassion for the downtrodden, ignored systemic and structural oppression, and blamed the oppressed for their own woes.[10] A new crop of judges and leaders built higher legal thresholds and barriers that were increasingly harder to surmount, blocking the advancement of human rights. Co-opting the civil rights movement's strategies, a coun-termovement gained more for the already privileged, including individual rights for corporations, without requiring the same responsibilities.[11] Nar-rowing access to courts, which had taken decades to develop, they cut short a rights revolution in the making—at least for now.

While all long-term complex litigation requires great endurance to respond to relentless motions meant to stall or stop cases or to wear advo-cates down and out, human rights lawyers face unique personal, physical, political, and professional risks, with fewer tangible rewards. Grisly truths, vicarious trauma, attacks on reputations, and dangerous, remote, and costly fact-finding compound a process already replete with procedural barriers that most lawyers take for granted—jurisdiction, process service, securing testimony from traumatized, remote witnesses, who, for safety, must often remain anonymous and who face travel restrictions based upon the prover-bial "accident of birth"—where and to whom they were born. But the com-bined shifts in the US—the attacks on domestic civil rights and the sharp narrowing of access for international human rights cases—came to divide the advocates' already scarce time. Reformulated strategies—turning to common law, state courts, or suing individual corporate executives—continued to advance a smattering of cases but only when advocates had requisite information to pass the court's higher thresholds.

As the US became less hospitable to human rights claims, the locus of the human rights strategy shifted. A local-global approach developed in the battle to confront the most difficult and protected defendants—powerful public officials and transnational corporations. For officials who escaped traditional routes of accountability, such as the international tribunals or the ICC, the principle of universal jurisdiction in cross-border strategies became one tool of choice. These new strategies yielded indictments, arrests, and judgments not thought possible before, including in Europe, the UK, and the Americas. Still, countless victims remain without remedy, their abusers without accountability.

In the current legal order, transnational corporations in particular pose a complicated problem. Having outgrown many nation-states' economies, power, and policy-making influence,[12] many have taken roles traditionally held by states—but without the same responsibilities, duties, or meaningful accountability measures.[13] With globalization came mutually beneficial partnerships between oppressive regimes and transnational corporations, the former shored up by the latter, the latter traversing the globe for greater profits and reduced costs.[14] Legal obligations to shareholders and the corporations themselves and missions to maximize profits incentivize using corporate might to gain more for themselves while escaping sanctions, despite damage often left in their wake. Excluded from mandates such as the International Criminal Court, or from punishments such as incarceration, and not subject to elections or related forms of political accountability, corporate power left fewer meaningful levers for the aggrieved to stop or repair their damage.[15] Still, when the courts protected the US and its top officials from civil liability, in a few cases survivors found redress by suing the for-profit military contractor.

Because ideas transcend borders, with creative advocacy, they are shaped to fit different legal regimes, cultures, and overcome legal barriers. When survivors and lawyers across the globe wrested information from the confines of secrecy and sequestration, they amalgamated classic and new ideas, applying them to local facts, institutions, customs, or jurisprudence in the courts of their own countries, interstate courts, and, more recently, the territory where the wrongs occurred, to find a remedy from the transnational corporation violator. Some used common law, others criminal law with goals to prevent, repair, and redress damage left unmitigated—winning some, losing others, while many cases are still pending.

Throughout this book, evidence affirms earlier studies about influences on case outcomes, including judicial ideology, structural support, and the movement's collective efforts[16] while the advocates' ethos reflects the morality-law connection that other scholars have noted.[17] These advocates use existing laws to stretch the law and challenge injustices within political-legal systems on behalf of their "entire client constituency" and for "future generations."[18] It affirms studies finding lawyers transforming human rights into an international movement and into "a more influential force."[19] But this book also revealed the central roles of ideas, information, and creative agency to find, combine, frame, and move them in persuasive ways: shaped by their own experiences and understandings, advocates discovered harrowing information that changed their thinking, and then advanced sometimes unconventional ideas—to colleagues, clients, courts, and beyond—to solve conscience-shocking problems. Often met with reticence, even resistance, each development emerged from information flowing to an advocate, followed by a decision to solve a terrible problem, and to put forward a new, unorthodox, or unpopular idea through persuasion.

Despite frustrations and risks, the intangible benefits—a sense of purpose, healing for client and self, a commitment to a more just world, and much-needed challenges and contests—kept many in the struggle. Many donate their time and skills;[20] others supplement human rights work with easier or more lucrative cases or with university positions; the rest work at NGOs funded through philanthropy, grants, and other contributions. And through the process, from discovery to resolution, both advocates and their clients often change.

In the contest of human rights arguments, the collective cases suggest both optimism and some pessimism, not as optimistic as scholars like Kathryn Sikkink, who argued that we are witnessing a human rights revolution, a "justice cascade" in which the purveyors of death, torture, and mass destruction who once sat at the pinnacles of power are no longer untouchable by courts of law. She points to the radical shift, in which Chilean dictator Augusto Pinochet, Uruguayan president Juan Maria Bordaberry Arocena, and Liberian president Charles Taylor were charged for human rights violations perpetrated during their reigns—an unthinkable phenomenon in their terrorized communities of past decades. Collectively, speckled all over the world, court by court, case by case, prosecutions of human rights abusers are weaving together a growing global fabric of justice, she wrote.[21]

While these developments are real, they are but a few wins among widespread violations of fundamental human rights—torture, genocide, slavery—that continue mostly unabated, unprosecuted, and unredressed. The impossibility of adjudicating all of the abuses gives many violators a pass and leaves their victims without remedy. Yet these realities don't mean that the doomsday predictions of scholars like Stephen Hopgood and Eric Posner are true. Some of these arguments suggest that we are in the twilight or the end-times for human rights and human rights law. Problematic international criminal tribunals, religious and ideological attacks on human rights norms, and shifts in global power damage progress, leave mass failures, and marginalize victims.[22]

But this is where agency, ideas, and information matter. Creative advocacy changes to fit the times and address systemic deficiencies, locally and internationally. Given the painstakingly slow political-legal processes, the fluidity, and transient wins and losses, it is too soon to declare the human rights contest either victorious, dying, or outdated. The struggle is alive and well and transforming to fit the challenges of the new era. With lessons from the US and beyond, cross-border collaborations are producing new systems and structures to build and buttress local and international rights revolutions, toward grand visions about a global, working rule of law that leaves no one above the law and no one below it.

Notes

Preface

1. See, for example, D. Cingranelli and D. Richards, "The Cingranelli and Richards (Ciri) Human Rights Data Project," *Human Rights Quarterly* 32 (2010). Eric A. Posner, *The Twilight of Human Rights Law* (Oxford: Oxford University Press, 2014); A. S. Chilton and M. Versteeg, "The Failure of Constitutional Torture Prohibitions," *Journal of Legal Studies* 44, no. 2 (2015); Human Rights Watch, "Human Rights World Reports, 2014–2019," (2019), https://www.hrw.org/world-report/2018; Amnesty International, "State of the World's Human Rights," (2018), https://www.amnesty.org/download/Documents/POL1067002018ENGLISH.PDF; Tony Evans, *The Politics of Human Rights: A Global Perspective* (London: Pluto Press, 2005); Mining Watch Canada, "Annual Report," (2016), https://miningwatch.ca/sites/default/files/mwcannualreport2016.pdf; J. Steyn, "Guantánamo Bay: The Legal Black Hole.," *International & Comparative Law Quarterly* 53, no. 1 (2004); Stephen Hopgood, *The Endtimes of Human Rights* (Ithaca, NY: Cornell University Press, 2013).

2. Charles Epp, *The Rights Revolution: Lawyers, Activists, and Supreme Courts in Comparative Perspectives* (Chicago: University of Chicago Press, 1998).

3. Kathryn Sikkink, *Evidence for Hope: Making Human Rights Work in the 21st Century* (Princeton: Princeton University Press, 2017); Michael McCann, *Rights at Work: Pay Equity Reform and the Politics of Legal Mobilization* (Chicago: University of Chicago Press, 1994).

4. Dataset originated by Cortelyou C. Kenney, "Measuring Transnational Human Rights," *Fordham Law Review* 84, no. 3 (2015).

Chapter 1

1. Personal interviews with human rights lawyers in the USA, UK, and Europe, 2016 and 2017.

2. Cindy Cohn, interview by author, 2018, Skype;

3. Judith Chomsky, interview by author, 2016, Skype.

4. Scott Gilmore, interview by author, 2016, Skype.

5. Gilmore interview.

6. Gilmore interview.

7. Katherine Gallagher, interview by author, 2017, New York.

8. Dataset originated by Kenney, "Measuring Transnational Human Rights."

9. Paul Hoffman, interview by author, 2017, Los Angeles; Hoffman, oral arguments in Doe v. Cisco, 2017, Ninth Circuit Court of Appeals.

10. Matt Eisenbrandt, interview by author, 2017, via Skype. Dismissal rates are in Kenney, "Measuring Transnational Human Rights." Beth Van Schaack, interview by author, 2017, Stanford University.

11. Van Schaack Interview.

12. William J. Aceves, *The Anatomy of Torture: A Documentary History of Filártiga v. Peña-Irala* (Leiden: Brill, 2007).; Albert Ruben, *The People's Lawyer: The Center for Constitutional Rights and the Fight for Social Justice, from Civil Rights to Guantánamo* (New York: Monthly Review Press, 2011), 8.

13. Alexander Hamilton, "Federalist No. 80: The Powers of the Judiciary" (1788); John Jay, "Federalist No. 3: Concerning Dangers from Foreign Force and Influence" (1787); Anthony D'Amato, "The Alien Tort Statute and the Founding of the Constitution," *American Journal of International Law* 82, no. 1 (1988).

14. Peter Weiss, interview by author, 2017, New York.

15. Dolly Filártiga, "American Courts, Global Justice," *New York Times*, March 30, 2004.

16. Filártiga, "American Courts, Global Justice."

17. Paul Hoffman, interview by author, 2016. Also interview by author with Paul Hoffman, 2017, and Hoffman's CV (accessed 2017).

18. Interviews with human rights lawyers (2016 and 2017).

19. Ronald Smothers, "3 Women Win Suit over Torture by an Ethiopian Official," *New York Times*, August 21, 1993.

20. Hoffman interview 2017. See also Gerald Gray, interview by author, San Francisco, 2017; Andrew Rice, "The Long Interrogation," *New York Times Magazine*, June 4, 2006.

21. Gray interview.

22. Interviews with Hoffman, Gray, and Van Schaack.

23. Chomsky interview.

24. Katie Redford and Beth Stephens, "The Story of Doe v. Unocal: Justice Delayed but Not Denied," in *Human Rights Advocacy Stories*, ed. Deena Hurwitz, Margaret Satterthwaite, and Doug Ford (New York: Thomson Reuters/Foundation Press, 2009).

25. Redford and Stephens, "The Story of Doe v. Unocal"; interviews (2016 and 2017) with counsel representing Doe: Dan Stormer; Katie Redford, Marco Simons, Anne Richardson; EarthRights International and Southeast Asian Information Network, "Total Denial: A Report on the Yadana Pipeline Project in Burma" (Washington, DC: EarthRights International and Southeast Asian Information Network, 1996); Milena Kaneva, *Total Denial* (2006).

26. Interviews (2016 and 2017) with Katie Redford, Dan Stormer, Marco Simons.

27. Interviews (2016 and 2017) with Katie Redford, Dan Stormer, Marco Simons.

28. Official court records of *John Doe I v. Unocal Corp.*, 395 F.3d 932 (2002).

29. Michael Goldhaber, "A Win for Wiwa, a Win for Shell, a Win for Corporate Human Rights," *Am Law Daily*, June 10, 2009, https://amlawdaily.typepad.com/amlawdaily/2009/06/a-win-for-wiwa-a-win-for-shell-a-win-for-corporate-human-rights.html

30. The total amount was reported in the media (i.e., Goldhaber, "A Win for Wiwa"). The use of the money from Anne Richardson, interview by author, 2016; Katie Redford, interview by author, 2017.

31. "The Curse of Oil in Ogoniland," http://umich.edu/~snre492/cases_03-04/Ogoni/Ogoni_case_study.htm

32. "Curse of Oil in Ogoniland."

33. "Curse of Oil in Ogoniland."

34. Shell and SPDC, its subsidiary, spilled 1.6 million gallons of oil in Ogoniland, representing approximately 40 percent of Shell's total worldwide spills, according to the original *Kiobel v. Royal Dutch Petroleum Co.*, 642 F.3d 268 (2011).

35. "Curse of Oil in Ogoniland"; *Wiwa v. Royal Dutch Petroleum Co.*, 226 F.3d 88 (2000).

36. "Curse of Oil in Ogoniland"; *Kiobel v. Royal Dutch Petroleum Co.*, (2004).

37. *Kiobel v. Royal Dutch Petroleum* (2004). https://ccrjustice.org/sites/default/files/assets/05.14.04%20Amended%20Complaint.pdf

38. *Kiobel v. Royal Dutch Petroleum* (2004).

39. "Curse of Oil in Ogoniland."

40. *Wiwa v. Royal Dutch Petroleum Co.* (2004){~?~MA: This is still from their complaint, referenced above.}.

41. Jad Mouawad, "Shell to Pay $15.5 Million to Settle Nigerian Case," *New York Times*, June 8, 2009.

42. *Wiwa v. Royal Dutch Petroleum Co.*

43. *Kiobel v. Royal Dutch Petroleum Co.*

44. Kerrie M. Taylor, "Thicker Than Blood: Holding Exxon Mobil Liable for Human Rights Violations Committed Abroad," *Syracuse Journal of International Law and Commerce* 31, no. 2 (2004).

45. Taylor, "Thicker Than Blood."

46. Privambudi Sulistiyanto, "Whither Aceh?," *Third World Quarterly* 22, no. 3 (2010).

47. Sulistiyanto, "Whither Aceh?"

48. Sulistiyanto, "Whither Aceh?"

49. Taylor, "Thicker Than Blood."

50. Additional plaintiffs filed a companion lawsuit and the cases were consolidated.

51. Taylor, "Thicker Than Blood"; *Doe v. Exxon Mobil Corp.*, 654 F.3d 11 (D.C. 2011). Also Laird Townsend and Ian Shearn, "Did ExxonMobil Pay Torturers?," *Mother Jones*, October 5, 2012. https://www.motherjones.com/environment/2012/10/did-exxon-pay-torturers/

52. *Doe v. Exxon Mobil Corp.*

53. *Doe v. Exxon Mobil Corp.*, 39–41, 46; Agnieszka Fryszman, interview by

author, 2017, Washington, DC; http://www.csrandthelaw.com/2015/07/31/alien
-tort-case-development-plaintiffs-in-exxon-mobil-case-survive-touch-aand-conce
rn-review/; "Exxon Human Rights Case Survives—on Claim That Execs Knew All
Along," *100 Reporters*, July 16, 2015, https://100r.org/2015/07/exxon-human-righ
ts-case-survives-claim-that-execs-knew-all-along/

54. Fryszman interview.
55. Fryszman interview.
56. Morton Sklar, interview by author, 2017.
57. Sklar interview.
58. Hoffman interview.
59. Hoffman interview 2017.
60. Beth Stephens, interview by author, 2017, telephone.
61. Sklar interview.
62. Interviews with human rights lawyers, 2016 and 2017.
63. Chomsky interview.
64. Cohn interview.
65. Richardson interview.
66. Fryszman interview.
67. Gray interview. Also Van Schaack interview.
68. *Jean v. Dorelien*, 431 F.3d 776 (2003).
69. *Jean v. Dorelien*, 431 F.3d 776 (2003); "Crimes against Humanity under
Haitian High Command, Jean v. Dorélian," Center for Justice & Accountability,
http://cja.org/what-we-do/litigation/jean-v-dorelien/; Andrew Buncombe, "The
Junta Fugitive, a Lottery Win and a Battle for Justice in Haiti," *Independent* (London), February 17, 2007, https://www.independent.co.uk/news/world/americas
/the-junta-fugitive-a-lottery-win-and-a-battle-for-justice-in-haiti-436664.html
70. Marco Simons, interview by author, 2016.
71. Gilmore interview.
72. Richardson interview.
73. Richardson interview
74. Richardson interview.
75. Simons interview.
76. Terry Collingsworth, interview by author, 2016, via Skype.
77. Collingsworth interview.
78. Dixon Osburn, interview by author, 2017, telephone.
79. Stephens interview.
80. Stormer interview.
81. Stormer interview.
82. Stephens interview.
83. Interview with human rights lawyers, 2016 and 2017.
84. Martyn Day, interview by author, 2017, London. Eisenbrandt interview.

Chapter 2

1. William J. Aceves, *The Anatomy of Torture: A Documentary History of Filártiga
v. Peña-Irala* (Leiden: Brill, 2007).
2. Aceves, *Anatomy of Torture.*

3. *Filártiga v. Peña-Irala*, 630 F.2d 876 (NY 1980). The quote is slightly differ-ent in the account of Richard Alan White, *Breaking Silence: The Case That Changed the Face of Human Rights* (Washington, DC: Georgetown University Press, 2004).

4. Carla Hall, "In Paraguay, a Death in the Family," *Washington Post*, March 25, 1982.

5. Filártiga, "American Courts, Global Justice."

6. Aceves, *Anatomy of Torture*.

7. Hall, "In Paraguay, a Death in the Family."

8. Filártiga, "American Courts, Global Justice."

9. Aceves, *Anatomy of Torture*; Stephens interview.

10. Aceves, *Anatomy of Torture*; Stephens interview.

11. Aceves, *Anatomy of Torture*; White, *Breaking Silence*.

12. Weiss interview 2017.

13. Weiss interview 2017.

14. Weiss interview 2017.

15. Weiss interview 2017.

16. "What Is a Crime against Humanity? An Interview with Peter Weiss" *Pin-kyshow*, December 11, 2006, http://www.pinkyshow.org/projectarchives/videos/what-is-a-crime-against-humanity-an-interview-with-peter-weiss

17. "What Is a Crime against Humanity? An Interview with Peter Weiss."

18. Weiss interview 2017.

19. Weiss interview 2017.

20. Weiss Interview 2017.

21. Weiss interview 2017.

22. Albert Ruben, *The People's Lawyer: The Center for Constitutional Rights and the Fight for Social Justice, from Civil Rights to Guantánamo* (New York: Monthly Review Press, 2011), 8.

23. Weiss interview 2017. Also, Peter Weiss, interview by author, via telephone, May 27, 2020.

24. Aceves, *Anatomy of Torture*.

25. *Filártiga v. Peña-Irala*.

26. White, *Breaking Silence*.

27. *Filártiga v. Peña-Irala*.

28. Edward Wong, "Following Up; Still Seeking Justice in a Brother's Death," *New York Times*, October 1, 2000.

29. *Tel-Oren v. Libyan Arab Republic*, 726 F.2d 774 (DC 1984).

30. Stephens interview.

31. Gus Yatron, "The Phenomenon of Torture: Hearings of the Subcommittee of Human Rights of the House Committee on Foreign Affairs," House of Repre-sentatives, Ninety-Eighth Congress, 1984.

32. See, for example, Associated Press, "Around the World: Panel Votes Dead-line on Arms to Turks," *New York Times*, May 11, 1983.

33. See, for example, "House Panel OK's Aid Program," *Boston Globe*, July 16, 1982.

34. Gus Yatron, "Declassified Letter to Honorable Ronald Reagan" (1983).

35. "Yatron Will Seek Reelection to Seat for Ninth Term," *Morning Call*, Janu-ary 10, 1984.

36. Yatron, "Phenomenon of Torture."

37. Larry Cox, deputy director of Amnesty International, in Yatron, "Phenomenon of Torture."

38. Yatron, "Phenomenon of Torture," 83–84.

39. United States Senate, Committee on Foreign Relations, "Practice of Torture by Foreign Governments and US Efforts to Oppose its Use," June 26, 1984.

40. Yatron, "Phenomenon of Torture."

41. Yatron, "Phenomenon of Torture."

42. Yatron, "Phenomenon of Torture."

43. United Nations General Assembly, "Resolution 39/46 Convention against Torture and Other Cruel, Inhuman or Degrading Treatment or Punishment" (1984).

44. Yatron said during 1988 hearings that he and his colleagues introduced the bill in the 99th Congress. He also said it amended the United Nations Participation Act of 1945, which included obligations of the US under the UN Charter. See Committee on Foreign Affairs, Subcommittee on Human Rights and International Organizations, "The Torture Victim Protection Act," March 23, 1988.

45. Alfred McCoy, "Dark Legacy: Human Rights under the Marcos Regime," in *Memory, Truth Telling and the Pursuit of Justice: A Conference on the Legacies of the Marcos Dictatorship* (Manila: Ateneo de Manila University: 1999).

46. Joan Fitzpatrick, "The Future of the Alien Tort Claims Act of 1789: Lessons from in Re Marcos Human Rights Litigation," *St. John's Law Review* 67, no. 3 (2012).

47. McCoy, "Dark Legacy."

48. *In Re Estate of Marcos Human Rights Litigation*, 978 F.2d 493 (1992).

49. McCoy, "Dark Legacy."

50. McCoy, "Dark Legacy."

51. *In Re Estate of Marcos Human Rights Litigation*.

52. Adrienne LaFrance, "Marcos Victims to Split $7.5m Settlement," *Civil Beat* (Honolulu) January 14, 2011. https://www.civilbeat.org/2011/01/8157-marcos-victims-to-split-75m-settlement/

53. *Hilao v. Estate of Marcos*, 103 F.3d 767 (1996). See also Ellen Lutz. "The Marcos Human Rights Litigation: Can Justice be Achieved in US Courts for Abuses that Occurred Abroad." *BC Third World LJ* 14 (1994): 43.

54. *Trajano v. Marcos* (1992).

55. Fitzpatrick, "The Future of the Alien Tort Claims Act of 1789: Lessons from in Re Marcos Human Rights Litigation," 491; *Trajano v. Marcos*.

56. Susan F. Quimpo and Nathan Gilbert Quimpo, *Subversive Lives: A Family Memoir of the Marcos Years* (Athens: Ohio University Press, 2016). Witnesses reported in books, articles, and memorial organizations. See, for example, Kate Pedroso and Marielle Medina, "Liliosa Hilao: First Martial Law Detainee Killed," https://newsinfo.inquirer.net/718061/liliosa-hilao-first-martial-law-detainee-killed

57. Gerard Clarke, *The Politics of NGOs in South-East Asia: Participation and Protest in the Philippines* (New York: Routledge, 1998).

58. David M. Giles, "Hitting a Home Run," *Litigation* 23, no. 3 (1997).

59. SELDA's full name is Society of Ex-Detainees for Liberation against Detention and for Amnesty, or Samahan ng Ex-Detainees Laban sa Detensyon at Aresto.

60. Nate Ela, "Litigation Dilemmas: Lessons from the Marcos Human Rights Class Action," *Law & Social Inquiry* 42, no. 2 (2016).

61. Ela, "Litigation Dilemmas."

62. SELDA Chronology retrieved from http://www.karapatan.org/files/Chronology%20of%20Events%20Related%20to%20the%20Human%20Rights%20Class%20Action%20Suit%20Against%20Marcos%20(1985%20%E2%80%93%202013).pdf

63. Accounts for the numbers have varied between 7,000 and more than 10,000 plaintiffs.

64. Ela, "Litigation Dilemmas."

65. Paul Hoffman, interview by author, 2018, Hermosa Beach.

66. Don Rosen, "Four, with Help of ACLU, Sue Marcos for $111 Million," *Los Angeles Times*, March 28, 1986.

67. Hoffman interview 2016, 2017.

68. Hoffman interview 2016, 2017.

69. Hoffman interview 2016, 2017.

70. Sklar interview.

71. Henry Weinstein, "Fight for Human Rights Ranges the World," *Los Angeles Times*, November 22, 2002; Hoffman interview 2016, 2017.

72. Hoffman interview 2016, 2017.

73. Samuel Walker, *In Defense of American Liberties: A History of the ACLU* (Carbondale: Southern Illinois University Press, 1999).

74. Hoffman interview 2016, 2017.

75. *In Re Estate of Marcos Human Rights Litigation.* See also Belinda A. Aquino, "Justice Finally Achieved for Victims of Marcos," *Honolulu Advertiser*, February 1, 2011. Trajano won by default when on May 29, 1986, Marcos-Manatoc failed to appear in court. The case was filed March 20, 1986; the act of state doctrine was announced from the US Supreme Court in the case *Underhill v. Hernandez*, discussion of its application in some of the Marcos cases is in Adam C. Robitaille, "The Marcos Cases: A Consideration of the Act of State Doctrine and the Pursuit of the Assets of Deposed Dictators," *Boston College Third World Law Journal* 9, no. 81 (1989).

76. Arguments rested on immunity questions. Trajano argued that Federal Sovereign Immunities Act does not immunize individuals when the acts are "outside the scope of their official duties and that the acts of torture and arbitrary killing . . . cannot be 'official acts' within whatever authority Marcos-Manotoc was given," p. 3. *In re Estate of Ferdinand E. Marcos Litigation*, 978 F.2d 493 (9th Cir. 1992).

77. *In re Estate of Ferdinand E. Marcos Litigation*, 978 F.2d 493 (9th Cir. 1992).

78. *Forti v. Suarez Mason*, 672 F. Supp. 1531 (CA 1987).

79. See, for example, Carlos Osario, "Kissinger to Argentines on Dirty War: The Quicker You Succeed, the Better," ed. Carlos Osario (Washington, DC: National Security Archive, 2003).

80. See Larry Rohter, "Argentina Charges Ex-Dictator and Others in 'Dirty War' Deaths," *New York Times*, July 11, 2002.

81. *Forti v. Suarez Mason*; Caryle Murphy, "The Disappeared," *Washington Post*, February 12, 1984.

82. *Washington Post* (Murphy, "The Disappeared") recounts this from her tell-

ing. The *New York Times* account also suggests her brother, Rubin, was shot at that time ("Freedom to Go Home Again," February 6, 1986, 33).

83. "Freedom to Go Home." *New York Times*, February 6, 1986, 33. Debora Benchoam became a human rights lawyer.

84. Robert Lindsey, "Argentine Officer Is Arrested in U.S.," *New York Times*, January 25, 1987.

85. Paul T. Friedman from Morrison & Foerster, William C. Gordon and Samuel Issacharoff were private lawyers in two cases, including Forti and Martinez-Baca; see Katherine Bishop, "3 Sue an Argentine General Held in U.S.," *New York Times*, May 4, 1987.

86. See, for example, *Forti v. Suarez Mason*.

87. Paul Ciotti, "A Victim Victorious Now," *Los Angeles Times*, May 3, 1988; Camille Peri, "Getting to Know the Lord," *Mother Jones*, September 1988.

88. Ciotti, "A Victim Victorious Now."

89. Dan Morain, "General Must Pay $21 Million in Torture Case," *Los Angeles Times*, April 26, 1988.

90. Morain, "General Must Pay $21 Million in Torture Case."

91. Morain, "General Must Pay $21 Million in Torture Case."

92. Morain, "General Must Pay $21 Million in Torture Case."

93. Lawyers indicated this was one of their motivations during interviews. In press accounts, Joanne Hoeper of Morrison & Foerster was one of Martinez-Baca's lawyers who made this argument to the *Los Angeles Times*. Also, Ciotti, "A Victim Victorious Now."

94. Hoeper cited in Ciotti, "A Victim Victorious Now."

95. "Argentine Military Killings/Widows Sue Ex-General in S.F.," *San Francisco Chronicle*, May 7, 1987.

96. The Torture Victim Protection Act.

97. The Torture Victim Protection Act.

98. Michael Posner at hearing for the Torture Victim Protection Act.

99. Michael Posner, at hearing of the U.S. Senate Committee on Foreign Affairs on March 23, 1988 on the Torture Victim Protection Act; formal written testimony of both the Association of the Bar of the City of New York, Committee on International Human Rights, and Robert Kapp, chairman of the board of directors of the International Human Rights Law Group.

100. Robert Kapp, written testimony submitted to Subcommittee on Human Rights and International Organization. April 29, 1988. Kapp was the chairman of the Board of Directors, International Human Rights law Group.

101. The Convention against Torture and other Cruel, Inhuman or Degrading Treatment or Punishment, http://www.ohchr.org/EN/ProfessionalInterest/Pages/CAT.aspx

102. The Torture Victim Protection Act, Hearing and markup before the committee on Foreign Affairs and its Subcommittee on Human Rights and International Organizations of the House of Representatives. Gerald Solomon, June 7, 1988. P. 80.

103. Dan Morain, "Ex-Argentine General Ordered to Pay $60 Million," *Los Angeles Times*, April 29, 1989; Katherine Bishop, "Ex-Argentine General Loses U.S. Extradition Case," *New York Times*, April 28, 1988.

104. "Ex-Argentine General Told to Pay Victims," *Gazette* (Montreal), May 2, 1990.

105. The Torture Victim Protection Act. Arlen Spector, Senate Judiciary Committee Subcommittee on Immigration and Refugee Affairs, June 22, 1990.

106. John McGinnis, "Testimony before the Subcommittee on Immigration of Refugee Affairs of the Committee on the Judiciary," United States Senate, 101st Congress, 1990, June 22, 1990. 8–14.

107. McGinnis, "Testimony before the Subcommittee on Immigration." The Torture Victim Protection Act. June 22, 1990

108. Arlen Specter, Subcommittee on Immigration of Refugee Affairs of the Committee on the Judiciary. June 22, 1990

109. David P. Stewart, "Testimony before the Subcommittee on Immigration of Refugee Affairs of the Committee on the Judiciary," United States Senate, 101st Congress, 1990.

110. Paul Simon, "Testimony before the Subcommittee on Immigration of Refugee Affairs of the Committee on the Judiciary," United States Senate, 101st Congress, June 22, 1990.

111. The Torture Victim Protection Act, 183.

112. Fitzpatrick, "The Future of the Alien Tort Claims Act of 1789."

113. Hoffman interview 2016, 2017.

114. Hoffman interview 2016, 2017.

115. Aquino, "Justice Finally Achieved for Victims of Marcos." See also Fitzpatrick, "The Future of the Alien Tort Claims Act of 1789."

116. Sources include Aceves, *Anatomy of Torture.*

117. John Roemer, "Philippines Dictator Estate Loses Appeal," *San Francisco Daily Journal*, October 26, 2012; Seth Mydans, "First Payments Are Made to Victims of Marcos Rule," *New York Times*, March 1, 2011; Robert Swift, "Holocaust Litigation and Human Rights Jurisprudence," in *Holocaust Restitution: Perspectives on the Litigation and Its Legacy*, ed. Michael Bazyler and Roger Alford (New York: New York University Press, 2005); Henry Weinstein, "Marcos' Victims Settle Case for $150 Million," *Los Angeles Times*, February 25, 1999.

118. Weinstein, "Marcos' Victims Settle Case for $150 Million." The judgment included $1.2 billion for "exemplary damages" based on Philippine law (on February 23, 1994), and $766 million for compensatory damages, according to media reports.

119. Robert Swift, "A Human Rights Class Action Distribution in the Philippines," *Philadelphia Lawyer* 74, no. 4 (2012); David Rosenzweig, "Merrill Lynch Releases $35 Million to Court in Marcos Case," *Los Angeles Times*, September 12, 2000.

120. Mydans, "First Payments Are Made to Victims of Marcos Rule"; Rosenzweig, "Merrill Lynch Releases $35 Million to Court in Marcos Case." It took years to find and liquidate assets. Merrill Lynch released another $35 million in funds set up in the name of a Panamanian company called Arelma, Inc.

121. Hoffman interview 2018.

Chapter 3

1. Gray interview.
2. Gray interview.
3. Gray interview.
4. Gray interview.
5. Gray interview.
6. Gray interview.
7. Gray interview.
8. Gerald Gray, "The Center for Justice and Accountability," *Health and Human Rights* 4, no. 1 (1999); Gray interview, 2017.
9. Gray, "Center for Justice and Accountability.".
10. Gray interview.
11. Gray interview. Also Hoffman interview 2017.
12. Smothers, "3 Women Win Suit over Torture by an Ethiopian Official." Another report in the *New York Times Magazine* (Rice, "The Long Interrogation"), said she was 22.
13. Lauran Neergaard, "Emigre Sued by Fellow Ethiopian Claiming Police Torture," *Associated Press*, October 12, 1990.
14. Rice, "Long Interrogation."
15. *Abebe-Jira v. Kelbessa Negewo*, 72 F.3d 844 (1996). United States Court of Appeals, Eleventh Circuit, No. 93–9133, January 10, 1996.
16. Neergaard, "Emigre Sued by Fellow Ethiopian Claiming Police Torture."
17. *Abebe-Jira v. Kelbessa Negewo*, 72 F.3d 844 (1996). United States Court of Appeals, Eleventh Circuit, No. 93–9133, January 10, 1996.
18. Ronald Smothers, "Nightmare of Torture in Ethiopia Is Relived," *New York Times*, May 22, 1993; Smothers, "3 Women Win Suit over Torture by an Ethiopian Official;; appellate opinion.
19. Smothers, "Nightmare of Torture in Ethiopia Is Relived"; Smothers, "3 Women Win Suit over Torture by an Ethiopian Official"; *Abebe-Jira v. Kelbessa Negewo*, 72 F.3d 844 (1996). United States Court of Appeals, Eleventh Circuit, No. 93–9133, January 10, 1996.
20. *Abebe-Jira v. Kelbessa Negewo*.
21. Smothers, "Nightmare of Torture in Ethiopia Is Relived"; Smothers, "3 Women Win Suit over Torture by an Ethiopian Official."
22. Associated Press, "Ethiopian Woman Sues Atlanta Man, Alleges Torture in Homeland," *Associated Press*, September 15, 1990.
23. Stephens interview.
24. Kilpatrick & Cody.
25. Smothers, "Nightmare of Torture in Ethiopia Is Relived."; "3 Women Win Suit over Torture by an Ethiopian Official."
26. Smothers, "3 Women Win Suit over Torture by an Ethiopian Official."
27. Ibid.
28. Hoffman interview, 2017.
29. Gray interview, 2016, 2017.
30. Gray interview, 2016, 2017.
31. Gray interview. Also Hoffman interview, 2017.

32. *Estate of Cabello v. Fernandez-Larios*, 157 F. Supp. 1345 (FL 2001). Lisa Lambert, "Obsessive Pursuit," *SF Weekly*, March 3, 2004. Gray email exchange 2017 and interview 2016.

33. Gray, 2016, 2017

34. Jamie O'Connell, "Gambling with the Psyche: Does Prosecuting Human Rights Violators Console Their Victims?" *Harvard International Law Journal* 46, no. 2 (2005).

35. O'Connell, "Gambling with the Psyche."

36. Rachel Barron, "From Foster City to Chile," *San Francisco Chronicle*, June 22, 2003.

37. Ann W. O'Neill, "Woman's Quest for Justice Spans Decades, Continents: Miami Ruling Brings Closure in Chilean Caravan of Death Killing," *South Florida Sun-Sentinel*, October 16, 2013.

38. See, for example, Metin Başoğlu, M. Paker, O. Paker, and E. Ozmen, "Psychological Effects of Torture: A Comparison of Tortured with Nontortured Political Activists in Turkey," *American Journal of Psychiatry* 151, no. 1 (1994); Z. Steel, Tien Chey, Derrick Silove, and Claire Marnane, "Association of Torture and Other Potentially Traumatic Events with Mental Health Outcomes among Populations Exposed to Mass Conflict and Displacement: A Systematic Review and Meta-Analysis," *JAMA* 302, no. 5 (2009).

39. *Estate of Cabello v. Fernandez-Larios*, 157 F. Supp. 2d 1345, Distr. Court, SD Florida 2001. In February 1987, Fernández pled guilty to being an "accessory after the fact" to the 1976 car bombing in Washington, DC, that killed the former Chilean ambassador to the United States and his assistant.

40. Douglas Grant Mine, "The Assassin Next Door," *Miami New Times*, November 18, 1999.

41. Lambert, "Obsessive Pursuit."

42. Sarah Conway, "For Torture Survivors, Kovler Center Offers Place of Peace," *Chicago Magazine*, May 2017, https://www.chicagomag.com/city-life/May-2017/Kovler-Center-Mario-Gonzalez/

43. Raul Romagoza Arce, "Written Testimony Submitted to the Subcommittee on Human Rights and the Law," Committee on the Judiciary, United States Senate, 2007.

44. Arce, "Written Testimony."

45. Arce, Written Testimony." Also "Journey to Justice: Carlos Mauricio's Story," Making Contact radio program, December 10, 2003, https://www.radiopr oject.org/sound/2003/MakingCon_031210_Ax.mp

46. Beth Van Schaack, "Romagoza v. García: Proving Command Responsibility under the Alien Tort Claims Act and the Torture Victim Protection Act," *Human Rights Brief* 10, no. 1 (2002).

47. Van Schaack, "Romagoza v. García."

48. "Journey to Justice: Carlos Mauricio's Story," Making Contact radio program, December 10, 2003. https://www.radioproject.org/2003/12/journey-to-justi ce-carlos-mauricios-story/

49. "Journey to Justice," Making Contact radio, December 10, 2003.

50. "Journey to Justice," Making Contact radio, December 10, 2003.

51. "Journey to Justice," Making Contact radio, December 10, 2003.

52. Julia Preston, "U.S. Deports Salvadoran General Accused in '80s Killings" *New York Times*, April 8, 2015.

53. Gray interview, 2016, 2017.

54. Gray interview, 2016, 2017.

55. *Mehinovic v. Vuckovic*, 198 F. Supp. 1322 (GA 2002). 198 F. Supp. 2d 1322—Dist. Court, ND Georgia 2002.

56. *Mehinovic v. Vuckovic*.

57. Hoffman interview.

58. Gray interview.

59. Gray interview.

60. Gray interview; Gerald Gray, "Some Notes Written during a Plague," email sent March 28, 2020.

61. Van Schaack interview.

62. Van Schaack interview.

63. Van Schaack interview. Also Kathy Roberts, interview by author, 2017, San Francisco.

64. Van Schaack interview.

65. Roberts interview.

66. Roberts interview.

67. Almudena Bernabeu, interview by author, 2017, London.

68. Cary Cordova, *The Heart of the Mission: Latino Art and Politics in San Francisco* (Philadelphia: University of Pennsylvania Press, 2017).

69. Marisa Gerber, "Arrests in 1989 El Salvador Priest Massacre Elicit Shock, Happiness—and a Hope for Justice," *Los Angeles Times*, February 7, 2016; Bernabeu interview.

70. Bernabeu interview; Almudena Bernabeu, email exchange, May 26, 2020.

71. Bernabeu interview.

72. Bernabeu interview.

73. Bernabeu interview.

74. Gilmore interview.

75. Gilmore interview.

76. Scott Gilmore, email exchange with author, March 28, 2019.

77. Gilmore email exchange.

78. Osburn interview.

79. Gilmore interview.

80. Osburn interview.

81. Gilmore,. email exchange, March 27, 2019.

82. Gilmore email exchange. Beth Van Schaack, "Syria Found Liable for the Death of War Correspondent Marie Colvin," *Just Security*, February 1, 2019, https://www.justsecurity.org/62459/breaking-news-syria-liable-death-war-correspondent-marie-colvin/

83. Osburn interview.

84. Naomi Roht-Arriaza and Almudena Bernabeu, "The Guatemalan Genocide Case in Spain" (Berkeley: Center for Latin American Studies, UC Berkeley, Fall 2008), Accessed May 26, 2020), https://cja.org/wp-content/uploads/downloads/Guatemala_U.C.Review_fall08.pdf

85. "Murder of Jesuit Priests and Civilians in El Salvador," Center for Justice & Accountability, https://cja.org/what-we-do/litigation/the-jesuits-massacre-case/. Accessed May 26, 2020.

86. Osburn interview.

87. Van Schaack interview.

88. See, for example, Başoğlu et al., "Psychological Effects of Torture"; Steel et al., "Association of Torture and Other Potentially Traumatic Events with Mental Health Outcomes among Populations Exposed to Mass Conflict and Displacement."

89. O'Connell, "Gambling with the Psyche."

90. Gilmore interview.

91. Gilmore interview.

92. Gray interview; O'Connell, "Gambling with the Psyche."

93. Gray interview.

94. Stephens interview.

95. Van Schaack interview.

96. Van Schaack interview.

97. Van Schaack interview.

98. Osburn interview.

99. Most studies are on the effects of truth and reconciliation commissions and criminal prosecutions.

100. O'Connell, "Gambling with the Psyche," 326.

101. Bishop, "3 Sue an Argentine General Held in U.S."

102. Roberts interview.

103. Van Schaack interview.

104. Benedict De Moerloose, interview by author, 2017, Geneva.

105. Lambert, "Obsessive Pursuit."

106. Lambert, "Obsessive Pursuit."

107. De Moerloose interview.

108. Chomsky interview.

109. Gilmore interview.

110. Osburn interview.

111. Gray interview, 2016, 2017.

112. Steven Watt, interview by author, New York, 2018.

Chapter 4

1. See, for example, Asia Watch, "Burma (Myanmar): Worsening Repression" (New York: Human Rights Watch, 1990); International Human Rights Law Group, "Human Rights in Burma (Myanmar): A Long Struggle for Freedom" (Washington, DC: International Human Rights Law Group, 1991); Amnesty International, "Myanmar (Burma). Continuing Killings and Ill Treatment of Minority Peoples" (London: Amnesty International, 1991); Eric Kolvig, "Burma Today: Land of Hope and Terror" (Washington, DC: International Burma Campaign, 1991). The US State Department also reported on these conditions in its 1991, 1994, and 1995 Country Reports on Human Rights Practices.

2. Redford and Stephens, "Story of Doe v. Unocal." Many had been farmers and herders who for generations lived in traditional villages, growing cashews, rice, and groundnuts.

3. Redford and Stephens, "The Story of Doe v. Unocal."

4. Redford and Stephens, "Story of Doe v. Unocal."

5. Redford and Stephens, "Story of Doe v. Unocal."

6. See "Ka Hsaw Wa—1999 Goldman Prize Recipient," http://www.goldma nprize.org/recipient/ka-hsaw-wa/, accessed December 17, 2018. Also, Richardson interview.

7. Redford and Stephens, "Story of Doe v. Unocal."

8. *"Total Denial."*

9. Redford and Stephens, "Story of Doe v. Unocal"; *Time*, "Consultant Warned Unocal in 1992 That Burmese Government 'Habitually Makes Use of Forced Labor,' Recently Unseaaled Court Documents Obtained by *Time* Reveal," November 9, 2003, http://content.time.com/time/nation/article/0,8599,538908,00.html

10. Jane Doe is a pseudonym.

11. *"Total Denial."*

12. *"Total Denial."*

13. *"Total Denial."*

14. EarthRights International and Southeast Asian Information Network, "Total Denial: A Report on the Yadana Pipeline Project in Burma" (Washington, DC: EarthRights International and Southeast Asian Information Network, 1996).

15. Redford interview.

16. Stephens, interview by author, May 25, 2020, Zoom conversation.

17. Stephens interview 2017, Chomsky interview.

18. Redford interview.

19. Redford interview. Stephens's recollection is that Redford may have actually called Jennifer Green.

20. Redford interview.

21. Simons interview. Also Redford and Stephens, "Story of Doe v. Unocal."

22. Simons interview.

23. Collingsworth interview.

24. Collingsworth interview.

25. Collingsworth interview.

26. Collingsworth interview.

27. Collingsworth interview.

28. Stephens interview 2017.

29. Beth Stephens, email exchange, April 22, 2019.

30. Richardson interview.

31. Hoffman interview, 2016, 2017.

32. Hoffman, Richardson, and Stormer interviews.

33. Stormer interview.

34. Stormer interview.

35. Stormer interview.

36. Stormer interview.

37. Richardson interview.

38. Richardson interview

39. Richardson interview.

40. Hoffman, Paul.

41. Unocal Corporation, "1999 Annual Report," https://www.chevron.com/-/media/chevron/investors/documents/unocal1999annualreport.pdf

42. *Doe v. Unocal Corp.*, 963 F. Supp. 880 (1997).

43. Lisa Girion, "Judge OKs Unocal Abuse Lawsuit," *Los Angeles Times*, June 12, 2002.

44. Susan Beck, "How O'Melveny & Myers Built a Litigation Powerhouse," *American Lawyer*, January 12, 2004.

45. *John Doe I v. Unocal Corp.*, Case No. CV 96–6959 RAP. Order of March 25, 1997, US District Court for the Central District of California, 963 F. Supp. 880.

46. Richardson interview.

47. Richardson interview.

48. Paul Hoffman and Daniel Zaheer, "The Rules of the Road: Federal Common Law and Aiding and Abetting under the Alien Tort Claims Act," *Loyola of Los Angeles International and Comparative Law Review* 26, no. 47 (2003): 47, warned about the memorandum from Control Risks to Unocal executives.

49. Stormer interview.

50. Unocal (C.D. Cal.2000), pp. 1306–07.

51. UPI, "Burma Plaintiffs to Appeal Dismissal of Unocal Suit," September 7, 2000.

52. Lisa Girion, "California Law to Govern Unocal Human Rights Case, Judge Rules," *Los Angeles Times*, August 1, 2003.

53. Center for Constitutional Rights, "C.C.R. Wins Significant Legal Motion in Unocal Case," (2011).

54. Center for Constitutional Rights, "C.C.R. Wins Significant Legal Motion in Unocal Case."

55. Beck, "How O'Melveny & Myers Built a Litigation Powerhouse."

56. Richardson interview.

57. Beck, "How O'Melveny & Myers Built a Litigation Powerhouse."

58. Stormer interview.

59. Stormer interview.

60. Richardson interview.

61. Lisa Girion, "One Legal Attack on Unocal Denied," *Los Angeles Times*, January 24, 2004.

62. "Unocal Must Face Abuse Suit," *Los Angeles Times*, September 15, 2004.

63. Stormer interview.

64. The amount of the settlement from Michael Goldhaber, "A Win for Wiwa, a Win for Shell, a Win for Corporate Human Rights," *Am Law Daily*, June 10, 2009, https://amlawdaily.typepad.com/amlawdaily/2009/06/a-win-for-wiwa-a-win-for-shell-a-win-for-corporate-human-rights.html

65. Richardson interview.

66. Redford interview.

67. Redford interview.

68. Redford interview.

69. Redford interview.

70. Redford interview.

71. Redford interview.

72. Norimitsu Onishi, "Not for a Nigerian Hero the Peace of the Grave," *New York Times*, March 22, 2000.

73. This has been widely documented in both academic and practitioner studies. See, for example, United Nations Environment Programme, "Environmental Survey of Ogoniland," (2007).

74. Onishi, "Not for a Nigerian Hero the Peace of the Grave"; *Wiwa v. Royal Dutch Petroleum Co.* Complaint; *Kiobel v. Royal Dutch Petroleum Co.*, Complaint.

75. Chomsky interview.

76. *Wiwa v. Royal Dutch Petroleum Co.*

77. Bob Herbert, "In America: Unholy Alliance in Nigeria," *New York Times*, January 26, 1996.

78. Paul Lewis, "Blood and Oil: A Special Report; after Nigeria Represses, Shell Defends Its Record," *New York Times*, February 13, 1996.

79. Jad Mouawad, "Oil Industry on Trial," *New York Times*, May 22, 2009.

80. *Wiwa v. Royal Dutch Petroleum Co.*

81. V. A. Oteri, "Memorandum to the Inspector General of Police" (Nigeria Police Force, 1994). Also Lewis, "Blood and Oil."

82. *Wiwa v. Royal Dutch Petroleum Co.*

83. Goldhaber, "A Win for Wiwa."

84. Mouawad, "Shell to Pay $15.5 Million to Settle Nigerian Case."

85. Hoffman interview, 2016, 2017.

86. Interviews with human rights lawyers.

87. Bowoto v. Chevron Trial Blog, "Day Two–Witnesses," October 28, 2008, https://bowotovchevron.wordpress.com/2008/10/28/day-two-witnesses/

88. Stormer interview.

89. A fax by Chevron to the US Embassy suggests this nonviolence was true, but defense counsel presented a photo in trial of a man with a sheathed knife.

90. *Bowoto v. Chevron Corp.*, 2009 U.S. Dist. LEXIS 38174 (2009).

91. Bert Voorhees, interview by author, 2017, via Skype.

92. Voorhees interview.

93. Cohn interview.

94. Cohn interview.

95. Bowoto v. Chevron Trial Blog, "Day Two–Witnesses."

96. Bowoto v. Chevron Trial Blog, "Day Two–Witnesses."

97. Bob Egelko, "Chevron Trial over Nigeria Protest Gets Started," *San Francisco Chronicle*, October 29, 2008; Bob Egelko, "Jurors Get Conflicting Accounts of Shootings," *San Francisco Chronicle*, November 26, 2008.

98. Bowoto v. Chevron Trial Blog, "Day Two–Witnesses."

99. Andrew Woods, "Landmark Human Rights Trial Continues in Bowoto v. Chevron—Opening Statements and More," *Huffington Post*, November 29, 2008; https://www.huffingtonpost.com/andrew-woods/landmark-human-rights-tri_b_138857.html; Andrew Woods, "Landmark Human Rights Trial Continues in Bowoto v. Chevron—Opening Statements and More," *Huffington Post*, May 25, 2011. Gilmore interview.

100. Egelko, "Chevron Trial over Nigeria Protest Gets Started"; Egelko, "Jurors Get Conflicting Accounts of Shootings."

101. Bowoto v. Chevron Trial Blog, Day Three, October 29, 2008.

102. CIC stands for Concerned Ilaje Citizens.

103. Bowoto v. Chevron Trial Blog, Day Three, October 29, 2008.

104. Bowoto v. Chevron Trial Blog, Day Four, October 30, 2008.

105. Bowoto v. Chevron Trial Blog, Day Five, November 3, 2008.

106. Bowoto v. Chevron Trial Blog, , Day Five, November 3, 2008.

107. Bowoto v. Chevron Trial Blog, Day Five, November 3, 2008.

108. Voorhees interview.

109. Voorhees interview.

110. Cohn interview.

111. Cohn interview.

112. Bowoto v. Chevron Trial Blog.

113. Bowoto v. Chevron Trial Blog.

114. Gilmore interview. Bowoto v. Chevron Trial Blog.

115. Voorhees interview.

116. *Bowoto v. Chevron Corp.*, 2009 U.S. Dist. LEXIS 38174 (2009).U.S. Dist. LEXIS 38174 (N.D. Cal. 2009).

117. *Bowoto v. Chevron Corp.*, 2009 U.S. Dist. LEXIS 38174 (2009). U.S. Dist. LEXIS 38174 (N.D. Cal. 2009).

118. Stormer interview.

119. Cohn interview.

120. Redford interview.

121. Bert Voorhees, interview by author, May 16, 2020, via Zoom.

122. Collingsworth interview.

123. Beth Stephens, Michael Ratner, Judith Chomsky, Jennifer Green, and Paul Hoffman, *International Human Rights Litigation in U.S. Courts.* (Martinus Nijhoff Publishers, 2008).

124. Jenny Strasburg, "Saipan Lawsuit Terms OKd," *SF Chronicle*, April 25, 2003.

125. Colin Woodward, "US Case Highlights Cuban 'Slaves' in Curacao," *Christian Science Monitor*, November 18, 2008.

126. "Drummond Hits Attys with RICO Suit over Murder Claims," *Law 360*, March 27, 2015, https://www.law360.com/articles/636779/drummond-hits-attys -with-rico-suit-over-murder-claims

127. Terry Collingsworth, email exchange, January 23, 2019.

Chapter 5

1. Michael Otterman, *American Torture: From the Cold War to Abu Ghraib and Beyond* (Melbourne: Melbourne University Press, 2007); Stephen Soldz, "Healers or Interrogators: Psychology and the United States Torture Program," *Psychoanalytic Dialogs* 8, no. 5 (2008).

2. Senate Torture Report.

3. Mark Denbeaux and Jonathan Hafetz, *The Guantánamo Lawyers* (New York: New York University Press, 2009), 7.

4. Lawrence B. Wilkerson, "Declaration by Lawrence B. Wilkerson in the Case of Adel Hamad" (2010).

5. Alberto R. Gonzales, "Memorandum for the President," January 25, 2002;

"Decision re Application of the Geneva Convention on Prisoners of War to the Conflict with Al Qaeda and the Taliban."

6. President George W. Bush, "Memorandum to the Vice President et al." February 7, 2002.

7. Jay Bybee, "Memorandum to Gonzales" August 1, 2002.

8. United States Department of Justice, Office of the Inspector General, "The September 11 Detainees: A Review of the Treatment of Aliens Held on Immigration Charges in Connection with the Investigation of the September 11 Attacks" (2003).

9. Department of Justice, Office of the Inspector General, "September 11 Detainees."

10. Watt interview.

11. Watt interview.

12. Department of Justice, Office of the Inspector General, "September 11 Detainees."

13. *Turkmen v. Ashcroft*, 2002. Complaint. https://ccrjustice.org/sites/default/fi les/attach/2016/08/Original%20Turkmen%20Complaint%20April%2017%2020 02.pdf; *Turkmen v. Ashcroft*, 589 F.3d 542 (2009).

14. The case, *Turkmen v. Ashcroft*, named Ibrahim Turkmen, French citizen Asif-Ur-Rehman Saffi, and Jaffri.

15. *Turkmen v. Ashcroft*, 589 F.3d 542 (2009).

16. *Turkmen v. Ashcroft*, 589 F.3d 542 (2009); Department of Justice, Office of the Inspector General, "September 11 Detainees," including supplemental report, pp. 10, 46 and 162.

17. *Elmaghraby and Iqbal v. Ashcroft et al.* (2004). Complaint filed in the US District Court for the Eastern District of New York, May 3, 2004.

18. *Elmaghraby and Iqbal v. Ashcroft et al.* (2004).

19. *Bivens v. Six Unknown Named Agents*, 403 U.S. 388 (1971). 403 U.S. 388 (1971).

20. Prohibitions on unlawful searches and seizures.

21. *Elmaghraby v. Ashcroft*, 2005 U.S. Dist LEXIS 21434 (2005). United States District Court, E.D. New York; *Turkmen v. Ashcroft*, 2006 WL 1662663 (E.D.N.Y., June 14, 2006, granting partial dismissal).

22. *Elmaghraby and Iqbal v. USA et al.* (2006). "Stipulation for Compromise Settlement and Release of Federal Tort Claims Act," February 27, 2006.

23. Roslynn Mauskopf, "Eleven Current and Former Federal Officers Indicted for Excessive Force and False Statements" (New York: Department of Justice, 2007).

24. Mauskopf, "Eleven Current and Former Federal Officers Indicted."

25. https://www.americanbar.org/content/dam/aba/publishing/preview/publi ced_preview_briefs_pdfs_07_08_07_1015_Respondent.pdf. Accessed October 19, 2018.

26. *Ashcroft v. Iqbal*, 566 U.S. 662 (2009).

27. Gregory Garre, "Ashcroft V Iqbal (Oral Argument)" (2008). https://www .americanbar.org/content/dam/aba/publishing/preview/publiced_preview_briefs _pdfs_07_08_07_1015_Petitioner.pdf. Accessed October 19, 2018.

28. Antonin Scalia, "Ashcroft v. Iqbal (Oral Argument)" (2008).

29. *Ashcroft v. Iqbal*, 129 S. Ct. 1937, 54 (2009). (both the ourt of Appeals and Supreme Court), Appeals Court here: https://law.justia.com/cases/federal/appell ate-courts/ca2/05-6352/05-6352-cv_opn-2011-03-27.html. Accessed October 2, 2018.

30. *Ashcroft v. Iqbal*, 129 S. Ct. 1937, 54 (2009). https://supreme.justia.com/cas es/federal/us/556/662/#tab-opinion-1962862

31. Alexander Reinhardt, interview at Cardozo Law. https://www.youtube.com /watch?v=e9nn-bhcBp0. Accessed March 27, 2019.

32. United States District Court, Eastern District of New York, "Exhibit A. Turkmen et al. v. Ashcroft et al." (2009). Filed November 16, 2009. https://ccr justice.org/sites/default/files/attach/2015/01/687%20exhibit%20a.pdf. Accessed September 28, 2018; Mauskopf, "Eleven Current and Former Federal Officers Indicted."

33. Fourth Amended Complaint, *Turkmen v. Ashcroft*, E.D.N.Y., 02-cv-2307, September. 13, 2010, https://ccrjustice.org/sites/default/files/assets/726%20Four th%20Amended%20Complaint_0.pdf Accessed October 2, 2018.

34. *Turkmen v. Ashcroft.* https://ccrjustice.org/sites/default/files/attach/2015 /06/Turkmen%20v.%20Ashcroft%20Second%20Circuit%20Ruling%206-17-15 .pdf. Accessed October 6, 2018.

35. *Turkmen v. Hasty*, et al. 789 F.3d 218 (2d Cir. 2015), 43.

36. Two justices recused themselves.

37. *Ziglar v. Abbasi*, 137 S. Ct. 1843 (2017).

38. Open Society Justice Initiative, "Globalizing Torture: C.I.A. Secret Detention and Extraordinary Rendition" (New York: Open Society Foundations, 2013), 14.

39. United States Senate Select Committee on Intelligence, "Committee Study of the Central Intelligence Agency's Detention and Interrogation Program" (Washington, DC: United States Senate, 2014), 23.

40. Katherine (Katie) Gallagher, email exchange, July 8, 2020.

41. *Maher Arar et al. v. Her Majesty the Queen et al.* (2004). Court file No. 04-CV-266499CM3, April 2, 2004, https://www.falconers.ca/wp-content/uploads /2016/09/Ara-Statement-of-Claim.pdf

42. Watt interview.

43. Watt interview.

44. Watt interview.

45. Commission of Inquiry into the Actions of Canadian Officials in Relation to Maher Arar, "Report of the Events Relating to Maher Arar," 2006.

46. *Arar v. Ashcroft*, 585 F 3d. 559 (2009).

47. Watt interview.

48. Watt interview.

49. Watt interview.

50. *Arar v. Ashcroft*, Complaint and Demand for Jury Trial, 04-cv-0249, E.D.N.Y., January 22, 2004, https://ccrjustice.org/sites/default/files/assets/Arar %20Complaint_FINAL.pdf

51. *Arar v. Ashcroft et al.*, Complaint and Demand for Jury Trial, 04-cv-0249, E.D.N.Y., January 22, 2004, https://ccrjustice.org/sites/default/files/assets/Arar %20Complaint_FINAL.pdf

52. Watt interview.

53. *Arar v. Ashcroft*, 414 F. Supp. 2d 250, 274 (E.D.N.Y. 2006), https://ccrjusti ce.org/sites/default/files/assets/EDNY%20Opinion%202.06.pdf; also Jules Lobel, "Extraordinary Rendition and the Constitution: The Case of Maher Arar," *Review of Litigation* 28, no. 2 (2008): 492.

54. Katie Gallagher, interview by author, July 10, 2020, by Zoom.

55. Katie Gallagher, email exchange, July 8, 2020.

56. *Arar v. Ashcroft*, 414 F. Supp, 2d 250; 2006 U.S. Dist. LEXIS 5803.

57. Reuters, "Rice Admits U.S. Erred in Deportation," *New York Times*, October 25, 2007; *Arar v. Ashcroft*, 130 S. Ct. 3409 (2010).

58. Katie Redford, email exchange, July 8, 2020.

59. Denbeaux and Hafetz, *Guantánamo Lawyers*, 8.

60. University of California, Davis, Center for the Study of Human Rights, "Lists of Guantanamo Prisoners (Organized by Last Name, Citizenship, ISN, Date of Birth"; James Ball, "Guantánamo Bay Files: Children and Senile Old Men among Detainees," *Guardian*, April 25, 2011.

61. Clive Stafford Smith, "Rule of Law Oral History Project" (New York: Columbia Center for Oral History, 2011), 8.

62. Smith, "Rule of Law Oral History Project", 7; Joseph Margulies, *Guantánamo and the Abuse of Presidential Power* (New York: Simon and Schuster, 2007).

63. Smith, "Rule of Law Oral History Project," 13.

64. Smith, "Rule of Law Oral History Project."

65. See, for example, attending attorneys at Guantánamo teach-in at Seton Hall Law and subheading, "Guantánamo Bay Bar Association," https://archive.is/2007 0810014117/http://law.shu.edu/guantanamoteachin/page8.htm. Accessed August 23, 2018. There were articles about this in the news media, including Deroy Murdock, "Gitmo Legal," *National Review*, January 25, 2006.

66. See, for example, attending attorneys at Guantánamo teach-in at Seton Hall Law and subheading, "Guantánamo Bay Bar Association," https://archive.is/2007 0810014117/http://law.shu.edu/guantanamoteachin/page8.htm. Accessed August 23, 2018. Articles about this included Stacy Sullivan, "The Minutes of the Guantánamo Bay Bar Association," *New York Magazine*, June 26, 2006, and Murdock, "Gitmo Legal."CCR suggested some 400 attorneys were working on these cases.

67. Murdock, "Gitmo Legal."

68. Peter Jan Honigsberg, *Our Nation Unhinged: The Human Consequences of the War on Terror* (Berkeley: University of California Press, 2009).

69. Thomas Wilner, "Rule of Law Oral History Project" (New York: Columbia Center for Oral History, 2009), 13.

70. Wilner, "Rule of Law Oral History Project," 10, The interviewer is Ronald J. Grele. file:///C:/Users/armou/Documents/Lawyers%20Beyond%20Borders/Ca se%20documents/thomas%20wilner%20oral%20history%20project%20re%20g uantanamo%20ccoh_8626509_transcript.pdf. Accessed August 23, 2018.

71. Wilner, "Rule of Law Oral History Project," 13.

72. Smith, "Columbia Oral History Project," 15-17.

73. Smith, "Rule of Law Oral History Project," 15-17.

74. Wilner, "Rule of Law Oral History Project," 25-27. He added that when people criticized him, Robert Mueller, head of the FBI at the time, toasted him.

75. *Rasul v. Bush*, 215 F. Supp. 2d 55 (D.D.C. 2002); *Rasul V Bush*, 215 F. Supp. 2d 55 (2004). 215 F. Supp. 2d 55—Distr. Court of Columbia 2002. https://scholar .google.co.nz/scholar_case?case=979153241978472781&hl=en&as_sdt=6&as_vis= 1&oi=scholarr. Accessed August 23, 2018.

76. *Al Odah v. United States*, 321 F.3d 1134 (D.C. Cir. 2003).

77. Wilner, "Rule of Law Oral History Project," 44-46.

78. Watt interview.

79. Watt interview.

80. Wilner, " Oral History Project," 50.

81. Honigsberg, *Our Nation Unhinged*, 90.

82. Wilner, "Rule of Law Oral History Project," 48-50.

83. United States Senate, Select Committee on Intelligence, "Committee Study of the Central Intelligence Agency's Detention and Interrogation Program," xxv.

84. *Rasul v. Bush*, Theodore Olson, Oral Arguments before the Supreme Court, April 20, 2004. https://apps.oyez.org/player/#/rehnquist10/oral_argument_audio /22545

85. *Rasul v. Bush*, https://www.oyez.org/cases/2003/03-334

86. *Rasul v. Bush*, 542 U.S. 466 (2004), 542 U.S. 466 (2004). No. 03–334. https://scholar.google.co.nz/scholar_case?case=13489903449749466109&hl=en& as_sdt=6&as_vis=1&oi=scholarr

87. *Al Odah v. United States*, 2009 U.S. App. LEXIS 25539 (2008), and *Boumediene v. Bush*, 553 U.S. 723 (2008).

88. Reports by NGOs including the ACLU, Human Rights First, and Human Rights Watch. The latter record is here, Human Rights Watch, "Guantánamo: Facts and Figures," https://www.hrw.org/video-photos/interactive/2017/03/30/gu antanamo-facts-and-figures

89. Honigsberg, *Our Nation Unhinged*, 90; numbers as of 2017 are found here: https://www.aclu.org/issues/national-security/detention/guantanamo-numbers. Human Rights Watch said six died in apparent suicide.

90. Associated Press, "23 Detainees Attempted Suicide in Protest at Base, Military Says," *New York Times*, January 25, 2005.

91. Reported in Murdock, "Gitmo Legal."

92. Eric Lewis, "The Last Word," *Legal Business*, March 2007.

93. David J. Parnell, "Eric Lewis of Lewis Baach, on the Polarizing Legal Market, Internationalism, and White Collar Trends," *Forbes*, January 3, 2017.

94. Parnell, "Eric Lewis of Lewis Baach."

95. Eric Lewis, 2004. As reported by the BBC, "Guantanamo Four Plan to Sue US," October 27, 2004, http://news.bbc.co.uk/2/hi/uk_news/3959635.stm. Accessed September 3, 2018.

96. Lewis, 2004.

97. Tom Freeman, "Eric Lewis, Truth, Justice and Guantanamo Bay." *Legal Business*, March 2007, 76.

98. *Rasul v. Rumsfeld*, 414 F. Supp. 2d 26 (2006). (D.D.C. 2006).

99. *Rasul v. Rumsfeld*, 414 F. Supp. 2d 26 (2006). (D.D.C. 2006).

100. *Rasul v. Rumsfeld* (which became *Rasul v. Myers*), p. 24.

101. *Rasul v. Rumsfeld* (which became *Rasul v. Myers*), p. 24.

102. *Rasul v. Myers*, 563 F.3d 527 (D.C. Cir. 2008), p. 14. (No. 06–5209 consolidated with 06–5222. No 04 cv 01864).

103. *Rasul v. Rumsfeld*, LEXIS 11134 2009 U.S. App. (2009), p. 43.

104. *Rasul v. Myers*, 130 S. Ct. 1013 (2009). 130 S. Ct. 1013. Supreme Court. 2009.

105. Eric Lewis, "Supreme Court Refused to Hear Suit Seeking Accountability for Guantánamo Torture" (Center for Constitutional Rights, 2009).

106. "Who Are 'We the People'?," *New York Times*, October 4, 2014.

107. *Celikgogus et al. v. Rumsfeld et al.* (2007). Amended Complaint filed in U.S. District Court for the District of Columbia, March 21, 2007. https://ccrjustice.org/sites/default/files/assets/CELIKGOGUS_AmendComplaint.pdf

108. *Celikgogus et al. v. Rumsfeld et al.* (2007). Amended Complaint filed in U.S. District Court for the District of Columbia, March 21, 2007. https://ccrjustice.org/sites/default/files/assets/CELIKGOGUS_AmendComplaint.pdf. Accessed on August 27, 2018.

109. *Al Laithi v. Rumsfeld*, 753 F.3d 1327 (2014). Center for Constitutional Rights, "Report on Torture and Cruel, Inhuman and Degrading Treatment of Prisoners at Guantánamo Bay, Cuba," July 2006, 20; *Al Laithi v. Rumsfeld at al.* (2008). Complaint. United States District Court for the District of Columbia. September 30, 2008. https://ccrjustice.org/sites/default/files/assets/2008-09-30%20Allaithi%20v.%20Rumsfeld%20-%20Complaint%20(court%20stamped).pdf

110. These statements were reported by Carol D Leonnig, "Guantánamo Detainee Says Beating Injured Spine," *Washington Post*, August 13, 2005. Filed in U.S. District Court for the District of Columbia, September 30, 2008.

111. *Celikgogus v. Rumsfeld*, (2010). *Al Laithi v. Rumsfeld*.

112. *Al Laithi v. Rumsfeld*.

113. *Al Laithi v. Rumsfeld*, p. 11.

114. Josh White, "Suicide on the Brink of Release; Families, Attorneys Push to Hold Guantanamo Officials Liable," *Washington Post*, August 29, 2008, https://www.atlanticphilanthropies.org/news/suicide-brink-release-families-attorneys-push-hold-guantanamo-officials-liable

115. He was also known as Manei al Otaibi, and Mane Shaman Al-Habartdi.

116. Denbeaux et al., "Uncovering the Cover Ups: Death in Camp Delta" (Seton Hall Public Law Research Paper No. 2437423, 2014).

117. The Defense Department ostensibly acknowledged 50 hunger strikers. The Al Zahrani complaint suggests 200 inmates went on hunger strike.

118. Pardiss Kabriaei, Rule of Law Oral History Project,"29.

119. Denbeaux et al., "Uncovering the Cover Ups."

120. Denbeaux et al., "Uncovering the Cover Ups."

121. Denbeaux et al., "Uncovering the Cover Ups"; see Scott Horton, "The Guantánamo 'Suicides': A Camp Delta Sergeant Blows the Whistle," *Harper's Magazine*, January 18, 2010.

122. *Al Zahrani v. Rumsfeld*, 684 F. Supp. 103 (2010). https://ccrjustice.org/sites/default/files/assets/Al-Zahrani%20v.%20Rumsfeld%20Amended%20Complaint.pdf; Carole Vann, "Suicides in Guantánamo: A Swiss Autopsy Reveals Troubling Facts," *InfoSud: Human Rights Tribune*, March 3, 2007.

123. *Al Zahrani v. Rumsfeld*, https://ccrjustice.org/sites/default/files/assets/Al-Zahrani%20v.%20Rumsfeld%20Amended%20Complaint.pdf

124. *Al-Zahrani et al. v. Rumsfeld et al.*, Amended Complaint, 2009, p. 35. https://ccrjustice.org/sites/default/files/assets/Al-Zahrani%20v%20Rumsfeld.pdf

125. *Al-Zahrani et al. v. Rumsfeld et al.*, Amended Complaint, 2009, p. 35. https://ccrjustice.org/sites/default/files/assets/Al-Zahrani%20v%20Rumsfeld.pdf

126. Jeff Davis, "Thoughts on Clients," http://dlib.nyu.edu/guantanamo/documents/pdfa/Davis_Thoughts.pdfa

127. Mario Kaiser, "Death in Camp Delta: On the Power of Silence, Submission to Force-Feeding, and the First Suicides in Guantánamo," *Guernica Magazine*, February 17, 2014.

128. Kaiser, "Death in Camp Delta."

129. Pardiss Kebriaei, "The Rule of Law Oral History Project" (New York: Columbia Center for Oral History, 2013), 20–21.

130. Kebriaei, "The Rule of Law Oral History Project," 20-21.

131. *Al Zahrani v. Rumsfeld.* Memorandum Opinion, https://ccrjustice.org/sites/default/files/assets/Memorandum%20Opinion.pdf. Accessed October 17, 2008.

132. The earlier iteration of Janko was "al-Ginco."

133. Some reports say it was Al Qaeda that tortured him.

134. *Janko v. Gates*, 741 F. 3d 136–2014. Complaint.

135. *Janko v. Gates*, 741 F. 3d 136–2014. Memorandum opinion. https://ecf.dcd.uscourts.gov/cgi-bin/show_public_doc?2010cv1702-20. Accessed October 18, 2018.

136. Sophia Brill, "The National Security Court We Already Have." *Yale L. & Pol'y Rev.* 28 (2009): 525.

137. *Al Janko v. Gates*, 831 F. Supp. 2d 272—Dist. Court, Dist. of Columbia 2011; Mike Doyle, "Judge Dismisses Ex-Captive's Damage Suit," *Miami Herald*, December 24, 2011 (updated February 9, 2014).

138. Kebriaei, "The Rule of Law History Project," 32–33.

139. Gene Johnson, "Sudanese Man Sues U.S. Government after Release from Guantánamo," *HeraldNet*, April 7, 2010. See also Adel Hamad, "Witnessing Guantánamo: Transcription of Adel Hamad's Interview," ed. Amy Goodman (Davis, CA: Center for the Study of Human Rights in the Americas, 2008).

140. *Hamad v. Gates*, 732 F. 3d 990—Court of Appeals, 9th Circuit, 2013.

141. Julie Sullivan, "Steven T. Wax, Oregon's Federal Public Defender, Has Created a Crack Legal Team to Follow the Rule of Law," *Oregonian*, June 11, 2011.

142. Scott Baldauf, "Former Guantanamo Prisoner Asks U.S. to Review Its Founding Ideals," *Christian Science Monitor*, February 6, 2008.

143. Hamad, "Witnessing Guantánamo."

144. Gene Johnson, "Sudanese Man Released from Guantánamo Sues," *Seattle Times*, April 7, 2010.

145. Julie Sabatier, "Guantánamo Lawsuits" (radio segment), *Think Out Loud*, Oregon Public Broadcasting, 2015.

146. Wilkerson, "Declaration by Lawrence B. Wilkerson in the Case of Adel Hamad."

147. "International Human Rights Clinic Files Second Guantanamo Lawsuit." *Willamette Lawyer* 12, no. 1 (Spring 2012).

148. *Hamad v. Gates* (2013).

149. *Al-Zahrani v. United States*. Petition. https://ccrjustice.org/sites/default/fi

les/assets/Talal%20Al-Zahrani%20et%20al%20%20v%20%20United%20States
_Petition%208-21-12.pdf

Chapter 6

1. Watt interview.
2. Peter Singer, "Outsourcing War," *Foreign Affairs* 84 (2005).
3. Susan Burke, interview by author, 2018.
4. Burke interview.
5. Amanda Aranowski, "Shereef Akeel – Huntington Woods," , 2004, *Michigan Lawyers Weekly*. March 2004.
6. Aranowski, "Shereef Akeel."
7. Aranowski, "Shereef Akeel."
8. Charles Hanley, "AP Enterprise: Former Iraqi Detainees Tell of Riots, Punishment in the Sun, Good Americans, and Pitiless Ones," *San Diego Union Tribune*, November 1, 2003.
9. The Taguba, Fay-Jones, and Church Reports (2004) each detailed different facets of the abuses and causes; see Maj. General Antonio M. Taguba, "Article 15–6 Investigation of the 800th Military Police Brigade" (May 2004), 16; LTG Anthony R. Jones, "AR 15–6 Investigation of the Abu Ghraib Prison and 205th Military Intelligence Brigade"; and MG George R. Fay, "AR 15–6 Investigation of the Abu Ghraib Detention Facility and 205th Military Intelligence Brigade (August 2004).
10. See, for example, Seymour Hersh, "Torture at Abu Ghraib," *New Yorker*, April 30, 2004, https://www.newyorker.com/magazine/2004/05/10/torture-at-abu-ghraib
11. CCR lawyers included Michael Rather, Barbara Oshansky, Jeff Fogel, Jennifer Green, Judith Chomsky, and Jules Lobel. Susan Feathers from the University of Pennsylvania, Joseph Margulies, and William Aceves were co-counsel.
12. Shereef Akeel, email exchange, March 3, 2019.
13. Some condolence payments have been made to some victims from the US government and have amounted to approximately $12,500 per person.
14. Susan Burke, interview by author, Skype, 2017.
15. *Saleh v. Titan* (2004). First Amended Complaint, 04-cv-114, S.D. Cal., June 30, 2004, https://ccrjustice.org/home/what-we-do/our-cases/saleh-et-al-v-titan-et-al
16. Gallagher, interview by author, 2017, New York.
17. Burke interview, 2017.
18. Akeel, 2019; Burke interview, 2017.
19. Ibid.
20. Ibid.
21. Akeel 2019.
22. Burke interview, 2017.
23. Burke interview 2017.
24. *Saleh v. Titan*, CACI motion to dismiss, September 10, 2004.
25. Burke interview, 2017.
26. Gallagher interview.
27. Burke interview, 2017.

28. *Ibraham v. Titan*, 556 F. Supp. 2d 1, 4 and 10, (D.D.C. 2007). https://ccrjustice.org/sites/default/files/assets/Saleh_summaryjudgmentdec_11_07.pdf; *Saleh v. Titan*, 436 F. Supp. 2d 55 (D.D.C. 2006), P. 23 Memorandum Order. https://ccrjustice.org/sites/default/files/assets/Saleh_summaryjudgmentdec_11_07.pdf; *Saleh v. Titan Corp.*, 580 F. 3d 1 (D.C. Cir. 2009).

29. Burke interview, 2017; Gallagher interview.

30. Burke interview, 2017.

31. *Saleh v. Titan Corp.*, 580 F. 3d 1 (D.C. Cir. 2009).

32. Gallagher interview.

33. *Saleh v. CACI* (2010). Brief of Amici Curiae Professors of Federal Courts, International Law, and U.S. Foreign Relations Law in Support of Petitioners, May 25, 2010, https://ccrjustice.org/sites/default/files/assets/05.25.10%20Brief%20of%20International%20Law%20Professors%20et%20al.pdf

34. "Abu Ghraib Torture Victims Challenge Corporate Impunity," CCR press release, December 20, 2011, https://ccrjustice.org/home/press-center/press-releases/abu-ghraib-torture-victims-challenge-corporate-impunity

35. *Saleh v. Titan*, Brief for the United States of America as Amicus Curiae, No. 09–1313, 2011 WL 2134985 (U.S.), at 19.

36. Burke interview, 2017.

37. *Al-Quraishi v. Nakhla*, 728 F. Spp. 2d 702 (D.Md. 2010); Memorandum opinion. https://ccrjustice.org/sites/default/files/assets/7.29.10%20%20Decision%20denying%20motion%20to%20dismiss.pdf.

38. Motion to dismiss; also reported at CBS News, "U.S. Contractor to Pay $5.8 Million to Abu Ghraib Prisoners," January 8, 2013, https://www.cbsnews.com/news/us-contractor-to-pay-528-million-to-abu-ghraib-prisoners/2/

39. Memorandum opinion. Al Quraishi. https://ccrjustice.org/sites/default/files/assets/7.29.10%20%20Decision%20denying%20motion%20to%20dismiss.pdf

40. See *Al-Quraishi v. Nakhla*, 657 F.3d 201 (4th Cir. 2011); *Al Shimari v. CACI Int'l*, 679 F.3d 205 (4th Cir. 2012) (en banc).

41. Burke interview, 2017.

42. Burke interview, 2017.

43. CBS News, "US Contractor to Pay $5.28 Million to Abu Ghraib Prisoners," January 8, 2013, https://www.cbsnews.com/news/us-contractor-to-pay-528-million-to-abu-ghraib-prisoners/

44. *Al Shimari v. CACI* (2008). Complaint. For background, visit *Al Shimari v. CACI* at https://ccrjustice.org/AlShimari

45. *Al Shimari v. CACI* (2012), p. 2. https://ccrjustice.org/sites/default/files/assets/files/US%20Brief%201.14.12_0.pdf

46. *Al Shimari v. CACI* (2016). 758 F. 3d 516. (E.D.Va. 2016).

47. *Al Shimari v. CACI* (2017). Transcript of Telephone Conference before the Honorable Leonie M. Brinkema, February 9, 2017, p. 4. https://ccrjustice.org/sites/default/files/attach/2017/02/Al%20Shimari%20v.%20CACI%202-9-17.pdf

48. John O'Connor, Transcript of oral arguments, *Al Shimari v. CACI*, September 22, 2017.

49. Judge Leonie Brinkema, Transcript of oral arguments, *Al Shimari v. CACI*.

50. Robert LoBue, Transcript of oral arguments, *Al Shimari v. CACI*.

51. *Al Shimari v. CACI.* Transcript of Motion Hearing before the Honorable Leonie M. Brinkema, September 22, 2017.

52. *Al Shimari v. CACI* (2018). Brinkema dismissed the third party complaint in March 2019.

53. *Al Shimari v. CACI* (2018). Memorandum order, pp. 3–7; Transcript.

54. *Al Shimari v. CACI* (2018). Memorandum order, p. 8.

55. *Al Shimari v. CACI* (2018). Transcript of Motion Hearing. June 18, 2018. https://ccrjustice.org/sites/default/files/attach/2018/06/Al%20Shimari%20v.%20 CACI%20transcript%206-15-18%20web.pdf

56. *Al Shimari v. CACI* (2018). Transcript of Motion Hearing. June 18, 2018.

57. *Al Shimari v. CACI* (2018). Transcript of Motion Hearing. June 18, 2018.

58. *Al Shimari v. CACI* (2018). Transcript of Motion Hearing. June 18, 2018.

59. *El-Masri v. Tenet et al.*, 479 F.3d 269 (VA 2007).

60. Central Intelligence Agency, "Report of Investigation: The Rendition and Detention of Khalid Al-Masri" (Central Intelligence Agency, 2007).

61. John L. Helgerson, "Report of Investigation: The Rendition and Detention of German Citizen Khalid Al-Masri" (Central Intelligence Agency, 2007).

62. *El-Masri v. Tenet et al.* Scott Shane, Stephen Grey, and Margot Williams, "C.I.A. Expanding Terror Battle under Guise of Charter Flights," *New York Times,* May 31, 2005.

63. Shane, Grey, and Williams, "C.I.A. Expanding Terror Battle under Guise of Charter Flights."

64. Watt interview.

65. Gerard Seenan and Giles Tremlett, "How Planespotters Turned into the Scourge of the CIA," *Guardian,* December 10, 2005; Shane, Grey, and Williams, "C.I.A. Expanding Terror Battle under Guise of Charter Flights."

66. Dana Priest, "Jet Is an Open Secret in Terror War," *Washington Post,* December 27, 2004.

67. Priest, "Jet Is an Open Secret in Terror War."

68. Shane, Grey, and Williams, "C.I.A. Expanding Terror Battle under Guise of Charter Flights."

69. Watt interview.

70. *El-Masri v. Tenet et al.* http://www.ca4.uscourts.gov/Opinions/Published /061667.P.pdf

71. "European Court Award for Rendition Victim Khaled Al-Masri," BBC News, December 13, 2012, https://www.bbc.com/news/world-europe-20712615

72. Matthew Schofield, "Yet No Apology: CIA's Mistaken Detention Destroyed German Man's Life," *Impact2020,* December 13, 2014, https://www.mcclatchydc .com/news/nation-world/world/article24777424.html

73. Watt interview.

74. Jane Mayer, "The CIA's Travel Agent," *New Yorker,* October 30, 2006.

75. Watt interview.

76. Watt interview.

77. Watt interview.

78. *Mohamed v. Jeppesen* (2008).

79. *Mohamed v. Jeppesen* (2008). Order Granting the United States' Motion to Intervene. February 13, 2008. https://scholar.google.co.nz/scholar_case?case=135 67719441242203463&hl=en&as_sdt=6&as_vis=1&oi=scholarr

80. Executive Orders 13491, 13492, 13493, January 27, 2009. https://www.gpo.gov/fdsys/pkg/FR-2009-01-27/pdf/E9-1885.pdf

81. Watt interview.

82. *Mohamed v. Jeppesen Dataplan, Inc.* (2009). 579 F. 3d 943—Court of Appeals, 9th Circuit.

83. *Mohamed v. Jeppesen Dataplan, Inc.* (2010). 614 F. 3d 1070—Court of Appeals, 9th Circuit 2010.

84. Watt interview.

85. Untited States House of Representatives, "Activities of the Committee on Oversight and Government Reform—Report 110–930," (2007–08); United States House of Representatives, Committee on Oversight and Government Reform, "Memorandum: Additional Information about Blackwater USA" (Washington, DC: United States Congress, 2007), http://graphics8.nytimes.com/packages/pdf/national/20071001121609.pdf; see also Sue Pleming, "Blackwater Involved in 195 Iraq Shootings," *Reuters*, October 2, 2007, https://www.reuters.com/article/us-iraq-usa-blackwater/blackwater-involved-in-195-iraq-shootings-idUSN2739989220071002.

86. Untited States House of Representatives, "Activities of the Committee on Oversight and Government Reform—Report 110–930," (2007–08); Untited States House of Representatives, Committee on Oversight and Government Reforms, "Memorandum: Additional Information about Blackwater USA"; Pleming, "Blackwater Involved in 195 Iraq Shootings," *Reuters*, October 1, 2007.

87. Paul Von Zielbauer, "Iraqi Inquiry Says Shooting Was Unprovoked," *New York Times*, October 7, 2007; David Johnston and John Broder, "F.B.I. Says Guards Killed 14 Iraqis without Cause," *New York Times*, November 14, 2007.

88. Spencer Hsu and Victoria St. Martin, "Four Blackwater Guards Sentenced in Iraq Shootings of 31 Unarmed Civilians," *Washington Post*, April 13, 2015; Peter W. Singer, "The Dark Truth about Blackwater," Brookings Institution, https://www.brookings.edu/articles/the-dark-truth-about-blackwater/. See also *Atban v. Blackwater* (2007).

89. Erik Prince, October 2, 2007 testimony. https://www.c-span.org/video/?201290-1/private-security-firms-iraq; John Broder, "Chief of Blackwater Defends His Employees," *New York Times*, October 3, 2007.

90. NBC News, "Blackwater Armory Raided in Firearms Inquiry," June 26, 2008, http://www.nbcnews.com/id/25394941/ns/us_news-crime_and_courts/t/blackwater-armory-raided-firearms-inquiry/#.XA8gGnQzbIV

91. BBC News, "Ex-Blackwater President Indicted on Firearms Charges," April 16, 2010.

92. Agence France-Presse, "Former Blackwater Guard Convicted for 2007 Massacre of Civilians in Baghdad," December 19, 2018.

93. *Abtan v. Blackwater Lodge and Training Center* (2009). Complaint; *Albazzaz v. Blackwater Lodge and Training Center* (2007). Complaint 2007.

94. In re: XE Services Alien Tort Litigation, Memorandum Opinion, October 21, 2009, https://ccrjustice.org/sites/default/files/assets/10.21.09%20Memorandum%20opinion%20re%20defendants%27%20motion%20to%20dismiss.pdf

95. In re: Blackwater. Motion to enjoin the parties.

96. In re: XE Services Alien Tort Litigation. "United States of America's Consolidated Brief in Opposition to Defendants' Motion to Substitute the United

States in Place of all Defendants Pursuant to the Westfall Act." https://ccrjustice
.org/sites/default/files/assets/10.8.09%20US%20government%27s%20brief%20
in%20opp%20to%20defendants%27%20motion%20under%20westfall%20to
%20substitute%20parties.pdf; In re: XE Services. Order on Defendants' Consolidated motion to Dismiss. October 21, 2009. https://ccrjustice.org/sites/default/fi
les/assets/10.21.09%20Memorandum%20opinion%20re%20defendants%27%20
motion%20to%20dismiss.pdf

97. Jeremy Scahill, "Blackwater Settles Massacre Lawsuit," *Nation*, January 6, 2010.

98. Liz Sly, "Iraqis Say They Were Forced to Take Blackwater Settlement," *Los Angeles Times*, January 11, 2010.

99. James Risen, "Blackwater Reaches Deal on US Export Violations," *New York Times*, August 20, 2010.

100. Debra Cassens Weiss, "DC Lawyer Pursues Suit to Unmask Authors Who Changed Her Wikipedia Page," *ABA Journal*, September 16, 2013, http://www.aba journal.com/news/article/dc_lawyer_pursues_suit_to_unmask_authors_who_chan ged_her_wikipedia_page/; Zoe Tillman, "Lawyer Wants Wikipedia Editor's Iden-tity Revealed," *National Law Journal*, September 9, 2013, https://www.law.com/na tionallawjournal/almID/1202618385256&Lawyer_Wants_Identity_of_Wikipedia _Editor_Revealed/?slreturn=20181104181153

101. Burke interview, 2017, 2018.

102. Weiss, "DC Lawyer Pursues Suit to Unmask Authors Who Changed Her Wikipedia Page"; Tillman, "Lawyer Wants Wikipedia Editor's Identity Revealed."

103. Weiss, "DC Lawyer Pursues Suit to Unmask Authors Who Changed Her Wikipedia Page"; Tillman, "Lawyer Wants Wikipedia Editor's Identity Revealed."

104. Paul Hoffman, "Lecture at University of California Irvine," 2017.

105. United States Senate Select Committee on Intelligence, "Committee Study of the Central Intelligence Agency's Detention and Interrogation Program," 13.

106. United States Senate Select Committee on Intelligence, "Committee Study of the Central Intelligence Agency's Detention and Interrogation Program," 2.

107. United States Senate Select Committee on Intelligence, "Committee Study of the Central Intelligence Agency's Detention and Interrogation Program," xiiiv–xx (9–11).

108. *Salim v. Mitchell* (2017).

109. Watt interview.

110. *Salim v. Mitchell* (2017). Complaint. Filed October 13, 2015.

111. *Salim v. Mitchell.*

112. Watt interview.

113. Watt interview.

114. Watt interview.

115. Hoffman interview 2017.

116. Ibid.

117. Watt interview.

118. Hoffman interview 2017.

119. Hoffman, "Lecture at University of California Irvine."

120. *Salim v. Mitchell.*

121. Steve Shapiro, "Letter to Honorable Loretta Lynch" (2015).

122. Eric Tucker, "Justice Department Appears Open to Interrogation Suit," *San Diego Union-Tribune*, April 21, 2016. Statement of Interest of the United States, *Salim v. Mitchell*, No 2:15-CV-286-JLQ. April 8, 2016.

123. Hoffman interview 2017.

124. Watt interview.

125. Watt interview.

126. *Salim v. Mitchell* Motion to Dismiss. January 8, 2016; November 18, 2016.

127. Thomas Clouse, "Federal Judge Questions Civil Torture Suit against Spokane Psychologists Mitchell and Jessen," *Spokesman-Review* (Spokane, WA), July 28, 2017. http://www.spokesman.com/stories/2017/jul/28/federal-judge-questions-civil-torture-suit-against/.

128. Thomas Clouse, "Judge Quackenbush Denies Motion to Dismiss Torture Suit against Mitchell and Jessen," AP News, January 19, 2017, https://apnews.com/article/46e68b17b8de450da6eacdeb5a988b12; Thomas Clouse, "Judge Clears Path for Torture Trial against Spokane Psychologists Involved in CIA Waterboarding," *Spokesman-Review* (Spokane, WA), August 7, 2017, http://www.spokesman.com/stories/2017/aug/07/judge-clears-path-for-civil-trial-against-mitchell/; Clouse, "Federal Judge Questions Civil Torture Suit against Spokane Psychologists Mitchell and Jessen."

129. "Mitchell and Jessen Attorneys Seek Judge to Unlock CIA Records of Torture Program," *Spokesman-Review* (Spokane, WA), March 23, 2017, http://www.spokesman.com/stories/2017/mar/23/mitchell-and-jessen-attorneys-seek-judge-to-unlock/

130. *Salim v. Mitchell*. "Order re: motion to compel medical exams and depositions." Filed December 20, 2016.

131. Watt interview.

132. Watt interview.

133. *Salim v. Mitchell*. "Order re: Motion to compel medical exams and depositions."

134. Hoffman interview 2017.

135. Watt interview. Hoffman interview 2017.

136. Watt interview.

137. Watt interview.

138. Jose Rodriguez, Deposition, *Salim v. Mitchell*.

139. *New York Times* (Editorial Board), "The Torturers Speak," *New York Times*, June 23, 2017.

140. Clouse, "Judge Clears Path for Torture Trial against Spokane Psychologists Involved in CIA Waterboarding."

141. Thomas Clouse, "Spokane Psychologists Turn to Nuremberg Trial Ruling on Nazi Gas Killings to Defend Role in Torture," *Spokesman-Review* (Spokane, WA), July 25, 2017.

142. Thomas Clouse, "Spokane Psychologists Mitchell and Jesen Called to Testify about 'Torture' Techniques in 9/11 Tribunals," *Spokesman-Review* (Spokane, WA), May 20, 2019; Thomas Clouse, "In What ACLU Calls 'Historic Victory,' Settlement Reached in CIA Interrogation Suit of 2 Former Spokane Psychologists," *Spokesman-Review* (Spokane, WA), August 17, 2017. http://www.spokesman.com/stories/2017/aug/17/alert-settlement-reach-in-mitchell-jessen-interrog/

143. Watt interview.

144. Thomas Clouse, "Testy Exchange over CIA Records Marks Hearing in Civil Torture Case against Mitchell and Jessen," *Spokesman-Review* (Spokane, WA), May 5, 2017. http://www.spokesman.com/stories/2017/may/05/testy-exchange-ov er-CIA-records-marks-hearing-in-c/

145. Watt interview.

146. Hoffman interview 2017.

147. Hoffman interview 2017.

148. Hoffman interview 2017.

149. Hoffman interview 2017.

150. BusinessWire, "Attorneys for Defendants in Salim v. Mitchell Announce Settlement," August 17, 2017, https://www.businesswire.com/news/home/20170 817005689/en/Attorneys-Defendants-Salim-v.-Mitchell-Announce-Settlement; Clouse, "In What ACLU Calls 'Historic Victory,' Settlement Reached in CIA Interrogation Suit of 2 Former Spokane Psychologists."

151. Hoffman interview 2017.

152. Watt interview.

153. Hoffman interview 2017.

154. Ray Downs, "ACLU Settles Suit against Psychologists Who Created CIA Interrogation Program," *UPI*, April 15, 2019, https://www.upi.com/ACLU-settl es-suit-against-psychologists-who-created-CIA-interrogation-program/75615030 22305/

Chapter 7

1. *Kiobel v. Royal Dutch Petroleum Co.* Complaint. 2004.

2. *Kiobel v. Royal Dutch Petroleum Co.* Complaint. 2004.

3. *Kiobel v. Royal Dutch Petroleum Co.* Complaint. 2004.

4. "One Women against Shell," Amnesty International, https://www.amnesty .org/en/latest/campaigns/2017/06/one-nigerian-widow-vs-shell/

5. *Kiobel v. Royal Dutch Petroleum Co.*

6. *Kiobel v. Royal Dutch Petroleum Co.*

7. Chief Justice John Roberts (oral argument) in *Kiobel v. Royal Dutch Petro-leum Co.* 2012. Transcript retrieved from "Kiobel v. Royal Dutch Petroleum," *Oyez*, April 8, 2018, www.oyez.org/cases/2011/10-1491

8. Stephen Breyer (oral argument) in *Kiobel v. Royal Dutch Petroleum Co.* 2012. Transcript retrieved from "Kiobel v. Royal Dutch Petroleum," *Oyez*, April 8, 2018, www.oyez.org/cases/2011/10-1491

9. Elena Kagan (oral argument) in *Kiobel v. Royal Dutch Petroleum Co.* Tran-script retrieved from "Kiobel v. Royal Dutch Petroleum," *Oyez*, April 8, 2018, www .oyez.org/cases/2011/10-1491

10. Edwin Kneeler (oral argument) in *Kiobel v. Royal Dutch Petroleum Co.* Tran-script retrieved from "Kiobel v. Royal Dutch Petroleum," *Oyez*, April 8, 2018, www .oyez.org/cases/2011/10-1491

11. Kathleen Sullivan (oral argument) in *Kiobel v. Royal Dutch Petroleum Co.* 2012. Transcript retrieved from "Kiobel v. Royal Dutch Petroleum," *Oyez*, April 8, 2012, www.oyez.org/cases/2011/10-1491

12. Paul Hoffman (oral argument) in *Kiobel v. Royal Dutch Petroleum Co.* Transcript retrieved from "Kiobel v. Royal Dutch Petroleum," *Oyez*, April 8, 2012, www.oyez.org/cases/2011/10-1491

13. Anthony Kennedy (oral argument) in *Kiobel v. Royal Dutch Petroleum Co.* 2012. Transcript retrieved from "Kiobel v. Royal Dutch Petroleum," *Oyez*, April 8, 2018, www.oyez.org/cases/2011/10-1491

14. Paul Hoffman (oral argument) in *Kiobel v. Royal Dutch Petroleum Co.* Transcript retrieved from "Kiobel v. Royal Dutch Petroleum." *Oyez*, April 8, 2012, www.oyez.org/cases/2011/10-1491

15. Samuel Alito (oral argument) in *Kiobel v. Royal Dutch Petroleum Co.* Transcript retrieved from "Kiobel v. Royal Dutch Petroleum," *Oyez*, April 8, 2012, www.oyez.org/cases/2011/10-1491

16. Paul Hoffman (oral argument) in *Kiobel v. Royal Dutch Petroleum Co.* Transcript retrieved from "Kiobel v. Royal Dutch Petroleum," *Oyez*, April 8, 2012, www.oyez.org/cases/2011/10-1491

17. Antonin Scalia (oral argument) in *Kiobel v. Royal Dutch Petroleum Co.* Transcript retrieved from "Kiobel v. Royal Dutch Petroleum." *Oyez*, October 1, 2012.

18. Anthony Kennedy (oral argument) in *Kiobel v. Royal Dutch Petroleum Co.* Transcript retrieved from "Kiobel v. Royal Dutch Petroleum." *Oyez*, October 1, 2012.

19. Kathleen Sullivan (oral argument) in *Kiobel v. Royal Dutch Petroleum Co.* Transcript retrieved from "Kiobel v. Royal Dutch Petroleum." *Oyez*, October 1, 2012.

20. Donald Verrilli (oral argument) in *Kiobel v. Royal Dutch Petroleum Co.* Transcript retrieved from "Kiobel v. Royal Dutch Petroleum." *Oyez*, October 1, 2012.

21. Donald Verrilli (oral argument) in *Kiobel v. Royal Dutch Petroleum Co.* Transcript retrieved from "Kiobel v. Royal Dutch Petroleum." *Oyez*, October 1, 2012.

22. Elena Kagan (oral argument) in *Kiobel v. Royal Dutch Petroleum Co.* Transcript retrieved from "Kiobel v. Royal Dutch Petroleum." *Oyez*, October 1, 2012.

23. Elena Kagan (oral argument) in *Kiobel v. Royal Dutch Petroleum Co.* Transcript retrieved from "Kiobel v. Royal Dutch Petroleum." *Oyez*, October 1, 2012.

24. Paul Hoffman (oral argument) in *Kiobel v. Royal Dutch Petroleum Co.* Transcript retrieved from "Kiobel v. Royal Dutch Petroleum." *Oyez*, October 1, 2012.

25. Paul Hoffman (oral argument) in *Kiobel v. Royal Dutch Petroleum Co.* Transcript retrieved from "Kiobel v. Royal Dutch Petroleum." *Oyez*, October 1, 2012.

26. Collingsworth interview.

27. Fryszman interview.

28. See, for example, the International Covenant on Civil and Political Rights, adopted by the UN in 1966.

29. See, for example, United Nations Human Rights, Office of the High Commissioner, "Basic Principles and Guidelines on the Right to a Remedy and Reparation for Victims of Gross Violations of International Human Rights Law and Serious Violations of International Humanitarian Law," https://www.ohchr.org/en/professionalinterest/pages/remedyandreparation.aspx. And also https://iccforum.com/background/reparations; see also "Report of the Special Representative of the Secretary-General on the Issue of Human Rights and Transnational Corporations and Other Business Enterprises," https://www.business-humanrights.org/si

tes/default/files/media/documents/ruggie/ruggie-guiding-principles-21-mar-2011
.pdf

30. Cindy Cohn, interview, 2018,

31. Cohn interview.

32. Simons interview.

33. Sklar interview.

34. Morton Sklar, email exchange, May 28, 2020.

35. Chomsky interview.

36. Wayne Arnold, "Exxon Mobil, in Fear Exits Indonesian Gas Fields," *New York Times*, March 24, 2001.

37. Anthony Smith, "Aceh: Democratic Times, Authoritarian Solutions," *New Zealand Journal of Asian Studies* 4 (2012).

38. UN Commission on Human Rights, Report of the Special Rapporteur on Torture and Cruel, Inhuman or Degrading Treatment or Punishment, UN Doc. E/CN.4/1993/31. http://hrlibrary.umn.edu/commission/torture94/cat-indonesia.htm; see also Steve Coll, *Private Empire: ExxonMobil and American Power* (London: Penguin, 2012). Mobil later merged with Exxon to become ExxonMobil. Michael Shari, "Indonesia: What Did Mobil Know?," *Bloomberg*, December 27, 1998, https://www.bloomberg.com/news/articles/1998-12-27/indonesia-what-did-mobil-know; Taylor, "Thicker Than Blood."

39. *Doe v. Exxon Mobil Corp.*, First Amended Complaint for Equitable Relief and Damages. Filed January 20, 2006, 32.

40. Kirsty Alfredson, "Exxonmobil Rejects Aceh Human Rights Abuse Claims," *CNN.com*, June 22, 2001, http://edition.cnn.com/2001/WORLD/asiapcf/southeast/06/22/indonesia.exxon.mobil/. *Doe v. Exxon Mobil Corp*, 393 F. Supp. 2d 20 (Dist. Court, Dist. of Columbia 2005). Arnold, "Exxon Mobil, in Fear Exits Indonesian Gas Fields."

41. *Doe v. Exxon Mobil Corp.*, 393 F. Supp. 2d 20 Dist. Court, Dist. of Columbia 2005. https://scholar.google.co.nz/scholar_case?case=16628283638041959457&hl=en&as_sdt=2006&as_vis=1

42. *Doe v. Exxon Mobil Corp.*, 473 F. 3d 345 Court of Appeals, Dist. of Columbia Circuit. 2007. https://scholar.google.co.nz/scholar_case?case=2898355848533048038&hl=en&as_sdt=6&as_vis=1&oi=scholarr

43. Fryszman interview.

44. *Doe v. Exxon Mobil Corp.*, 473 F. 3d 345 Court of Appeals, Dist. of Columbia Circuit. 2007. https://scholar.google.co.nz/scholar_case?case=2898355848533048038&hl=en&as_sdt=6&as_vis=1&oi=scholarr

45. *Doe v. Exxon Mobil Corp.*, 473 F. 3d 345 Court of Appeals, Dist. of Columbia Circuit. 2007. https://scholar.google.co.nz/scholar_case?case=2898355848533048038&hl=en&as_sdt=6&as_vis=1&oi=scholarr

46. *Doe v. Exxon Mobil Corp.*, 473 F. 3d 345 Court of Appeals, Dist. of Columbia Circuit. 2007. https://scholar.google.co.nz/scholar_case?case=2898355848533048038&hl=en&as_sdt=6&as_vis=1&oi=scholarr

47. Mike Scarcella, "Exxon Wants Rehearing in Corporate Liability Dispute," Business & Human Righs Centre, August 10, 2011, https://www.business-humanrights.org/en/exxon-wants-rehearing-in-corporate-liability-dispute-usa. *Exxon Mobil Corporation v. John Doe I*, Petition for a Writ of Certiorari, July 20, 2007, https://www.scotusblog.com/archives/07-81_pet.pdf

48. Mike Scarcella, "Judge Rejects Summary Judgment in Human Rights Lawsuit against Exxon," *Legal Times*, August 28, 2008.

49. *John Doe VIII v. Exxon Mobil Corp.*, 658 F. Supp. 2d 131—Dist. Court, Dist. of Columbia. 2009.

50. *John Doe VIII v. Exxon Mobil Corp.*, 658 F. Supp. 2d 131 (Dist. Court, Dist. of Columbia 2009). *John Doe VIII v. Exxon Mobil Corp.*, 658 F. Supp. 2d 131—Dist. Court, Dist. of Columbia. 2011.

51. *John Doe VIII v. Exxon Mobil Corp.*, 658 F. Supp. 2d 131 (Dist. Court, Dist. of Columbia 2009). *John Doe VIII v. Exxon Mobil Corp.*, 658 F. Supp. 2d 131—Dist. Court, Dist. of Columbia. 2011.

52. *Doe v. Exxon Mobil Corp.*

53. Fryszman interview.

54. Bill Mears, "Exxon Mobile to Face Lawsuit over Alleged Human Rights Violations," *CNN*, July 8, 2011, http://edition.cnn.com/2011/CRIME/07/08/exxon.mobil.lawsuit/index.html?hpt=hp_t2

55. *John Doe VIII v. Exxon Mobil Corp.*, 658 F. Supp. 2d 131—Dist. Court, Dist. of Columbia. 2009. Fryszman interview.

56. *Doe v. Exxon Mobil Corp.*, Case No: 01-cv-1357-RCL (D.D.C., December 6, 2016).

57. Fryszman interview.

58. *Doe v. Exxon Mobil Corporation.* 2015. Dist. Court, Dist. of Columbia. Civil No. 01–1357 (RCL). July 6, 2015. https://scholar.google.com/scholar_case?case=2878410930854783539

59. *John Doe v. Exxon Mobil Corporation*, "Declaration of Terrence P. Collingsworth," https://amlawdaily.typepad.com/0000collingsworth.pdf

60. Fryszman interview.

61. Douglas Frantz, "Chiquita Still under Cloud after Newspaper's Retreat," *New York Times*, July 17, 1998.

62. *John Doe v. Exxon Mobil Corporation.* 2015. Dist. Court, Dist. of Columbia. Civil No. 01–1357 (RCL). July 6, 2015. https://scholar.google.com/scholar_case?case=2878410930854783539

63. Frantz, "Chiquita Still under Cloud after Newspaper's Retreat."

64. Frantz, "Chiquita Still under Cloud after Newspaper's Retreat."

65. Olga Martin-Ortega, "Business and Human Rights in Conflict," *Ethics & International Affairs* 22, no. 3 (2008). ibid.

66. Reuters, "Colombia Civil Conflict Has Killed 'Nearly a Quarter of a Million': Study," July 25, 2013, https://www.telegraph.co.uk/news/worldnews/southamerica/colombia/10201512/Colombia-civil-conflict-has-killed-nearly-a-quarter-of-a-million-study.html; Reuters, "Colombia Calls Drummond Coal Officials to Testify on Paramilitaries: Source," *Reuters*, October 31, 2018.

67. Martin-Ortega, "Business and Human Rights in Conflict," also citing Amnesty International. Ibid.

68. Curt Anderson, "Bananas, Colombian Death Squads, and a Billion Dollar Lawsuit," *NBC News*, May 31, 2011, http://www.nbcnews.com/id/43221200/ns/world_news-americas/t/bananas-colombian-death-squads-billion-dollar-lawsuit/; States News Service, "Para-Business Gone Bananas: Chiquita Brands in Colombia," August 18, 2011.

69. Adriaan Alsema, "Colombia Charges 13 Former Chiquita Executives over

Hundreds of Murders," *Colombia Reports*, September 1, 2018, https://colombiarepo
rts.com/terror-for-profit-colombia-charges-14-former-chiquita-executives/

70. Toby Muse, "Chiquita to Pay $2m Fine in Terror Case," *Associated Press*,
March 15, 2007. ibid.

71. Name withheld for security of the family.

72. *Doe v. Chiquita*. First Amended Class Action Complaint filed in US District
Court, Southern District of Florida. February 26, 2010. https://earthrights.org/wp
-content/uploads/Chiquita-1st-amended-complaint.pdf

73. *Doe v. Chiquita*; Aviva Chomsky, "Globalization, Labor, and Violence in
Colombia's Banana Zone," *International Labor and Working-Class History* 72, no. 1
(2007).

74. Sibylla Brodzinsky, "Chiquita Case Puts Big Firms on Notice," *Christian
Science Monitor*, April 11, 2007. ibid.

75. Martin-Ortega, "Business and Human Rights in Conflict"; Michael Evans,
"'Para-Politics' Goes Bananas," *Nation*, April 4, 2007.

76. Al Jazeera America, "Court Tosses Out Cases against Chiquita over Colombia Killings," July 24, 2014, http://america.aljazeera.com/articles/2014/7/24/chiq
uita-lawsuitcolombia.html; Mike Gallagher and Cameron McWhirter, "Chiquita
Secrets Revealed," *Cincinnati Enquirer*, May 3, 1998; Frantz, "Chiquita Still under
Cloud after Newspaper's Retreat."

77. Montse Ferrer, "Prosecuting Extortion Victims: How Counter-Terrorist
Finance Measure Executive Order 13224 Is Going Too Far," *Journal of Financial
Crime* 16, no. 3 (2009): 262.

78. Josh Meyer, "Chiquita to Pay Fine for Deals with Militants," *Los Ange-
les Times*, March 15, 2007; Department of Justice, "Chiquita Brands International
Pleads Guilty to Making Payments to a Designated Terrorist Organization and
Agrees to Pay $25 Million Fine" (Washington, DC: Department of Justice, 2007);
States News Service, "Para-Business Gone Bananas."

79. Jane Bussey, "Fort Lauderdale Law Firm Sues Chiquita," *Tribune Business
News*, June 14, 2007; Sarah Altschuller, Dan Feldman, and Lara Blecher, "Cor-
porate Social Responsibility," *International Lawyer* 42 (Summer 2008): 489; Sarah
Altschuller and Amy Lehr, "Corporate Social Responsibility," *International Lawyer*
43, no. 2 (2008). Includes *Carrizosa v. Chiquita Brands Int'l* in the Southern District
Court of Florida (June 13, 2007), *Doe v. Chiquita Brands Int'l* in the Federal District
Court of New Jersey (July 19, 2007), and *Doe v. Chiquita Brands Int'l* in the Southern District Court of New York, *Doe v. Chiquita* filed June 2007 in Washington,
DC, *Montes v. Chiquita*, and *Valencia v. Chiquita*. In the New York case representing
393 AUC victims, New York-based Jonathan Reiter, Ramon Rasco, and Gary Osen
sued Chiquita in Manhattan federal court, asking for $7.86 billion to compensate
each victim, among which was a student killed while waiting for a bus. *In re: Chiquita*. 2008. June 6, 2008; Carrizosa; *Doe v. Chiquita*. 2008. Amended Complaint.
Filed June 6 2008. https://www.law.du.edu/documents/corporate-governance/inte
rnational-corporate-governance/in-re-chiquita-third-amended.pdf

80. *Doe v. Chiquita Brands International, Inc.* June 6, 2008 Third Amended Complaint,, 172. https://www.law.du.edu/documents/corporate-governance/internatio
nal-corporate-governance/in-re-chiquita-third-amended.pdf

81. Doe v. Chiquita Brands International, Inc. June 6, 2008 Third Amended

Complaint, 193. https://www.law.du.edu/documents/corporate-governance/inter national-corporate-governance/in-re-chiquita-third-amended.pdf

82. *Carrizosa v. Chiquita Brands International, Inc.* 2007. United States District Court, S.D. Florida. "Opinion and Order." November 13, 2007.

83. *Doe v. Chiquita.* June 6, 2008 amended complaint; *Cardona et al v. Chiquita.* 2014. Circuit Court decision.

84. John Lyons and David Luhnow, "Chiquita Sued by Relatives of Five Slain Missionaries," *Wall Street Journal*, March 12, 2008; Jane Musgrave, "All Chiquita Lawsuits in Colombia Slayings Shift to West Palm," *Palm Beach Post*, April 30, 2008.

85. "New Lawsuit Claims Chiquita Transported Weapons," *Palm Beach Post*, May 14, 2008.

86. Musgrave, "All Chiquita Lawsuits in Colombia Slayings Shift to West Palm."

87. *Doe v. Chiquita.* 2008. Motion to Dismiss, July 11, 2008, p. 1 (document 93).

88. *Doe v. Chiquita.* Motion. September 19, 2008; Opinion and order, 2011. https://cases.justia.com/federal/district-courts/florida/flsdce/0:2010cv60573/3556 47/40/0.pdf?ts=1411532329

89. *Doe v. Chiquita.* 2008. Opposition to Motion to Dismiss. August 19, 2008, pp. 21–22. https://EarthRights.org/wp-content/uploads/Pls-consolidated-opp-to -MTD.pdf

90. *In re: Chiquita Brands International.* 2011. "Opinion and Order." June 11, 2011. https://cases.justia.com/federal/district-courts/florida/flsdce/0:2010cv60573 /355647/40/0.pdf?ts=1411532329

91. Brief of Appellants, Chiquita Brands International, Inc. and Chiquita Fresh North America LLC, https://EarthRights.org/wp-content/uploads/Chiquita-Me rits-Brief-on-Interlocutory-Appeal-5.28.13.pdf; "Business Briefs," *Telegram & Gazette*, B10, April 25, 2014.

92. Anderson, Curt, "Chiquita Asks Court to Toss Terror Payments Case," *Daily Mail*, April 24, 2014, https://www.dailymail.co.uk/wires/ap/article-2612130 /Chiquita-asks-court-toss-terror-payments-case.html

93. *Doe v. Chiquita Brands Int.* https://EarthRights.org/wp-content/uploads /chq_11th_cir_opinion_072414.pdf

94. *Doe v. Chiquita.* Also in Jane Musgrave, "Families Fight to Sue Chiquita in U.S," *Palm Beach Post*, January 21, 2015.

95. *In re: Chiquita.* Eleventh Circuit Court Opinion. August 14, 2014. https:// EarthRights.org/wp-content/uploads/chiquita_pfr_-_final_8.14_as_filed.pdf

96. *In re: Chiquita.* Eleventh Circuit Court Opinion. August 14, 2014. https:// EarthRights.org/wp-content/uploads/chiquita_pfr_-_final_8.14_as_filed.pdf

97. Katherine Gallagher, interview by author, 2018, New York.

98. Michael Evans, interview by author, 2017, Washington, DC.

99. Evans interview.

100. Evans interview.

101. Collingsworth interview; Brodzinsky, "Chiquita Case Puts Big Firms on Notice."

102. *In Re: Chiquita Brands International.* 2016. Order granting in part and denying in part defendants' joint consolidated motion to dismiss. (Case 0:07-cv-60821-KAM. Document 267). June 1, 2016.

103. *In re: Chiquita.* Order granting in part and denying in part defendants' joint consolidated motion to dismiss. June 1, 2016. http://iradvocates.org/sites/iradvoca tes.org/files/06.01.16%20Order%20re%20MTD.pdf

104. Reuters, "Chiquita Settles with Families of US Victims of Colombia's FARC," February 5, 2018, https://www.voanews.com/a/chiquita-settles-with-fam ilies-of-us-victims-of-colombia-farc-/4240697.html

105. *In Re: Chiquita Brands International Inc.* September 5, 2019 Summary Judgment. United States District Court Southern District of Florida. https://earthrigh ts.org/wp-content/uploads/Summary-Judgement-Decision-September-2019.pdf

106. *Jane Doe. v. Chiquita International Brands.* 2020. Complaint.

107. France 24, "Colombia: 13 Ex-Chiquita Aides Face Trial on Paramilitary Funding," August 31, 2018. https://www.france24.com/en/20180831-colombia-13 -ex-chiquita-aides-face-trial-paramilitary-funding

108. Sue Reisinger, "3 Us Execs Indicted in Chiquita Terrorist Funding Probe in Colombia," September 10, 2018, https://www.law.com/corpcounsel/2018/09 /10/three-u-s-execs-indicted-in-chiquita-terrorist-funding-probe-in-colombia/

109. International Human Right Clinic, Harvard Law School, "The Contribution of Chiquita Corporate Officials to Crimes against Humanity in Colombia" (2017): 5–6.

110. Fryszman interview.

111. *Doe v. Nestle,* 906 F.3d 1120 (2018;. *Doe v. NESTLE, SA,* 906 F. 3d 1120— Court of Appeals, 9th Circuit 2018.

Chapter 8

1. Stuart Scheingold, *The Politics of Rights: Lawyers, Public Policy, and Political Change* (Ann Arbor: University of Michigan Press, 2010).

2. Chomsky interview.

3. Gallagher interview.

4. Weiss interview, 2017, New York; Kenneth C. Randall, "Universal Jurisdiction under International Law," *Texas Law Review* 66 (1987).

5. Weiss interview; Randall, "Universal Jurisdiction under International Law."

6. Wolfgang Kaleck and Patrick Kroker, "Syrian Torture Investigations in Germany and Beyond: Breathing New Life into Universal Jurisdiction in Europe?," *Journal of International Criminal Justice* 16, no. 1 (2018); Council of the European Union, "Council Decision of 13 June 2002: Setting Up a European Network of Contact Points in Respect of Persons Responsible for Genocide, Crimes against Humanity and War Crimes" (Official Journal of the European Communities, 2002).

7. Weiss interview.

8. Andreas Schüller, interview by author, 2017, Berlin.

9. Schüller interview.

10. Kaleck and Kroker, "Syrian Torture Investigations in Germany and Beyond."

11. Schüller interview.

12. Schüller interview.

13. Schüller interview.

14. Gallagher interview.

15. See Center for Constitutional Rights, "Accountability for International Crimes in Afghanistan," November 20, 2017, https://ccrjustice.org/home/what-we -do/our-cases/accountability-international-crimes-afghanistan

16. Katie Gallagher, email exchange, July 9, 2020.

17. See Center for Constitutional Rights, "Accountability for International Crimes in Afghanistan," November 20, 2017, https://ccrjustice.org/home/what-we -do/our-cases/accountability-international-crimes-afghanistan

18. Day interview.

19. FIDH has approximately 180 member organizations worldwide.

20. Worldwide Movement For Human Rights, "Syria, Iraq, Rwanda: Universal Jurisdiction Has Gathered Unprecedented Momentum in 2016," March 27, 2017, https://www.fidh.org/en/issues/international-justice/universal-jurisdiction/syria -iraq-rwanda-universal-jurisdiction-has-gathered-unprecedented; TRIAL International, "Make Way for Justice #4: Momentum Towards Accountability" (Geneva: TRIAL International, 2018).

21. Watt interview. His Macedonian lawyer is Filip Medarski. Global Legal Monitor, "European Court of Human Rights: Decision Issued in Rendition Case," March 4, 2013, http://www.loc.gov/law/foreign-news/article/european-court-of -human-rights-decision-issued-in-rendition-case/

22. James L. Cavallaro and Stephanie Erin Brewer, "Reevaluating Regional Human Rights Litigation in the Twenty-First Century: The Case of the Inter-American Court," *American Journal of International Law* 102, no. 4 (2008).

23. Gallagher interview.

24. John Vidal, "Lawyers Leigh Day: Troublemakers Who Are a Thorn in the Side of Multinationals," *Guardian*, August 2, 2015.

25. Day interview.

26. Day interview.

27. Day interview.

28. Day interview.

29. Vidal, "Lawyers Leigh Day."

30. Vidal, "Lawyers Leigh Day."

31. Robert Verkaik, "BP Pays Out Millions to Colombian Farmers," *Independent*, July 22, 2006.

32. Voice of America, "British Finally Agree to Help Kenyans Injured by Their Munitions," July 25, 2002, https://www.voanews.com/amp/a-13-a-2002-07-25-52 -british-67276632/268335.html

33. Voice of America, "British Finally Agree to Help Kenyans Injured by Their Munitions."

34. Voice of America, "British Finally Agree to Help Kenyans Injured by Their Munitions."

35. Voice of America, "British Finally Agree to Help Kenyans Injured by Their Munitions."

36. Day interview.

37. Day interview.

38. Press Association, "Kenyan Torture Victims Give Evidence in High Court Compensation Case," *Guardian*, January 30, 2019.

39. Afua Hirsch, "UK 'Using Obscure Legal Principle' to Dismiss Torture Claims in Colonial Kenya," *Guardian*, January 25, 2010.

40. Day interview.

41. Day interview.

42. Press Association, "UK to Compensate Kenya's Mau Mau Torture Victims," *Guardian*, June 6, 2013.

43. Jo Moore, "Kenyan 'Mau Mau' Claim Dismissed: Fair Trial Not Possible Because of Half Century Delay," August 6, 2018, https://ukhumanrightsblog.com /2018/08/06/kenyan-mau-mau-claim-dismissed-fair-trial-not-possible-because-of -half-century-delay/.

44. Helena Smith, "UK to Pay 1 M to Greek Cypriots over Claims of Human Rights Abuses," *Guardian*, January 23, 2019.

45. Day interview.

46. Day interview.

47. James Courtright, "In Sierra Leone–UK Mining Case, a New Attempt to Measure the Arm of the Law," *Christian Science Monitor*, June 19, 2018, https:// www.csmonitor.com/World/Africa/2018/0619/In-Sierra-Leone-UK-mining-case -a-new-attempt-to-measure-the-arm-of-the-law; Human Rights Watch, "Whose Development? Human Rights Abuses in Sierra Leone's Mining Boom" (New York: Human Rights Watch, 2014); Shafi Musaddique, "UK Mining Company Faces Landmark High Court Case over Alleged Worker Abuse in Sierra Leone," *Independent*, January 29, 2018, https://www.independent.co.uk/news/business/news/to nkolili-iron-ore-uk-mining-company-sierra-leone-high-court-case-worker-abuse -villagers-a8179891.html; "Landmark Case against British Mining Firm Begins in Sierra Leone," *Guardian*, February 7, 2018.

48. Regina Pratt, "British Judge Ends AML Trial in Sierra Leone," *Concord Times*, February 14, 2018.

49. Pratt, "British Judge Ends AML Trial in Sierra Leone"; *Kadie Kalma & Ors v African Minerals Ltd & Ors* [2018] EWHC 3506 (QB). Author: UK High Court of Justice, Queen's Bench Division, Published on December 19, 2018.

50. Day interview.

51. Day interview.

52. Kenyan Human Rights Commission, "High Court Rejects LSK Mau Mau Claim against KHRC, Leigh Day & MMWVA," December 2, 2015.

53. Jamie Grierson, "Law Firm at Centre of Al-Sweady Inquiry to Close Down, Say Reports," *Guardian*, August 15, 2016.

54. Owen Bowcott, "Lawyer 'Used Sensationalist Language in Iraq Torture Case'," *Guardian*, July 17, 2018.

55. Bowcott, "Lawyer 'Used Sensationalist Language in Iraq Torture Case'."

56. Bowcott, "Lawyer 'Used Sensationalist Language in Iraq Torture Case'."

57. Eisenbrandt interview.

58. https://www.international.gc.ca/world-monde/international_relations-rela tions_internationales/icc-cpi/index.aspx?lang=eng. Accessed: December 19, 2020. Accessed January 18, 2019.

59. Eisenbrandt interview.

60. Gray interview; Eisenbrandt interview.

61. Eisenbrandt interview.

62. Commission of Inquiry into the Actions of Canadian Officials in Relation to Maher Arar, "Report of the Events Relating to Maher Arar" (2006).

63. Associated Press, "Canada Charges Syrian Officer over Torture of Engineer Mistaken for Terrorist," *Guardian*, September 1, 2015; Ian Austen, "Canada to Pay $9.75 Million to Man Tortured in Syria," *New York Times*, January 27, 2007; Amnesty International, "The Case of Maher Arar," https://www.amnesty.ca/legal-brief/case-maher-arar; CBC News, "RCMP Charges Syrian Officer in Maher Arar Torture Case." Arar's lawyers in Canada are Paul Champ, Julian Falconer, Julian Roy, and Michael Edelson.

64. Eisenbrandt interview.

65. "Transnational Lawsuits in Canada against Extractive Companies" Above Ground, February 17, 2016, updated August 22, 2017, https://www.aboveground.ngo/wp-content/uploads/2016/02/Cases_Aug2017.pdf

66. *Anvil Mining Limited v. Canadian Association Against Impunity.* No. 500-09-021701-115. Court of Appeal. Canada, province of Quebec. January 24, 2012. https://www.ccij.ca/content/uploads/2015/07/Anvil-Judgment-QCA-English-translation.pdf

67. *Anvil Mining Limited v. Canadian Association Against Impunity.* No. 500-09-021701-115. Court of Appeal. Canada, province of Quebec. January 24, 2012.

68. The concessions were later ruled to violate international law by the United Nations Labor Organization. And in 2011, the Constitutional Court of Guatemala granted the indigenous Mayans legal rights to their ancestral homeland, overruling the concession.

69. Peter McFarlane, *Northern Shadows: Canadians and Central America* (Toronto: Between the Lines, 1989).

70. Dawn Paley, "This Is What Development Looks Like," *Dominion*, January 11, 2007.

71. McFarlane, *Northern Shadows*; *Choc v. Hudbay Minerals Inc.*, ONSC 1414—2013 (2013). *Angelica Choc v. Hudbay Minerals Inc. et al.* 2013. Third Amended Statement of Claim. October 10, 2013; Suzanne Daley, "Guatemalan Women's Claims Put Focus on Canadian Firms' Conduct Abroad," *New York Times*, April 2, 2016.

72. *Angelica Choc v. Hudbay Minerals Inc. et al.* 2013. Third Amended Statement of Claim. October 10, 2013.

73. Marina Jimenez, "The Mayans vs. the Mine," *Toronto Star*, June 18, 2016.

74. *Choc v. Hudbay Minerals Inc.*, https://www.ccij.ca/content/uploads/2015/07/HudBay-Judgment-July-22-2013-Hudbays-motion-to-strike.pdf. The cases include *Choc v. HudBay*, *Caal v. HudBay*, and *Chub v. HudBay*.

75. Hudbay Minerals, "Press Release" (2009).

76. Hudbay Minerals, "Press Release" (2009); https://www.ccij.ca/content/uploads/2015/07/HudBay-Judgment-July-22-2013-Hudbays-motion-to-strike.pdf. Accessed January 7, 2019.

77. http://www.chocversushudbay.com/wp-content/uploads/2020/02/2020-01-22-Decision-re-motion-to-amend-pleadings.pdf, *Choc v. Hudbay Minerals Inc.*, 2013 ONSC 1414. Court File no. CV-10-411159 CV-11-423077 and CV-11-435841. July 22, 2013; Shin Imai, Bernadette Maheandiran, and Valerie Crystal,

"Access to Justice and Corporate Accountability: A Legal Case Study of Hudbay in Guatemala," *Canadian Journal of Development Studies* 35, no. 2 (2014). Amnesty International Canada, granted intervenor status, argued that the Canadian government had endorsed these international norms and standards of conduct. In 2011, Hudbay sold its interest in the mine. Andrew Findlay, "Rocked: Canadian Mining Companies Deal with Fallout from Supreme Court Ruling," *BC Business*, January 8, 2019, https://www.bcbusiness.ca/Rocked-Canadian-mining-companies-deal-wi th-fallout-from-Supreme-Court-ruling

78. Findlay, "Rocked." Also, *Garcia v. Tahoe Resources Inc.*, BCCA 39—2017 (2017). https://www.ccij.ca/content/uploads/2015/07/Tahoe-Notice-Civil-Claim .pdf. Accessed January 13, 2019.

79. Greg Rasmussen, "Tahoe Resources, Vancouver Mining Firm, in Court Today over Guatemalan Workers' Lawsuit," *CBC*, April 8, 2015, https://www.cbc .ca/news/canada/british-columbia/tahoe-resources-vancouver-mining-firm-in-co urt-today-over-guatemalan-workers-lawsuit-1.3024121

80. Rasmussen, "Tahoe Resources, Vancouver Mining Firm, in Court Today over Guatemalan Workers' Lawsuit."

81. Rasmussen, "Tahoe Resources, Vancouver Mining Firm, in Court Today over Guatemalan Workers' Lawsuit."

82. *Garcia v. Tahoe Resources Inc.* BCCA 39. January 26, 2017. Docket CA 43295. https://www.ccij.ca/content/uploads/2015/11/SCBC-judgment-on-FNC-Nov-20 15.pdf. Accessed January 13, 2019; https://www.ccij.ca/content/uploads/2017/01 /2017-BCCA-39-Garcia-v.-Tahoe-Resources-Inc.pdf. Accessed January 15, 2019.

83. *Garcia v. Tahoe Resources Inc.*; https://globalfreedomofexpression.columbia .edu/cases/garcia-v-tahoe-resources-inc/.

84. https://globalfreedomofexpression.columbia.edu/cases/garcia-v-tahoe-reso urces-inc/.

85. Findlay, "Rocked."

86. Michael Swan, "Probe Sought into Canadian-Owned Mine in Guatemala," *Catholic Register*, January 9, 2019.

87. Creamer Media Reporter, "Court Case Sets Precedent for Claims Arising from Overseas Activities of Canadian Miners," *Mining Weekly*, July 30, 2019. https://m.miningweekly.com/article/court-case-sets-precedent-for-claims-arising -from-overseas-activities-of-canadian-miners-2019-07-30

88. United Nations Human Rights (Office of the High Commissioner), "UN Inquiry Finds Crimes against Humanity in Eritrea," https://www.ohchr.org/EN /NewsEvents/Pages/DisplayNews.aspx?NewsID=20067&LangID=E; also, *Araya v. Nevsun Resources Ltd.*, BCCA 401—2017 (2017); Human Rights Watch, "Hear No Evil" (New York: Human Rights Watch, 2013). *Araya v. Nevsun Resources Ltd.*, 2017. https://www.courts.gov.bc.ca/jdb-txt/ca/17/04/2017BCCA0401.htm. Accessed January 17, 2019; Allison Martell and Edmund Blair, "We Were Forced to Work for Western-Run Mine," *Reuters Special Reports*, September 27, 2016.

89. Scott Anderson, "Mine Workers Suing Nevsun Resources over Allegations of Forced Labour," *CBC News*, January 22, 2019, https:// www.cbc.ca/news/business/nevsun-resources-mining-eritrea-1.4980530; Human Rights Watch, "Eritrea: Events of 2017," https://www.hrw.org/world-report/2018/country-chapters/eritrea#. *Araya v. Nevsun Resources Ltd.*, https://

www.ccij.ca/content/uploads/2015/07/Nevsun-Notice-of-Civil-Claim-Nov-20-2014.pdf. Accessed January 16, 2019.

90. *Araya v. Nevsun Resources Ltd.* 2016 BCSC 1856 (CanLII). https://www.canlii.org/en/bc/bcsc/doc/2016/2016bcsc1856/2016bcsc1856.html

91. *2016 BCSC 1856—2016* (2016); *Araya v. Nevsun Resources Ltd.* 2016; *Araya v. Nevsun Resources, Ltd.* 2014. Notice of Civil Claim. November 20, 2014. In the Supreme Court of British Columbia. https://www.ccij.ca/content/uploads/2015/07/Nevsun-Notice-of-Civil-Claim-Nov-20-2014.pdf. Accessed January 6, 2019. https://www.ccij.ca/content/uploads/2016/10/BCSC-Nevsun-judgment-Oct-2016.pdf. Accessed January 13, 2019.

92. Eisenbrandt interview.

93. Anderson, "Mine Workers Suing Nevsun Resources over Allegations of Forced Labour."

94. Martell and Blair, "We Were Forced to Work for Western-Run Mine."

95. *Araya v. Nevsun Resources Ltd.* 2014. Notice of Civil Claim. November 20, 2014. In the Supreme Court of British Columbia. https://www.ccij.ca/content/uploads/2015/07/Nevsun-Notice-of-Civil-Claim-Nov-20-2014.pdf. Accessed January 6, 2019.

96. *Araya v. Nevsun Resources Ltd.* 2014. Notice of Civil Claim. November 20, 2014. In the Supreme Court of British Columbia.

97. *Araya v. Nevsun Resources Ltd.* 2017. BCCA 401. November 21, 2017. Docket CA 44025. https://www.courts.gov.bc.ca/jdb-txt/ca/17/04/2017BCCA0401.htm

98. Agence France-Presse in Ottawa, "Canada Mining Firm Accused of Slavery Abroad Can Be Sued at Home, Supreme Court Rules," *Guardian*, February 28, 2020, https://www.theguardian.com/world/2020/feb/28/canada-nevsun-eritrea-lawsuit-human-rights-slavery

99. European Center for Constitutional and Human Rights, "Criminal Complaint Filed Accuses Senior Manager of Danzer Group of Responsibility over Human Rights Abuses against Congolese Community" (2013). Edmund Smyth and Emily Elliott, "Private Prosecutions for Crimes of Universal Jurisdiction," Kingsley Napley, April 9, 2015, https://www.kingsleynapley.co.uk/insights/blogs/criminal-law-blog/private-prosecutions-for-crimes-of-universal-jurisdiction; Human rights group SMX Collective filed the criminal complaint against Rabobank and its directors, TRIAL International against Argor Hereaus, the ECCHR and a Colombian trade union, Sinantrainal, against Nestle for the onsite murder of its employee, Luciano Romero, also a union leader. European Center for Constitutional and Human Rights, "Are Arms Manufacturers and Italian Authorities Complicit in Deadly Saudi-Coalition Airstrike in Yemen?" (2018).

100. Benedict De Moerloose, email exchange, May 18, 2020.

101. De Moerloose, email exchange, May 18, 2020; Kerry Dolan, "Swiss Gold Refiner Accused of Abetting Congo War via Money Laundering," *Forbes*, November 4, 2013.

102. Agence France-Presse, "Swiss Slammed for Closing DR Congo 'Dirty Gold' Case," *Daily Mail*, June 2, 2015.

103. Agence France-Presse, "Swiss Slammed for Closing DR Congo 'Dirty Gold' Case," *Daily Mail*, June 2, 2015.

104. Agence France-Presse, "Swiss Slammed for Closing DR Congo 'Dirty Gold' Case," *Daily Mail*, June 2, 2015.

105. The executives included Bruno Lafont, Bruno Pescheux, and Frederic Jolibois. David Keohane and Ralph Atkins, "Syrian Operation: Lafarge Faces Probe over ISIS Payments," *Financial Times*, May 16, 2018.

106. European Center for Constitutional and Human Rights, "Lafarge in Syria: Accusations of Complicity in War Crimes and Crimes against Humanity" (Berlin: European Center for Constitutional and Human Rights, 2016); Liz Alderman, "French Cement Giant Lafarge Indicted on Terror Financing Charge in Syria," *New York Times*, June 28, 2018.

107. European Center for Constitutional and Human Rights, "Lafarge in Syria"; Agence France-Presse, "Lafarge Charged with Complicity in Syria Crimes against Humanity," June 28, 2018.

108. LafargeHolcim, "Lafargeholcim Responds to Syria Review," March 2, 2017, https://www.lafargeholcim.com/LafargeHolcim-responds-syria-review

109. Liz Alderman, "Terrorism Financing Charge Upheld against French Company Lafarge," *New York Times*, November 7, 2019.https://www.nytimes.com/2019/11/07/business/lafarge-terrorism-syria.html

110. Agence France-Presse, "French Firm Amesys Probed over 'Complicity in Torture," May 22, 2012, https://www.france24.com/en/20120522-libya-france-gaddafi-amesys-war-crimes-technology-firm-court-justice; Reuters, "France Investigates Tech Firm Accused of Aiding Syria," July 26, 2012, https://www.reuters.com/article/syria-france-qosmos/france-investigates-tech-firm-accused-of-aiding-syria-idUSL6E8IQN9520120726?feedType=RSS&feedName=technologySector

111. Middle East Monitor, "Palestinian Family Sues French Technology Company for Complicity in War Crimes," June 20, 2016, https://www.middleeastmonitor.com/20160630-palestinian-family-sues-french-technology-company-for-complicity-in-war-crimes/; Smyth and Elliott, "Private Prosecutions for Crimes of Universal Jurisdiction."

112. Dieneke de Vos, "Corporate Criminal Accountability for International Crimes," *Just Security*, November 30, 2017, https://www.justsecurity.org/47452/corporate-criminal-accountability-international-crimes/

113. Adriaan Alsema, "Dole and Del Monte Also Facing Crimes against Humanity Charges for Financing Death Squads in Colombia: Report," *Colombia Reports*, September 1, 2018, https://colombiareports.com/dole-belmonte-also-accused-crimes-humanity-financing-banana-death-squads-colombia-report/

114. "Volkswagen 'Allowed Torture' under Brazil Military Rule," *BBC*, September 23, 2015, https://www.bbc.com/news/world-latin-america-34335094; "Brazil: Torture Lawsuit against VW," *DW.com*, September 23, 2015, https://www.dw.com/en/brazil-torture-lawsuit-against-vw/a-18731165

115. Uki Goñi, "Argentina: Two Ex-Ford Executives Convicted in Torture Case," *Guardian*, December 12, 2018; Gaston Chillier, "Prosecuting Corporate Complicity in Argentina's Dictatorship," *Open Democracy*, December 19, 2014, https://www.opendemocracy.net/openglobalrights-blog/gast%C3%B3n-chillier/prosecuting-corporate-complicity-in-argentina%E2%80%99s-dictatorship

116. Gallagher.

117. Gallagher.

118. Bibi Van der Zee, "Global Injustices," *Guardian*, January 21, 2015.

119. Ben Chapman, "Shell and ENI Face One of the Biggest Corruption Cases in Corporate History over $1.3bn Nigerian Oil Field," *Independent*, September 16, 2018.

120. Chapman, "Shell and ENI Face One of the Biggest Corruption Cases in Corporate History."

121. Marco Simons, email and document mark-up via EarthRights, May 21, 2020.

122. Simons email and document mark-up.

123. Simons email and document mark-up.

124. Simons email and document mark-up.

125. Chomsky interview. Redford interview.

126. Bernabeu interview.

127. Bernabeu interview.

128. Kaleck and Kroker, "Syrian Torture Investigations in Germany and Beyond." These include the Independent Commission of Inquiry into Human Rights Violations on the Syrian Arab Republic, which published at least 20 reports, and the Investigation and Prosecution of those Responsible for the Most Serious Crimes under International Law Committed in the Syrian Arab Republic (IIIM) to document, analyze, and preserve evidence of human rights violations.

129. A pseudonym.

130. Garance Le Caisne, "'They Were Torturing to Kill': Inside Syria's Death Machine," *Guardian*, October 1, 2015.

131. Le Caisne, "'They Were Torturing to Kill'."

132. Human Rights Watch counted 53,275 photographs. See https://www.hrw.org/news/2015/12/16/syria-stories-behind-photos-killed-detainees

133. Le Caisne, "They Were Torturing to Kill."

134. Le Caisne, "They Were Torturing to Kill."

135. Le Caisne, "They Were Torturing to Kill."

136. Le Caisne, "They Were Torturing to Kill."

137. Nick Cumming-Bruce, "High-Ranking Syrian Officials Could Face Reckoning in Landmark Spain Case," *New York Times*, March 27, 2017.

138. Bernabeu interview.

139. Schüller interview.

140. Bernabeu interview.

141. Bernabeu interview.

142. Schüller interview.

143. European Center for Constitutional and Human Rights, "Survivors of Assad's Torture Regime Demand Justice—German Authorities Issue First International Arrest Warrant" (Berlin: European Center for Constitutional and Human Rights, 2018).

144. United Nations, "Country Update: Germany Q1 2018," ed. UN Refugee Agency (2018).

145. Schüller interview.

146. Schüller interview.

147. Kaleck and Kroker, "Syrian Torture Investigations in Germany and Beyond"; Melinda Rankin, "The Future of International Criminal Evidence

in New Wars? The Evolution of the Commission for International Justice and Accountability (Cija)," *Journal of Genocide Research* (2018): 1–20. Marlise Simons, "Investigators in Syria Seek Paper Trails That Could Prove War Crimes," *New York Times*, October 7, 2014. Asylum-seekers were routinely asked about experiencing and witnessing atrocities.

148. Rankin, "The Future of International Criminal Evidence in New Wars?." Some groups include the Commission for Justice and Accountability, the Syrian Network for Human Rights, the Violations Documentation Center, the Syrian Observatory for Human Rights, and the Syrian Center for Statistics and Research. Office of the UN High Commissioner for Human Rights, "Updated Statistical Analysis of Documentation of Killings in the Syrian Arab Republic," August 2014, https://ohchr.org/Documents/Countries/SY/HRDAGUpdatedReportAug2014 .pdf

149. ABC News, "Germany to Start Trials over Syrian War Crimes, as Refugee Influx Brings Suspects into Country," May 1, 2016, https://www.abc.net.au/news /2016-05-01/refugee-influx-spurs-germany-to-tackle-syrian-war-crimes/7374152

150. Ana Carbajosa, "Building the Case against Assad's Regime," *El Pais*, June 15, 2018.

151. European Center for Constitutional and Human Rights, "Survivors of Assad's Torture Regime Demand Justice."

152. Lousia Loveluck, "Germany Seeks Arrest of Leading Syrian General on War Crimes Charges," *Washington Post*, June 8, 2018.

153. Philip Olterman, "Germany Charges Two Syrians with Crimes against Humanity," *Guardian*, October 29, 2019, https://www.theguardian.com/law/2019 /oct/29/germany-charges-two-syrians-with-crimes-against-humanity; Kate Connolly, "Germany Arrests Two Syrians Suspected of Crimes against Humanity," *Guardian*, February 13, 2019, https://www.theguardian.com/world/2019/feb/13 /germany-arrests-two-suspected-syrian-secret-service-officers

154. "The Path to Justice leads through Europe—E.G. Austria," European Center for Constitutional and Human Rights, https://www.ecchr.eu/en/case/the-path -to-justice-leads-through-europe-eg-austria/

155. TRIAL International, "Evidentiary Challenges in Universal Jurisdiction Cases" (Geneva: TRIAL International, 2019).

156. Maria Mattar, "France Seeks Three High-Ranking Syrian Officials in the Deaths of French-Syrian Nationals," *Global Voices*, December 6, 2018, https://glo balvoices.org/2018/12/06/france-seeks-three-high-ranking-syrian-officials-in-the -deaths-of-french-syrian-nationals/#; Lamija Grebo, "Lawyers Take Fight for Syrian Reparations to Dutch Courts," *Balkan Insight*, January 4, 2019, http://www.bal kaninsight.com/en/article/lawyers-take-fight-for-syrian-reparations-to-dutch-cou rts-01-04-2019

157. France24, "France Issues Arrest Warrants for Three Syrian Security Officials over Prison Torture," May 11, 2018, https://www.france24.com/en/20181 105-france-syria-arrest-warrants-security-officials-french-prisoners; Naharnet, "France Opens Murder Probe of Attack on Syria Media Center," March 3, 2012, http://www.naharnet.com/stories/en/32023-france-opens-murder-probe-of-atta ck-on-syria-media-center; Van Schaack, "Syria Found Liable for the Death of War Correspondent Marie Colvin." The NGO lawyers working on the prosecutions

related to these cases included Clemence Bectarte and Patrick Baudoin, and the NGOs included the Syrian Center for Media and Freedom of Expression, the Syrian Center for Legal Research and Studies and the Syrian Center for Media and Freedom of Speech.

158. Beth Van Schaak, "Evidence Unsealed in Colvin v. Syria," *Just Security*, April 10, 2018, https://www.justsecurity.org/54653/important-sources-evidence -unsealed-lawsuit-syria-killing-marie-colvin-case/

159. Van Schaack, "Syria Found Liable for the Death of War Correspondent Marie Colvin."

160. Gilmore interview.

161. France24, "France Issues Arrest Warrants for Three Syrian Security Officials over Prison Torture."

162. Radio Sweden, "Syrian Man Sentenced to Five Years for War Crime," February 26, 2015, https://sverigesradio.se/sida/artikel.aspx?programid=2054&artikel =6103548; Anne Barnard, "Syrian Soldier Is Guilty of War Crime, a First in the 6-Year Conflict," *New York Times*, October 3, 2017.

163. https://www.ecchr.eu/en/case/sweden-criminal-complaint-against-assads -intelligence-officials/

164. Human Rights Watch, "Q&A: First Cracks to Impunity in Syria, Iraq: Refugee Crisis and Universal Jurisdiction Cases in Europe," October 20, 2016, https:// www.hrw.org/news/2016/10/20/qa-first-cracks-impunity-syria-iraq; Worldwide Movement For Human Rights, "Q&A on the Dabbagh Case: French Judges Issue 3 International Arrest Warrants against Top Syrian Officials," May 11, 2018, https://www.fidh.org/en/issues/litigation/q-a-on-the-dabbagh-case-french-judges -issue-3-international-arrest

165. ABC News, "Germany to Start Trials over Syrian War Crimes."

166. Human Rights Watch, "The Long Arm of Justice: Lessons from the Specialized War Crimes Units in France, Germany and the Netherlands" (New York City: Human Rights Watch, 2014); Adam Dieng, keynote address, "Project of a New Multilateral Treaty for Mutual Legal Assistance and Extradition for Domestic Prosecution of Crimes of Genocide, Crimes against Humanity and War Crimes," 2015, https://www.iap-association.org/getattachment/Conferences/Annual-Confe rences/Annual-Conference-2015/Wednesday-16-September-2015/20AC_SIGM _SB_Annex2.pdf.aspx

167. Agence France-Presse, "Switzerland Investigates Syrian President's Uncle for War Crimes," September 26, 2017, https://www.thelocal.ch/20170926/switz erland-investigates-syrian-presidents-uncle-for-war-crimes; TRIAL International, "Revelations about TRIAL International's Investigation," September 25, 2017, https://trialinternational.org/latest-post/in-switzerland-proceedings-for-war-crim es-against-rifaat-al-assad/

168. BBC News, "CIA Agents Guilty of Italy Kidnap," November 4, 2009, http://news.bbc.co.uk/2/hi/europe/8343123.stm. The European Centre for Constitutional and Human Rights and Guantánamo detainee Abd al-Rahim al-Nashiri also filed a complaint in Germany against CIA director Gina Haspel who headed the Thailand black site were al-Nashiri was tortured, according to ECCHR publications.

169. Gilmore interview.

170. Bernabeu interview.
171. Roberts interview.
172. Roberts interview.

Chapter 9

1. United States Senate, Select Committee on Intelligence, "Committee Study of the Central Intelligence Agency's Detention and Interrogation Program" (Washington, DC: United States Senate, 2014). Deposition of Suleiman Salim.
2. *Salim v. Mitchell.* Deposition, p. 56.
3. *Salim v. Mitchell.* Deposition, p. 66.
4. Watt interview.
5. Watt interview, and email exchange.
6. Watt interview and email exchange.
7. Oscar Avila, "Torture Survivors Relive the Horrors," *Chicago Tribune,* May 14, 2004.
8. Gray interview.
9. Thomas G. Gutheil, Harold Bursztajn, Archie Brodsky, and Larry H. Strasburge, "Preventing 'Critogenic' Harms: Minimizing Emotional Injury from Civil Litigation," *Journal of Psychiatry & Law* 28, no. 1 (2000): 5–18.
10. Bernabeu interview.
11. Day interview.
12. Gray interview.
13. Gray interview.
14. Van Schaack interview.
15. Day interview.
16. Stephens interview.
17. Personal interviews revealed this in at least three NGOs; Inter-American Institute of Human Rights, "Comprehensive Attention to Victims of Torture in Cases under Litigation" (San José, Costa Rica, 2009). Mary Fabri, Marianne Joyce, Mary Black, and Mario Gonzalez, "Caring for Torture Survivors: The Marjorie Kovler Center," in *The New Humanitarians: Inspiration, Innovations, and Blueprints for Visionaries,* ed. Chris Stout (Westport, CT: Praeger, 2009).
18. Osburn.
19. Van Schaack interview.
20. Watt interview.
21. De Moerloose interview.
22. Watt interview.
23. Watt interview.
24. Hoffman, "Lecture at University of California Irvine."
25. Collingsworth.
26. Collingsworth.
27. Day interview.
28. Day interview.
29. Day interview.
30. Simons interview.

31. Voorhees interview 2017.

32. Collingsworth.

33. Gallagher.

34. Sharon Rae Jenkins and Stephanie Baird, "Secondary Traumatic Stress and Vicarious Trauma: A Validational Study," *Journal of Traumatic Stress* 15, no. 5 (2005): 423–32.

35. Watt interview.

36. Watt interview.

37. Hoffman, "Lecture at University of California Irvine."

38. Burke interview.

39. Burke interview.

40. Burke interview.

41. Stephens interview.

42. Gray interview.

43. Pilar Hernández, David Gangsei, and David Engstrom, "Vicarious Resilience: A New Concept in Work with Those Who Survive Trauma," *Family Process* 46, no. 2 (2007): 229–41; Margaret Satterthwaite, Sarah Knuckey, and Adam Brown, "Trauma, Depression, and Burnout in the Human Rights Field: Identifying Barriers and Pathways to Resilient Advocacy," *Columbia Human Rights Law Review* 49, no. 3 (2018): 267–323.

44. I found this to occur also with war correspondents, in Maria Armoudian, *Reporting from the Danger Zone: Frontline Journalists, Their Jobs and an Increasingly Perilous Future* (New York: Routledge, 2016); Hernández, Gangsei, and Engstrom, "Vicarious Resilience."

45. Hernández, Gangsei, and Engstrom, "Vicarious Resilience."

46. Stephens interview.

47. Sarah Conway, "For Torture Survivors, Kovler Center Offers Place of Peace," *Chicago Magazine*, May 15, 2017.

48. Hoffman interview 2017.

49. Gray interview.

50. Gray interview.

51. Gallagher.

52. Roberts interview.

53. Gallagher.

54. Cohn interview; Watt interview.

55. Cohn interview.

56. Day interview.

57. Roberts interview.

58. Fryszman interview.

59. Watt interview.

60. Day interview.

61. Stephens interview.

62. Stephens interview.

63. Cohn interview.

64. Stormer interview.

65. Day interview.

66. Day interview.
67. Richardson interview.
68. Cohn interview.

Chapter 10

1. Charles R. Epp, *The Rights Revolution: Lawyers, Activists, and Supreme Courts in Comparative Perspective* (Chicago: University of Chicago Press, 1998).

2. Epp, *The Rights Revolution*; Stuart Scheingold, *The Politics of Rights: Lawyers, Public Policy, and Political Change* (Ann Arbor: University of Michigan Press, 2010).

3. Epp, *The Rights Revolution*; Scheingold, *The Politics of Rights*; Michael W. McCann, *Rights at Work: Pay Equity Reform and the Politics of Legal Mobilization* (Chicago: University of Chicago Press, 1994); Kathryn Sikkink, *The Justice Cascade: How Human Rights Prosecutions Are Changing World Politics* (New York: W. W. Norton, 2011).

4. Hopgood, *The Endtimes of Human Rights*; Posner, *The Twilight of Human Rights Law*.

5. See, for example, Epp, *The Rights Revolution*; McCann, *Rights at Work*; Jonathan Goldberg-Hiller, *The Limits of Union: Same-Sex Marriage and the Politics of Civil Rights* (Ann Arbor: University of Michigan Press, 2002).

6. Interviews including Weiss.

7. Ruben, *The People's Lawyer*.

8. Weiss interview.

9. See, for example, Scheingold, *The Politics of Rights*; McCann, *Rights at Work*.

10. See, for example, David Redlawsk, "Donald Trump, Contempt, and the 2016 GOP Iowa Caucuses," *Journal of Elections, Public Opinion and Parties* 28, no. 2 (2018)): 173–89.

11. Adam Winkler, *We the Corporations: How American Businesses Won Their Civil Rights* (New York: W. W. Norton, 2018); Scheingold, *The Politics of Rights*.

12. Sarah Joseph, *Corporations and Transnational Human Rights Litigation* (Portland, OR: Hart Publishing, 2004); Michael K. Addo, *Human Rights Standards and the Responsibility of Transnational Corporations* (The Hague: Kluwer, 1999).

13. Joseph, *Corporations and Transnational Human Rights Litigation*; Addo, *Human Rights Standards and the Responsibility of Transnational Corporations*.

14. Matthew Lippman, "Transnational Corporatations and Repressive Regimes: The Ethical Dilemma," *Cal Western International Law Journal* 15 (1985).

15. Joseph, *Corporations and Transnational Human Rights Litigation*; Addo, *Human Rights Standards and the Responsibility of Transnational Corporations*.

16. Epp, *The Rights Revolution*; McCann, *Rights at Work*; Scheingold, *The Politics of Rights*; Gerald Rosenberg, *The Hollow Hope: Can Courts Bring about Social Change?* (Chicago: University of Chicago Press, 2008).

17. See, for example, Austin Sarat and Stuart Scheingold, *Cause Lawyering: Political Commitments and Professional Responsibilities* (Oxford: Oxford University Press, 1998); Carrie Menkel-Meadow, "The Causes of Cause Lawyering: Toward an Understanding of the Motivation and Commitment of Social Justice Lawyers," in *Cause Lawyering*, ed. Sarat and Scheingold, 31–68; Lisa Hajjar, "From the Fight for Legal Rights to the Promotion of Human Rights: Israeli and Palestinian Cause

Lawyers in the Trenches of Globalization," in Austin Sarat and Stuart Scheingold, eds., *Cause Lawyering and the State in a Global Era* (Oxford: Oxford University Press, 2001), 68–95.

18. Deborah Rohde, "Class Conflicts in Class Actions," *Stanford Law Review* 34, no. 6 (July 1982) 1183–1262, quote at 1240.

19. Hajjar, "From the Fight for Legal Rights to the Promotion of Human Rights."

20. For example, Judith Chomsky works full-time on many cases on a volunteer basis.

21. Sikkink, *The Justice Cascade.*

22. Hopgood, *The Endtimes of Human Rights.*

Bibliography

2016 BCSC 1856—2016 (2016).

ABC News. "Germany to Start Trials over Syrian War Crimes, as Refugee Influx Brings Suspects into Country." May 1, 2016. https://www.abc.net.au/news/20 16-05-01/refugee-influx-spurs-germany-to-tackle-syrian-war-crimes/7374152

Abebe-Jira v. Kelbessa Negewo, 72 F.3d 844 (1996).

Abtan v. Blackwater Lodge and Training Center (2009).

Aceves, William J. *The Anatomy of Torture: A Documentary History of Filártiga v. Peña-Irala*. Leiden: Brill, 2007.

Addo, Michael K. *Human Rights Standards and the Responsibility of Transnational Corporations*. The Hague: Kluwer, 1999.

Agence France-Presse. "French Firm Amesys Probed over 'Complicity in Torture.'" May 22, 2012. https://www.france24.com/en/20120522-libya-france-ga ddafi-amesys-war-crimes-technology-firm-court-justice

Agence France-Presse. "Lafarge Charged with Complicity in Syria Crimes against Humanity." June 28, 2018.

Agence France-Presse. "Swiss Slammed for Closing DR Congo 'Dirty Gold' Case." *Daily Mail*, June 2, 2015.

Agence France-Presse. "Switzerland Investigates Syrian President's Uncle for War Crimes." September 26, 2017. https://www.thelocal.ch/20170926/switzerland -investigates-syrian-presidents-uncle-for-war-crimes

Akeel, Shereef. Email exchange with author. email exchange, March 3, 2019..

Albazzaz v. Blackwater Lodge and Training Center (2007).

Alderman, Liz. "French Cement Giant Lafarge Indicted on Terror Financing Charge in Syria." *New York Times*, June 28, 2018.

Alfredson, Kirsty. "ExxonMobil Rejects Aceh Human Rights Abuse Claims." *CNN*, June 22, 2001. http://edition.cnn.com/2001/WORLD/asiapcf/southeast/06/22 /indonesia.exxon.mobil/

Al Jazeera America. "Court Tosses Out Cases against Chiquita over Colombia Killings." July 24, 2014. http://america.aljazeera.com/articles/2014/7/24/chiquita -lawsuitcolombia.html

Al Laithi v. Rumsfeld, 753 F.3d 1327 (2014).

Al Laitthi v. Rumsfeld et al., (2008).

Al Odah v. United States, 2009 U.S. App. LEXIS 25539 (2008).

Al-Quraishi, et al. v. Adel Nakhla, et al. (2010).

Alsema, Adriaan. "Colombia Charges 13 Former Chiquita Executives over Hundreds of Murders." September 1, 2018. https://colombiareports.com/terror-for -profit-colombia-charges-14-former-chiquita-executives/

Alsema, Adriaan. "Dole and Del Monte Also Facing Crimes against Humanity Charges for Financing Death Squads in Colombia: Report." *Colombia Reports*, February 4, 2017. https://colombiareports.com/dole-belmonte-also-accused -crimes-humanity-financing-banana-death-squads-colombia-report/

Al Shimari v. CACI (2008).

Al Shimari v. CACI (2012).

Al Shimari v. CACI (2016).

Al Shimari v. CACI (2017).

Al Shimari v. CACI (2018).

Altschuller, Sarah, and Amy Lehr. "Corporate Social Responsibility." *International Lawyer* 43, no. 2 (2008).

Al Zahrani v. Rumsfeld, 684 F. Supp. 103 (2010).

Al-Zahrani v. United States.

Amnesty International. "The Case of Maher Arar." https://www.amnesty.ca/legal -brief/case-maher-arar

Amnesty International. "Myanmar (Burma). Continuing Killings and Ill Treatment of Minority Peoples." London: Amnesty International, 1991.

Amnesty International. "State of the World's Human Rights." 2018. https://www .amnesty.org/download/Documents/POL1067002018ENGLISH.PDF

Anderson, Curt. "Bananas, Colombian Death Squads, and a Billion Dollar Lawsuit." *NBC News*, May 31, 2011. http://www.nbcnews.com/id/43221200/ns/wo rld_news-americas/t/bananas-colombian-death-squads-billion-dollar-lawsuit/

Anderson, Scott. "Mine Workers Suing Nevsun Resources over Allegations of Forced Labour." *CBC News*, January 22, 2019. https://www.cbc.ca/news/busin ess/nevsun-resources-mining-eritrea-1.4980530

Aquino, Belinda A. "Justice Finally Achieved for Victims of Marcos." *Honolulu Advertiser*, February 1, 2011.

Aranowski, Amanda "Shereef Akeel—Huntington Woods." *Michigan Lawyers Weekly*. March 2004.

Arar v. Ashcroft, 585 F 3d. 559 (2009).

Araya v. Nevsun Resources Ltd., BCCA 401—2017 (2017).

"Argentine Military Killings/Widows Sue Ex-General in S.F." *San Francisco Chronicle*, May 7, 1987.

Armoudian, Maria. *Reporting from the Danger Zone: Frontline Journalists, Their Jobs and an Increasingly Perilous Future.* New York: Routledge, 2016.

Arnold, Wayne. "Exxon Mobil, in Fear, Exits Indonesian Gas Fields." *New York Times,* March 24, 2001.

Ashcroft v. Iqbal, 566 U.S. 662 (2009).

Ashcroft v. Iqbal, 129 S. Ct. 1937, 54 (2009).

Asia Watch. "Burma (Myanmar): Worsening Repression." New York: Human Rights Watch, 1990.

Associated Press. "23 Detainees Attempted Suicide in Protest at Base, Military Says." *New York Times,* January 25, 2005.

Associated Press. "Around the World: Panel Votes Deadline on Arms to Turks." *New York Times,* May 11, 1983.

Associated Press. "Canada Charges Syrian Officer over Torture of Engineer Mistaken for Terrorist." *Guardian,* September 1, 2015.

Associated Press. "Ethiopian Woman Sues Atlanta Man, Alleges Torture in Homeland." *Associated Press,* September 15, 1990.

Associated Press. "House Panel OK's Aid Program." *Boston Globe,* July 16, 1982.

Atban v. Blackwater (2007).

Austen, Ian. "Canada to Pay $9.75 Million to Man Tortured in Syria." *New York Times,* January 27, 2007.

Avila, Oscar. "Torture Survivors Relive the Horrors." *Chicago Tribune,* May 14, 2004.

Baldauf, Scott. "Former Guantánamo Prisoner Asks U.S. to Review Its Founding Ideals." *Christian Science Monitor,* February 6, 2008.

Ball, James. "Guantánamo Bay Files: Children and Senile Old Men among Detainees." *Guardian,* April 25, 2011.

Barnard, Anne. "Syrian Soldier Is Guilty of War Crime, a First in the 6-Year Conflict." *New York Times,* October 3, 2017.

Barron, Rachel. "From Foster City to Chile." *San Francisco Chronicle,* June 22, 2003.

Başoğlu, Metin, M. Paker, O. Paker, and E. Ozmen. "Psychological Effects of Torture: A Comparison of Tortured with Nontortured Political Activists in Turkey." *American Journal of Psychiatry* 151, no. 1 (1994): 76–81.

BBC News. "CIA Agents Guilty of Italy Kidnap." November 4, 2009. http://news.bbc.co.uk/2/hi/europe/8343123.stm

BBC News. "Ex-Blackwater President Indicted on Firearms Charges." April 16, 2010. http://news.bbc.co.uk/2/hi/americas/8626585.stm

Beck, Susan. "How O'Melveny & Myers Built a Litigation Powerhouse." *American Lawyer,* January 12, 2004.

Bernabeu, Almudena. Interview by author, 2017, London.

Bishop, Katherine. "3 Sue an Argentine General Held in U.S." *New York Times,* May 4, 1987.

Bishop, Katherine. "Ex-Argentine General Loses U.S. Extradition Case." *New York Times,* April 28, 1988.

Bivens v. Six Unknown Named Agents, 403 U.S. 388 (1971).

Boumediene v. Bush (2008).

Bowcott, Owen. "Lawyer 'Used Sensationalist Language in Iraq Torture Case'." *Guardian*, July 17, 2018.

Bowoto v. Chevron Corp, 2009 U.S. Dist. LEXIS 38174 (2009).

Bowoto v. Chevron Trial Blog. "Day Two–Witnesses." October 28, 2008. https://bowotovchevron.wordpress.com/2008/10/28/day-two-witnesses/

"Brazil: Torture Lawsuit against VW." *DW.com*, September 23, 2015. https://www.dw.com/en/brazil-torture-lawsuit-against-vw/a-18731165

Brill, Sophia. "The National Security Court We Already Have." *Yale L. & Pol'y Rev.* 28 (2009): 525.

Broder, John. "Chief of Blackwater Defends His Employees." *New York Times*, October 3, 2007.

Brodzinsky, Sibylla. "Chiquita Case Puts Big Firms on Notice." *Christian Science Monitor*, April 11, 2007.

Buncombe, Andrew. "The Junta Fugitive, a Lottery Win and a Battle for Justice in Haiti." *Independent* (London), February 17, 2007. https://www.independent.co.uk/news/world/americas/the-junta-fugitive-a-lottery-win-and-a-battle-for-justice-in-haiti-436664.html

Burke, Susan. Interview by author, 2017, Skype.

Burke, Susan. Edited by Maria Armoudian, 2018.

Bush, President George W. "Memorandum to the Vice President et al." February 7, 2002.

"Business Briefs." *Telegram & Gazette*, April 25, 2014.

BusinessWire. "Attorneys for Defendants in Salim v. Mitchell Announce Settlement." August 17, 2017. https://www.businesswire.com/news/home/20170817005689/en/Attorneys-Defendants-Salim-v.-Mitchell-Announce-Settlement

Bussey, Jane. "Fort Lauderdale Law Firm Sues Chiquita." *Tribune Business News*, June 14, 2007.

Bybee, Jay. "Memorandum to Gonzalez." August 1, 2002.

Carbajosa, Ana. "Building the Case against Assad's Regime." *El Pais*, June 15, 2018.

Cavallaro, James L., and Stephanie Erin Brewer. "Reevaluating Regional Human Rights Litigation in the Twenty-First Century: The Case of the Inter-American Court." *American Journal of International Law* 102, no. 4 (2008): 768–827.

CBS News. "US Contractor to Pay $5.28 Million to Abu Ghraib Prisoners." January 8, 2013. https://www.cbsnews.com/news/us-contractor-to-pay-528-million-to-abu-ghraib-prisoners/

Celikgogus et al. v. Rumsfeld et al. (2007).

Celikgogus v. Rumsfeld (2010).

Center for Constitutional Rights. "C.C.R. Wins Significant Legal Motion in Unocal Case." 2011.

Center for Constitutional Rights. "Report on Torture and Cruel, Inhuman and Degrading Treatment of Prisoners at Guantánamo Bay, Cuba." July 2006, 20.

Central Intelligence Agency. "Report of Investigation: The Rendition and Detention of Khalid Al-Masri." 2007.

Chapman, Ben. "Shell and ENI Face One of the Biggest Corruption Cases in Corporate History over $1.3bn Nigerian Oil Field." *Independent*, September 16, 2018.

Chillier, Gaston. "Prosecuting Corporate Complicity in Argentina's Dictatorship." *Open Democracy*, December 19, 2014. https://www.opendemocracy.net/openg lobalrights-blog/gast%C3%B3n-chillier/prosecuting-corporate-complicity-in -argentina%E2%80%99s-dictatorship

Chilton, A. S., and M. Versteeg. "The Failure of Constitutional Torture Prohibitions." *Journal of Legal Studies* 44, no. 2 (2015): 417–52.

Choc v. Hudbay Minerals Inc., ONSC 1414—2013 (2013).

Chomsky, Aviva. "Globalization, Labor, and Violence in Colombia's Banana Zone." *International Labor and Working-Class History* 72, no. 1 (2007): 90–115.

Chomsky, Judith. Interview by author, 2016.

Cingranelli, D., and D. Richards. "The Cingranelli and Richards (Ciri) Human Rights Data Project." *Human Rights Quarterly* 32 (2010): 401.

Ciotti, Paul. "A Victim Victorious Now." *Los Angeles Times*, May 3, 1988.

Clarke, Gerard. *The Politics of NGOs in South-East Asia: Participation and Protest in the Philippines*. New York: Routledge, 1998.

Clouse, Thomas. "Federal Judge Questions Civil Torture Suit against Spokane Psychologists Mitchell and Jessen." *Spokesman-Review* (Spokane, WA), July 28, 2017. http://www.spokesman.com/stories/2017/jul/28/federal-judge-questions -civil-torture-suit-against/

Clouse, Thomas. "In What ACLU Calls 'Historic Victory,' Settlement Reached in CIA Interrogation Suit of 2 Former Spokane Psychologists." *Spokesman-Review* (Spokane, WA), August 17, 2017. http://www.spokesman.com/stories/2017 /aug/17/alert-settlement-reach-in-mitchell-jessen-interrog/

Clouse, Thomas. "Judge Clears Path for Torture Trial against Spokane Psychologists Involved in CIA Waterboarding." *Spokesman-Review* (Spokane, WA), August 7, 2017. http://www.spokesman.com/stories/2017/aug/07/judge-clears -path-for-civil-trial-against-mitchell/

Clouse, Thomas. "Judge Quackenbush Denies Motion to Dismiss Torture Suit against Mitchell and Jessen." AP News, January 19, 2017. https://apnews.com /article/46e68b17b8de450da6eacdeb5a988b12

Clouse, Thomas. "Mitchell and Jessen Attorneys Seek Judge to Unlock CIA Records of Torture Program." *Spokesman-Review* (Spokane, WA), March 23, 2017. http://www.spokesman.com/stories/2017/mar/23/mitchell-and-jessen -attorneys-seek-judge-to-unlock/

Clouse, Thomas. "Testy Exchange over CIA Records Marks Hearing in Civil Torture Case against Mitchell and Jessen." *Spokesman-Review* (Spokane, WA), May 5, 2017. http://www.spokesman.com/stories/2017/may/05/testy-exchange-ov er-CIA-records-marks-hearing-in-c/

Cohn, Cindy. Interview by author, 2018, via Skype.

Cohn, Cindy. Interview by author, 2018.

Coll, Steve. *Private Empire: ExxonMobil and American Power.* London: Penguin, 2012.

Collingsworth, Terry. Email exchange, January 23, 2019

Collingsworth, Terry. Interview by author, 2016, via Skype.

Commission of Inquiry into the Actions of Canadian Officials in Relation to Maher Arar. "Report of the Events Relating to Maher Arar." 2006.

Connolly, Kate. "Germany Arrests Two Syrians Suspected of Crimes against Humanity." *Guardian*, February 13, 2019. https://www.theguardian.com/wor ld/2019/feb/13/germany-arrests-two-suspected-syrian-secret-service-officers

Conway, Sarah. "For Torture Survivors, Kovler Center Offers Place of Peace." *Chicago Magazine*, May 15, 2017.
https://www.chicagomag.com/city-life/May-2017/Kovler-Center-Mario-Gonza lez/

Cordova, Cary. *The Heart of the Mission: Latino Art and Politics in San Francisco.* Philadelphia: University of Pennsylvania Press, 2017.

Council of the European Union. "Council Decision of 13 June 2002: Setting Up a European Network of Contact Points in Respect of Persons Responsible for Genocide, Crimes against Humanity and War Crimes." Official Journal of the European Communities, 2002.

Courtright, James. "In Sierra Leone–UK Mining Case, a New Attempt to Measure the Arm of the Law." *Christian Science Monitor*, June 19, 2018. https://www.csm onitor.com/World/Africa/2018/0619/In-Sierra-Leone-UK-mining-case-a-n ew-attempt-to-measure-the-arm-of-the-law

Cumming-Bruce, Nick. "High-Ranking Syrian Officials Could Face Reckoning in Landmark Spain Case." *New York Times*, March 27, 2017.

"The Curse of Oil in Ogoniland." http://umich.edu/~snre492/cases_03-04/Ogoni /Ogoni_case_study.htm

Daley, Suzanne. "Guatemalan Women's Claims Put Focus on Canadian Firms' Conduct Abroad." *New York Times*, April 2, 2016.

D'Amato, Anthony. "The Alien Tort Statute and the Founding of the Constitution." *American Journal of International Law* 82, no. 1 (1988): 62–67.

Davis, Jeff. "Thoughts on Clients." http://dlib.nyu.edu/guantanamo/documents /pdfa/Davis_Thoughts.pdfa

Day, Martyn. Interview by author, 2017, London.

De Moerloose, Benedict. Interview by author, 2017, Geneva.

Denbeaux, Mark, Charles Church, Ryan Gallagher, Adam Kirchner, Joshua Wirt-shafter, Chrystal Loyer, Bahadir Ekiz, Kelly Ann Taddonio, and Michael J. Ricciardelli. "Uncovering the Cover Ups: Death in Camp Delta." Seton Hall Public Law Research Paper No. 2437423, 2014.

Denbeaux, Mark, and Jonathan Hafetz. *The Guantánamo Lawyers.* New York: New York University Press, 2009.

de Vos, Dieneke. "Corporate Criminal Accountability for International Crimes." *Just Security*, November 30, 2017. https://www.justsecurity.org/47452/corpora te-criminal-accountability-international-crimes/

Doe v. Exxon Mobil Corp., 393 F. Supp. 2d 20 (Dist. Court, Dist. of Columbia 2005).

Doe v. Exxon Mobil Corp., 654 F.3d 11 (D.C. 2011).

Doe v. Nestle, 906 F.3d 1120 (2018).

Doe v. Unocal Corp., 963 F. Supp. 880 (1997).

Dolan, Kerry. "Swiss Gold Refiner Accused of Abetting Congo War via Money Laundering." *Forbes*, November 4, 2013.

Downs, Ray. "ACLU Settles Suit against Psychologists Who Created CIA Interrogation Program." *UPI*, April 15, 2019.

Doyle, Mike. "Judge Dismisses Ex-Captive's Damage Suit." *Miami Herald*, December 24, 2011 (updated February 9, 2014).

EarthRights International and Southeast Asian Information Network. "Total Denial: A Report on the Yadana Pipeline Project in Burma." Washington, DC: EarthRights International and Southeast Asian Information Network, 1996.

Egelko, Bob. "Chevron Trial over Nigeria Protest Gets Started." *San Francisco Chronicle*, October 29, 2008.

Egelko, Bob. "Jurors Get Conflicting Accounts of Shootings." *San Francisco Chronicle*, November 26, 2008.

Eisenbrandt, Matt. Interview by author, 2017, via Skype.

Ela, Nate. "Litigation Dilemmas: Lessons from the Marcos Human Rights Class Action." *Law & Social Inquiry* 42, no. 2 (2016): 479–508.

Elmaghraby and Iqbal v. Ashcroft et al. (2004).

Elmaghraby and Iqbal v. USA et al. (2006).

Elmaghraby v. Ashcroft, 2005 U.S. Dist. LEXIS 21434 (2005).

El-Masri v. Tenet et al., 479 F.3d 269 (VA 2007).

Epp, Charles. *The Rights Revolution: Lawyers, Activists, and Supreme Courts in Comparative Perspectives.* Chicago: University of Chicago Press, 1998.

Estate of Cabello v. Fernandez-Larios, 157 F. Supp. 1345 (FL 2001).

European Center for Constitutional and Human Rights. "Are Arms Manufacturers and Italian Authorities Complicit in Deadly Saudi-Coalition Airstrike in Yemen?" 2018.

European Center for Constitutional and Human Rights. "Criminal Complaint Filed Accuses Senior Manager of Danzer Group of Responsibility over Human Rights Abuses against Congolese Community." 2013.

European Center for Constitutional and Human Rights. "Lafarge in Syria: Accusations of Complicity in War Crimes and Crimes against Humanity." Berlin: European Center for Constitutional and Human Rights, 2016.

European Center for Constitutional and Human Rights. "Survivors of Assad's Torture Regime Demand Justice—German Authorities Issue First International Arrest Warrant." Berlin: European Center for Constitutional and Human Rights, 2018.

"European Court Award for Rendition Victim Khaled Al-Masri." Edited by BBC News, 2012.

Evans, Michael. Interview by author, 2017, Washington, DC.

Evans, Michael. "'Para-Politics' Goes Bananas." *Nation*, April 4, 2007.

Evans, Tony. *The Politics of Human Rights: A Global Perspective*. London: Pluto Press, 2005.

"Ex-Argentine General Told to Pay Victims." *Gazette* (Montreal), May 2, 1990.

Fabri, Mary, Marianne Joyce, Mary Black, and Mario Gonzalez. "Caring for Torture Survivors: The Marjorie Kovler Center." In *The New Humanitarians: Inspiration, Innovations, and Blueprints for Visionaries*, edited by Chris Stout. Westport, CT: Praeger, 2009.

Ferrer, Montse. "Prosecuting Extortion Victims: How Counter-Terrorist Finance Measure Executive Order 13224 Is Going Too Far." *Journal of Financial Crime* 16, no. 3 (2009).

Filártiga, Dolly. "American Courts, Global Justice." *New York Times*, March 30, 2004.

Filártiga v. Peña-Irala, 630 F.2d 876 (NY 1980).

Findlay, Andrew. "Rocked: Canadian Mining Companies Deal with Fallout from Supreme Court Ruling." *BC Business*, January 8, 2019. https://www.bcbusiness.ca/Rocked-Canadian-mining-companies-deal-with-fallout-from-Supreme-Court-ruling

Fitzpatrick, Joan. "The Future of the Alien Tort Claims Act of 1789: Lessons from in Re Marcos Human Rights Litigation." *St. John's Law Review* 67, no. 3 (2012).

Forti v. Suarez Mason, 672 F. Supp. 1531 (CA 1987).

France24. "France Issues Arrest Warrants for Three Syrian Security Officials over Prison Torture." May 11, 2018. https://www.france24.com/en/20181105-france-syria-arrest-warrants-security-officials-french-prisoners

Frantz, Douglas. "Chiquita Still under Cloud after Newspaper's Retreat." *New York Times*, July 17, 1998.

Freeman, Tom. "Eric Lewis, Truth, Justice and Guantanamo Bay." *Legal Business*, March 2007, 76.

Fryszman, Agnieszka. Interview by author, 2017, Washington, DC.

Gallagher, Katherine. Interview by author, 2017.

Gallagher, Katherine. Interview by author, 2018.

Gallagher, Mike, and Cameron McWhirter. "Chiquita Secrets Revealed." *Cincinnati Enquirer*, May 3, 1998.

Garcia v. Tahoe Resources Inc., BCCA 39—2017 (2017).

Garre, Gregory. "Ashcroft v. Iqbal (Oral Argument)." 2008.

Gerber, Marisa. "Arrests in 1989 El Salvador Priest Massacre Elicit Shock, Happiness—and a Hope for Justice." *Los Angeles Times*, February 7, 2016.

Giles, David M. "Hitting a Home Run." *Litigation* 23, no. 3 (1997): 22–24.

Gilmore, Scott. Interview by author, 2016, Skype.

Girion, Lisa. "California Law to Govern Unocal Human Rights Case, Judge Rules." *Los Angeles Times*, August 1, 2003.

Girion, Lisa. "Judge OKs Unocal Abuse Lawsuit." *Los Angeles Times*, June 12, 2002.

Girion, Lisa. "One Legal Attack on Unocal Denied." *Los Angeles Times*, January 24, 2004.

Girion, Lisa. "Unocal Must Face Abuse Suit." *Los Angeles Times*, September 15, 2004.

Global Legal Monitor. "European Court of Human Rights: Decision Issued in Rendition Case." http://www.loc.gov/law/foreign-news/article/european-court-of-human-rights-decision-issued-in-rendition-case/

Goldhaber, Michael. "A Win for Wiwa, a Win for Shell, a Win for Corporate Human Rights." *Am Law Daily*, June 10, 2009. https://amlawdaily.typepad.com/amlawdaily/2009/06/a-win-for-wiwa-a-win-for-shell-a-win-for-corporate-human-rights.html

Goñi, Uki. "Argentina: Two Ex-Ford Executives Convicted in Torture Case." *Guardian*, December 12, 2018.

Gonzales, Alberto R. "Memorandum for the President." January 18, 2002.

Gray, Gerald. "The Center for Justice and Accountability." *Health and Human Rights* 4, no. 1 (1999): 277–83.

Gray, Gerald. Interview by author, 2017, San Francisco.

Grebo, Lamija. "Lawyers Take Fight for Syrian Reparations to Dutch Courts." *Balkan Insight*, January 1, 2019. http://www.balkaninsight.com/en/article/lawyers-take-fight-for-syrian-reparations-to-dutch-courts-01-04-2019

Grierson, Jamie. "Law Firm at Centre of Al-Sweady Inquiry to Close Down, Say Reports." *Guardian*, August 15, 2016.

Gutheil, Thomas G., Harold Bursztajn, Archie Brodsky, and Larry H. Strasburge. "Preventing 'Critogenic' Harms: Minimizing Emotional Injury from Civil Litigation." *Journal of Psychiatry & Law* 28, no. 1 (2000): 5–18.

Hall, Carla. "In Paraguay, a Death in the Family." *Washington Post*, March 25, 1982.

Hamad, Adel. "Witnessing Guantánamo: Transcription of Adel Hamad's Interview." Edited by Amy Goodman. Davis, CA: Center for the Study of Human Rights in the Americas, 2008.

Hamad v. Gates (2013).

Hamilton, Alexander. "Federalist No. 80: The Powers of the Judiciary." 1788.

Hanley, Charles. "AP Enterprise: Former Iraqi Detainees Tell of Riots, Punishment in the Sun, Good Americans, and Pitiless Ones." *San Diego Union Tribune*, November 1, 2003.

Helgerson, John L. "Report of Investigation: The Rendition and Detention of German Citizen Khalid Al-Masri." Washington, DC: Central Intelligence Agency, 2007.

Herbert, Bob. "In America: Unholy Alliance in Nigeria." *New York Times*, January 26, 1996.

Hernández, Pilar, David Gangsei, and David Engstrom. "Vicarious Resilience: A New Concept in Work with Those Who Survive Trauma." *Family Process* 46, no. 2 (2007): 229–41.

Hilao v. Estate of Marcos, 103 F.3d 767 (1996).

Hirsch, Afua. "UK 'Using Obscure Legal Principle' to Dismiss Torture Claims in Colonial Kenya." *Guardian*, January 25, 2010.

Hoffman, Paul. Interview by author, 2016.

Hoffman, Paul. Interview by author, 2017.

Hoffman, Paul. Interview by author, 2018, Hermosa Beach.

Hoffman, Paul. "Lecture at University of California Irvine." 2017.

Hoffman, Paul, and Daniel Zaheer. "The Rules of the Road: Federal Common Law and Aiding and Abetting under the Alien Tort Claims Act." *Loyola of Los Angeles International and Comparative Law Review* 26, no. 47 (2003).

Honigsberg, Peter Jan. *Our Nation Unhinged: The Human Consequences of the War on Terror*. Berkeley: University of California Press, 2009.

Hopgood, Stephen. *The Endtimes of Human Rights*. Ithaca, NY: Cornell University Press, 2013.

Horton, Scott. "The Guantánamo 'Suicides': A Camp Delta Sergeant Blows the Whistle." *Harper's Magazine*, January 18, 2010.

Hsu, Spencer, and Victoria St. Martin. "Four Blackwater Guards Sentenced in Iraq Shootings of 31 Unarmed Civilians." *Washington Post*, April 13, 2015.

Hudbay Minerals. "Press Release." 2009.

Human Rights Watch. "Eritrea: Events of 2017." https://www.hrw.org/world-report/2018/country-chapters/eritrea#

Human Rights Watch. "Guantanamo: Facts and Figures." March 30, 2017. https://www.hrw.org/video-photos/interactive/2017/03/30/guantanamo-facts-and-figures

Human Rights Watch. "Hear No Evil." New York: Human Rights Watch, 2013.

Human Rights Watch. "Human Rights World Reports, 2014–2019." 2019.

Human Rights Watch. "The Long Arm of Justice: Lessons from the Specialized War Crimes Units in France, Germany, and the Netherlands." New York City: Human Rights Watch, 2014.

Human Rights Watch. "Q&A: First Cracks to Impunity in Syria, Iraq: Refugee Crisis and Universal Jurisdiction Cases in Europe." October 20, 2016. https://www.hrw.org/news/2016/10/20/qa-first-cracks-impunity-syria-iraq

Human Rights Watch. "Whose Development? Human Rights Abuses in Sierra Leone's Mining Boom." New York: Human Rights Watch, 2014.

Imai, Shin, Bernadette Maheandiran, and Valerie Crystal. "Access to Justice and Corporate Accountability: A Legal Case Study of Hudbay in Guatemala." *Canadian Journal of Development Studies* 35, no. 2 (2014).

In Re Estate of Marcos Human Rights Litigation, 978 F.2d 493 (1992).

Inter-American Institute of Human Rights. "Comprehensive Attention to Victims of Torture in Cases under Litigation." San José, Costa Rica, 2009.

"International Human Rights Clinic Files Second Guantanamo Lawsuit." *Willamette Lawyer* 12, no. 1 (Spring 2012).

International Human Right Clinic, Harvard Law School. "The Contribution of Chiquita Corporate Officials to Crimes against Humanity in Colombia." 2017.

International Human Rights Law Group. "Human Rights in Burma (Myanmar): A Long Struggle for Freedom." Washington, DC: International Human Rights Law Group, 1991.

Jay, John. "Federalist No. 3: Concerning Dangers from Foreign Force and Influence." 1787.

Jean v. Dorelien, 431 F.3d 776 (2003).

Jenkins, Sharon Rae, and Stephanie Baird. "Secondary Traumatic Stress and Vicarious Trauma: A Validational Study." *Journal of Traumatic Stress* 15, no. 5 (2005): 423–32.

Jimenez, Marina. "The Mayans vs. the Mine." *Toronto Star*, June 18, 2016.

John Doe I v. Unocal Corp., 395 F.3d 932 (2002).

John Doe VIII v. Exxon Mobil Corp, 658 F. Supp. 2d 131 (Dist. Court, Dist. of Columbia 2009).

Johnson, Gene. "Sudanese Man Released from Guantánamo Sues." *Seattle Times*, April 7, 2010.

Johnson, Gene. "Sudanese Man Sues U.S. Government after Release from Guantánamo." *HeraldNet*, April 7, 2010.

Johnston, David, and John Broder. "F.B.I. Says Guards Killed 14 Iraqis without Cause." *New York Times*, November 14, 2007.

Joseph, Sarah. *Corporations and Transnational Human Rights Litigation*. Portland, OR: Hart Publishing, 2004.

Kaiser, Mario. "Death in Camp Delta: On the Power of Silence, Submission to Force-Feeding, and the First Suicides in Guantánamo." *Guernica Magazine*, February 17, 2014.

Kaleck, Wolfgang, and Patrick Kroker. "Syrian Torture Investigations in Germany and Beyond: Breathing New Life into Universal Jurisdiction in Europe?" *Journal of International Criminal Justice* 16, no. 1 (2018): 165–91.

Kaneva, Milena, director. *Total Denial*. 2006. Documentary film about the *Doe v. Unocal* suit brought by Burmese villagers.

Kebriaei, Pardiss. "The Rule of Law History Project." New York: Columbia Center for Oral History, 2013.

Kenney, Cortelyou C. "Measuring Transnational Human Rights." *Fordham Law Review* 84, no. 3 (2015): 1053–1115.

Kenyan Human Rights Commission. "High Court Rejects LSK Mau Mau Claim against KHRC, Leigh Day & MMWVA." December 2, 2015.

Keohane, David, and Ralph Atkins. "Syrian Operation: Lafarge Faces Probe over ISIS Payments." *Financial Times*, May 16, 2018.

Kiobel v. Royal Dutch Petroleum (2004). Complaint, https://ccrjustice.org/sites/default/files/assets/05.14.04%20Amended%20Complaint.pdf

Kiobel v. Royal Dutch Petroleum Co., 642 F.3d 268 (2011).

Kiobel v. Royal Dutch Petroleum Co., 569 U.S. 108 (2013).

Kolvig, Eric. "Burma Today: Land of Hope and Terror." Washington, DC: International Burma Campaign, 1991.

LafargeHolcim. "Lafargeholcim Responds to Syria Review." March 2, 2017. https://www.lafargeholcim.com/LafargeHolcim-responds-syria-review

LaFrance, Adrienne. "Marcos Victims to Split $7.5m Settlement." *Civil Beat* (Honolulu) January 14, 2011. https://www.civilbeat.org/2011/01/8157-marcos -victims-to-split-75m-settlement/

Lambert, Lisa. "Obsessive Pursuit." *SF Weekly*, March 3, 2004.

"Landmark Case against British Mining Firm Begins in Sierra Leone." *Guardian*, February 7, 2018.

Le Caisne, Garance. "'They Were Torturing to Kill': Inside Syria's Death Machine." *Guardian*, October 1, 2015.

Leonnig, Carol D. "Guantanamo Detainee Says Beating Injured Spine." *Washington Post*, August 13, 2005.

Lewis, Eric. "The Last Word." *Legal Business*, March 2007.

Lewis, Eric. "Supreme Court Refused to Hear Suit Seeking Accountability for Guantanamo Torture." Center for Constitutional Rights, 2009.

Lewis, Eric. "Who Are 'We the People'?" *New York Times*, October 4, 2014.

Lewis, Paul. "Blood and Oil: A Special Report; after Nigeria Represses, Shell Defends Its Record." *New York Times*, February 13, 1996.

Lindsey, Robert. "Argentine Officer Is Arrested in U.S." *New York Times*, January 25, 1987.

Lippman, Matthew. "Transnational Corporations and Repressive Regimes: The Ethical Dilemma." *Cal Western International Law Journal* 15 (1985): 542.

Lobel, Jules. "Extraordinary Rendition and the Constitution: The Case of Maher Arar." *Review of Litigation* 28, no. 2 (2008).

Loveluck, Louisa. "Germany Seeks Arrest of Leading Syrian General on War Crimes Charges." *Washington Post*, June 8, 2018.

Lutz, Ellen L. "The Marcos Human Rights Litigation: Can Justice be Achieved in US Courts for Abuses that Occurred Abroad." *BC Third World LJ* 14 (1994): 43.

Lyons, John, and David Luhnow. "Chiquita Sued by Relatives of Five Slain Missionaries." *Wall Street Journal*, March 12, 2008.

Maher Arar et al. v. Her Majesty the Queen et al. (2004).

Margulies, Joseph. *Guantanamo and the Abuse of Presidential Power.* New York: Simon and Schuster, 2007.

Martell, Allison, and Edmund Blair. "We Were Forced to Work for Western-Run Mine." *Reuters Special Reports*, September 27, 2016.

Martin-Ortega, Olga. "Business and Human Rights in Conflict." *Ethics & International Affairs* 22, no. 3 (2008): 273–83.

Mattar, Maria. "France Seeks Three High-Ranking Syrian Officials in the Deaths of French-Syrian Nationals." *Global Voices*, December 6, 2018. https://global

voices.org/2018/12/06/france-seeks-three-high-ranking-syrian-officials-in-the
-deaths-of-french-syrian-nationals/#

Mauskopf, Roslynn. "Eleven Current and Former Federal Officers Indicted for Excessive Force and False Statements." New York: Department of Justice, 2007.

Mayer, Jane. "The CIA's Travel Agent." *New Yorker*, October 30, 2006.

McCann, Michael. *Rights at Work: Pay Equity Reform and the Politics of Legal Mobilization*. Chicago: University of Chicago Press, 1994.

McCoy, Alfred. "Dark Legacy: Human Rights under the Marcos Regime." In *Memory, Truth Telling and the Pursuit of Justice: A Conference on the Legacies of the Marcos Dictatorship*. Manila: Ateneo de Manila University, 1999.

McFarlane, Peter. *Northern Shadows: Canadians and Central America*. Toronto: Between the Lines, 1989.

McGinnis, John. "Testimony before the Subcommittee on Immigration of Refugee Affairs of the Committee on the Judiciary." United States Senate, 101st Congress, 1990.

Mears, Bill. "ExxonMobil to Face Lawsuit over Alleged Human Rights Violations." *CNN*, July 8, 2011. http://edition.cnn.com/2011/CRIME/07/08/exxon.mobil .lawsuit/index.html?hpt=hp_t2

Mehinovic v. Vuckovic, 198 F. Supp. 1322 (GA 2002).

Meyer, Josh. "Chiquita to Pay Fine for Deals with Militants." *Los Angeles Times*, March 15, 2007.

Middle East Monitor. "Palestinian Family Sues French Technology Company for Complicity in War Crimes." June 20, 2016. https://www.middleeastmonitor .com/20160630-palestinian-family-sues-french-technology-company-for-com plicity-in-war-crimes/

Mine, Douglas Grant. "The Assassin Next Door." *Miami New Times*, November 18, 1999.

Mining Watch Canada. "Annual Report." 2016.

Mohamed v. Jeppesen (2008).

Mohamed v. Jeppesen Dataplan, Inc. (2009).

Mohamed v. Jeppesen Dataplan (2010).

Moore, Jo. "Kenyan 'Mau Mau' Claim Dismissed: Fair Trial Not Possible Because of Half Century Delay." *UK Human Rights* blog, August 6, 2018. https://ukh umanrightsblog.com/2018/08/06/kenyan-mau-mau-claim-dismissed-fair-trial -not-possible-because-of-half-century-delay/

Morain, Dan. "Ex-Argentine General Ordered to Pay $60 Million." *Los Angeles Times*, April 29, 1989.

Morain, Dan. "General Must Pay $21 Million in Torture Case." *Los Angeles Times*, 26 April, 1988.

Mouawad, Jad. "Oil Industry on Trial." *New York Times*, May 22, 2009.

Mouawad, Jad. "Shell to Pay $15.5 Million to Settle Nigerian Case." *New York Times*, June 8, 2009.

Murdock, Deroy. "Gitmo Legal." *National Review*, January 25, 2006.

Murphy, Caryle. "The Disappeared." *Washington Post*, February 12, 1984.

Musaddique, Shafi. "UK Mining Company Faces Landmark High Court Case over Alleged Worker Abuse in Sierra Leone." *Independent*, January 29, 2018. https://www.independent.co.uk/news/business/news/tonkolili-iron-ore-uk-mining-company-sierra-leone-high-court-case-worker-abuse-villagers-a8179891.html

Muse, Toby. "Chiquita to Pay $2m Fine in Terror Case." *Associated Press*, March 15, 2007.

Musgrave, Jane. "All Chiquita Lawsuits in Colombia Slayings Shift to West Palm." *Palm Beach Post*, April 30, 2008.

Musgrave, Jane. "Families Fight to Sue Chiquita in U.S." *Palm Beach Post*, January 21, 2015.

Musgrave, Jane. "New Lawsuit Claims Chiquita Transported Weapons." *Palm Beach Post*, May 14, 2008.

Mydans, Seth. "First Payments Are Made to Victims of Marcos Rule." *New York Times*, March 1, 2011.

NBC News. "Blackwater Armory Raided in Firearms Inquiry." June 26, 2008. http://www.nbcnews.com/id/25394941/ns/us_news-crime_and_courts/t/blackwater-armory-raided-firearms-inquiry/#.XA8gGnQzbIV

Neergaard, Lauran. "Emigre Sued by Fellow Ethiopian Claiming Police Torture." *Associated Press*, October 12, 1990.

New York Times (Editorial Board). "The Torturers Speak." *New York Times*, June 23, 2017.

O'Connell, Jamie. "Gambling with the Psyche: Does Prosecuting Human Rights Violators Console Their Victims?" *Harvard International Law Journal* 46, no. 2 (2005): 295–345.

Office of the High Commissioner, United Nations Human Rights Commission. "UN Inquiry Finds Crimes against Humanity in Eritrea." June 8, 2016. https://www.ohchr.org/EN/NewsEvents/Pages/DisplayNews.aspx?NewsID=20067&LangID=E

O'Neill, Ann W. "Woman's Quest for Justice Spans Decades, Continents: Miami Ruling Brings Closure in Chilean Caravan of Death Killing." *South Florida Sun-Sentinel*, October 16, 2013.

Onishi, Norimitsu. "Not for a Nigerian Hero the Peace of the Grave." *New York Times*, March 22, 2000.

Open Society Justice Initiative. "Globalizing Torture: C.I.A. Secret Detention and Extraordinary Rendition." New York: Open Society Foundations, 2013.

Osario, Carlos. "Kissinger to Argentines on Dirty War: The Quicker You Succeed, the Better." Edited by Carlos Osario. Washington, DC: National Security Archive, 2003.

Osburn, Dixon. Interview by author, 2017, by telephone.

Oteri, V. A. "Memorandum to the Inspector General of Police." Nigeria Police Force, 1994.

Otterman, Michael. *American Torture: From the Cold War to Abu Ghraib and Beyond.* Melbourne: Melbourne University Press, 2007.

Paley, Dawn. "This Is What Development Looks Like." *Dominion*, January 11, 2007.

Parnell, David J. "Eric Lewis of Lewis Baach, on the Polarizing Legal Market, Internationalism, and White Collar Trends." *Forbes*, January 3, 2017.

Pedroso, Kate, and Marielle Medina. "Liliosa Hilao: First Martial Law Detainee Killed." *Inquirer.Net*, September 1, 2015, https://newsinfo.inquirer.net/718061 /liliosa-hilao-first-martial-law-detainee-killed

Peri, Camille. "Getting to Know the Lord." *Mother Jones*, September 1988.

Pleming, Sue. "Blackwater Involved in 195 Iraq Shootings." *Reuters*, October 1, 2007. https://www.reuters.com/article/us-iraq-usa-blackwater/blackwater-inv olved-in-195-iraq-shootings-idUSN2739989220071002

Posner, Eric A. *The Twilight of Human Rights Law.* Oxford: Oxford University Press, 2014.

Pratt, Regina. "British Judge Ends AML Trial in Sierra Leone." *Concord Times*, February 14, 2018.

Press Association. "Kenyan Torture Victims Give Evidence in High Court Compensation Case." *Guardian*, January 30, 2019.

Press Association. "UK to Compensate Kenya's Mau Mau Torture Victims." *Guardian*, June 6, 2013.

Preston, Julia. "U.S. Deports Salvadoran General Accused in '80s Killings" *New York Times*, April 8, 2015.

Priest, Dana. "Jet Is an Open Secret in Terror War." *Washington Post*, December 27, 2004.

Quimpo, Susan F., and Nathan Gilbert Quimpo. *Subversive Lives: A Family Memoir of the Marcos Years.* Athens: Ohio University Press, 2016.

Radio Sweden. "Syrian Man Sentenced to Five Years for War Crime." February 26, 2015. https://sverigesradio.se/sida/artikel.aspx?programid=2054&artikel=6 103548

Randall, Kenneth C. "Universal Jurisdiction under International Law." *Texas Law Review* 66 (1987): 785.

Rankin, Melinda. "The Future of International Criminal Evidence in New Wars? The Evolution of the Commission for International Justice and Accountability (Cija)." *Journal of Genocide Research* (2018): 1–20.

Rasmussen, Greg. "Tahoe Resources, Vancouver Mining Firm, in Court Today over Guatemalan Workers' Lawsuit." *CBC*, April 8, 2015. https://www.cbc.ca /news/canada/british-columbia/tahoe-resources-vancouver-mining-firm-in-co urt-today-over-guatemalan-workers-lawsuit-1.3024121

Rasul v. Bush, 215 F. Supp. 2d 55 (2004).

Rasul v. Bush, 542 U.S. 466 (2004).

Rasul v. Myers, 563 F.3d 527 (2008).

Rasul v. Myers, 130 S. Ct. 1013 (2009).

Rasul v. Rumsfeld, 414 F. Supp. 2d 26 (2006).

Redford, Katie. Interview by author, 2017.

Redford, Katie, and Beth Stephens. "The Story of Doe v. Unocal: Justice Delayed but Not Denied." In *Human Rights Advocacy Stories*, edited by Deena Hurwitz, Margaret Satterthwaite, and Doug Ford. New York: Thomson Reuters Foundation, 2009.

Redlawsk, David. "Donald Trump, Contempt, and the 2016 GOP Iowa Caucuses." *Journal of Elections, Public Opinion and Parties* 28, no. 2 (2018): 173–89.

Reisinger, Sue. "3 Us Execs Indicted in Chiquita Terrorist Funding Probe in Colombia." *Law.com*, September 10, 2018. https://www.law.com/corpcounsel /2018/09/10/three-u-s-execs-indicted-in-chiquita-terrorist-funding-probe-in -colombia/

Reuters. "Chiquita Settles with Families of US Victims of Colombia's FARC." *VOA News*, February 15, 2018. https://www.voanews.com/a/chiquita-settles -with-families-of-us-victims-of-colombia-farc-/4240697.html

Reuters. "Colombia Calls Drummond Coal Officials to Testify on Paramilitaries: Source." *Reuters*, October 31, 2018.

Reuters. "Colombia Civil Conflict Has Killed 'Nearly a Quarter of a Million': Study." *Telegraph*, July 25, 2013. https://www.telegraph.co.uk/news/worldnews /southamerica/colombia/10201512/Colombia-civil-conflict-has-killed-nearly -a-quarter-of-a-million-study.html

Reuters. "France Investigates Tech Firm Accused of Aiding Syria." July 26, 2012. https://www.reuters.com/article/syria-france-qosmos/france-investigates-tech -firm-accused-of-aiding-syria-idUSL6E8IQN9520120726?feedType=RSS&f eedName=technologySector

Reuters. "Rice Admits U.S. Erred in Deportation." *New York Times*, October 25, 2007.

Rice, Andrew. "The Long Interrogation." *New York Times Magazine*, June 4, 2006.

Richardson, Anne. Interview by author, 2016.

Risen, James. "Blackwater Reaches Deal on US Export Violations." *New York Times*, August 20, 2010.

Roberts, Kathy. Interview by author, 2017.

Robitaille, Adam C. "The Marcos Cases: A Consideration of the Act of State Doctrine and the Pursuit of the Assets of Deposed Dictators." *Boston College Third World Law Journal* 9, no. 81 (1989).

Roemer, John. "Philippines Dictator Estate Loses Appeal." *San Francisco Daily Journal*, October 26, 2012.

Rohter, Larry. "Argentina Charges Ex-Dictator and Others in 'Dirty War' Deaths." *New York Times*, July 11, 2002.

Romagoza Arce, Raul. "Written Testimony Submitted to the Subcommittee on Human Rights and the Law." Committee on the Judiciary, United States Senate, 2007.

Rosen, Don. "Four, with Help of ACLU, Sue Marcos for $111 Million." *Los Angeles Times*, March 28, 1986.

Rosenberg, Gerald. *The Hollow Hope: Can Courts Bring about Social Change?* Chicago: University of Chicago Press, 2008.

Rosenzweig, David. "Merrill Lynch Releases $35 Million to Court in Marcos Case." *Los Angeles Times*, September 12, 2000.

Ruben, Albert. *The People's Lawyer: The Center for Constitutional Rights and the Fight for Social Justice, from Civil Rights to Guantánamo*. New York: Monthly Review Press, 2011.

Sabatier, Julie. "Guantanamo Lawsuits" (radio report). *Think Out Loud*, Oregon Public Broadcasting, 2015.

Saleh v. Titan (2004).

Salim v. Mitchell (2017).

Satterthwaite, Margaret, Sarah Knuckey, and Adam Brown. "Trauma, Depression, and Burnout in the Human Rights Field: Identifying Barriers and Pathways to Resilient Advocacy." *Columbia Human Rights Law Review* 49, no. 3 (2018): 267–323.

Scarcella, Mike. "Exxon Wants Rehearing in Corporate Liability Dispute." Business & Human Rights Resource Centre, August 10, 2011. https://www.business-humanrights.org/en/exxon-wants-rehearing-in-corporate-liability-dispute-usa

Scarcella, Mike. "Judge Rejects Summary Judgment in Human Rights Lawsuit against Exxon." *Legal Times*, August 28, 2008.

Scheingold, Stuart. *The Politics of Rights: Lawyers, Public Policy, and Political Change*. Ann Arbor: University of Michigan Press, 2010.

Schofield, Matthew. "Yet No Apology: CIA's Mistaken Detention Destroyed German Man's Life." *McClatchy*, December 13, 2014. https://www.mcclatchydc.com/news/nation-world/world/article24777424.html

Schüller, Andreas. Interview by author, 2017, Berlin.

Seenan, Gerard, and Giles Tremlett. "How Planespotters Turned into the Scourge of the CIA." *Guardian*, December 10, 2005.

Shafiq Rasul v. Rumsfeld, LEXIS 11134 2009 U.S. App. (2009).

Shane, Scott, Stephen Grey, and Margot Williams. "C.I.A. Expanding Terror Battle under Guise of Charter Flights." *New York Times*, May 31, 2005.

Shapiro, Steve. "Letter to Honorable Loretta Lynch." 2015.

Shari, Michael. "Indonesia: What Did Mobil Know?" *Bloomberg.com*, December 27, 1998. https://www.bloomberg.com/news/articles/1998-12-27/indonesia-what-did-mobil-know

Sikkink, Kathryn. *Evidence for Hope: Making Human Rights Work in the 21st Century*. Princeton: Princeton University Press, 2017.

Sikkink, Kathryn. *The Justice Cascade: How Human Rights Prosecutions Are Changing World Politics*. New York: W. W. Norton, 2011.

Simon, Paul. "Testimony before the Subcommittee on Immigration of Refugee

Affairs of the Committee on the Judiciary." Washington, DC: United States Senate, 101st Congress, 1990.

Simons, Marco. Interview by author, 2016.

Simons, Marlise. "Investigators in Syria Seek Paper Trails That Could Prove War Crimes." *New York Times*, October 7, 2014.

Singer, Peter. "Outsourcing War." *Foreign Affairs* 84 (2005).

Singer, Peter W. "The Dark Truth about Blackwater." Brookings Institution, October 2, 2007. https://www.brookings.edu/articles/the-dark-truth-about-bl ackwater/

Sklar, Morton. Interview by author, 2017.

Sly, Liz. "Iraqis Say They Were Forced to Take Blackwater Settlement." *Los Angeles Times*, January 11, 2010.

Smith, Anthony. "Aceh: Democratic Times, Authoritarian Solutions." *New Zealand Journal of Asian Studies* 4 (2012).

Smith, Clive Stafford. "Columbia Oral History Project." New York: Columbia Center for Oral History, 2011.

Smith, Helena. "UK to Pay 1 M to Greek Cypriots over Claims of Human Rights Abuses." *Guardian*, January 23, 2019.

Smothers, Ronald. "3 Women Win Suit over Torture by an Ethiopian Official." *New York Times*, August 21, 1993.

Smothers, Ronald. "Nightmare of Torture in Ethiopia Is Relived." *New York Times*, May 22, 1993.

Smyth, Edmund, and Emily Elliott. "Private Prosecutions for Crimes of Universal Jurisdiction." Kingsley Napley, April 9, 2015. https://www.kingsleynapley.co .uk/insights/blogs/criminal-law-blog/private-prosecutions-for-crimes-of-univ ersal-jurisdiction

Soldz, Stephen. "Healers or Interrogators: Psychology and the United States Torture Program." *Psychoanalytic Dialogs* 8, no. 5 (2008): 592–613.

States News Service. "Para-Business Gone Bananas: Chiquita Brands in Colombia." August 18, 2011.

Steel, Z., Tien Chey, Derrick Silove, and Claire Marnane. "Association of Torture and Other Potentially Traumatic Events with Mental Health Outcomes among Populations Exposed to Mass Conflict and Displacement: A Systematic Review and Meta-Analysis." *JAMA* 302, no. 5 (2009): 537–49.

Stephens, Beth. Interview by author, 2017, by telephone.

Stephens, Beth. Interview by author, May 25, 2020, Zoom conversation.

Stewart, David P. "Testimony before the Subcommittee on Immigration of Refugee Affairs of the Committee on the Judiciary." United States Senate, 101st Congress, 1990.

Steyn, J. "Guantanamo Bay: The Legal Black Hole." *International & Comparative Law Quarterly* 53, no. 1 (2004): 1–15.

Stormer, Dan. Interview by author, 2016.

Sulistiyanto, Privambudi. "Whither Aceh?" *Third World Quarterly* 22, no. 3 (2010): 437–52.

Sullivan, Julie. "Steven T. Wax, Oregon's Federal Public Defender, Has Created a Crack Legal Team to Follow the Rule of Law." *Oregonian*, June 11, 2011.

Sullivan, Stacy. "The Minutes of the Guantanamo Bay Bar Association." *New York Magazine*, June 26, 2006.

Swan, Michael. "Probe Sought into Canadian-Owned Mine in Guatemala." *Catholic Register*, January 9, 2019.

Swift, Robert. "Holocaust Litigation and Human Rights Jurisprudence." In *Holocaust Restitution: Perspectives on the Litigation and Its Legacy*, edited by Michael Bazyler and Roger Alford. New York: New York University Press, 2005.

Swift, Robert. "A Human Rights Class Action Distribution in the Philippines." *Philadelphia Lawyer* 74, no. 4 (2012): 37–41.

Taylor, Kerrie M. "Thicker Than Blood: Holding Exxon Mobil Liable for Human Rights Violations Committed Abroad." *Syracuse Journal of International Law and Commerce* 31, no. 2 (2004): 273–97.

Tel-Oren v. Libyan Arab Republic, 726 F.2d 774 (DC 1984).

Tillman, Zoe. "Lawyer Wants Wikipedia Editor's Identity Revealed." *Law.com*, September 9, 2013. https://www.law.com/nationallawjournal/almID/1202618385256&Lawyer_Wants_Identity_of_Wikipedia_Editor_Revealed/?slreturn=20181104181153

Time. "Consultant Warned Unocal in 1992 That Burmese Government 'Habitually Makes Use of Forced Labor,' Recently Unsealed Court Documents Obtained by *Time* Reveal." November 9, 2003. http://content.time.com/time/nation/article/0,8599,538908,00.html

Townsend, Laird, and Ian Shearn. "Did ExxonMobil Pay Torturers?" *Mother Jones*, October 5, 2012. https://www.motherjones.com/environment/2012/10/did-exxon-pay-torturers/

Trajano v. Marcos (1992).

"Transnational Lawsuits in Canada against Extractive Companies." Above Ground, February 17, 2016, updated August 22, 2017, https://www.aboveground.ngo/wp-content/uploads/2016/02/Cases_Aug2017.pdf

TRIAL International. "Evidentiary Challenges in Universal Jurisdiction Cases." Geneva: TRIAL International, 2019.

TRIAL International. "Make Way for Justice #4: Momentum towards Accountability." Geneva: TRIAL International, 2018.

TRIAL International. "Revelations about TRIAL International's Investigation." September 26, 2017. https://trialinternational.org/latest-post/in-switzerland-proceedings-for-war-crimes-against-rifaat-al-assad/

Tucker, Eric. "Justice Department Appears Open to Interrogation Suit." *San Diego Union-Tribune*, April 21, 2016.

Turkmen v. Ashcroft, 589 F.3d 542 (2009).

Turkmen v. Hasty, et al. 789 F.3d 218 (2d Cir. 2015).

United Nations. "Country Update: Germany Q1 2018." Edited by the UN Refugee Agency, 2018.

United Nations Environment Programme. "Environmental Survey of Ogoniland." 2007.

United Nations General Assembly. "Resolution 39/46 Convention against Torture and Other Cruel, Inhuman or Degrading Treatment or Punishment." 1984.

United States Department of Justice. "Chiquita Brands International Pleads Guilty to Making Payments to a Designated Terrorist Organization and Agrees to Pay $25 Million Fine." Washington, DC: Department of Justice, 2007.

United States Department of Justice, Office of the Inspector General. "The September 11 Detainees: A Review of the Treatment of Aliens Held on Immigration Charges in Connection with the Investigation of the September 11 Attacks." 2003.

United States District Court. Eastern District of New York. "Exhibit A. Turkmen et al. v. Ashcroft et al." 2009.

United States House of Representatives. "Activities of the Committee on Oversight and Government Reform—Report 110–930." 2007–8.

United States House of Representatives, Committee on Oversight and Government Reform. "Memorandum: Additional Information about Blackwater USA." Washington, DC: United States Congress, 2007.

United States Senate, Committee on Foreign Relations, "Practice of Torture by Foreign Governments and US Efforts to Oppose its Use," June 26, 1984

United States Senate, Committee on Foreign Affairs, Subcommittee on Human Rights and International Organizations. "The Torture Victim Protection Act." March 23, 1988.

United States Senate, Select Committee on Intelligence. "Committee Study of the Central Intelligence Agency's Detention and Interrogation Program." Washington, DC: United States Senate, 2014.

University of California, Davis, Center for the Study of Human Rights, "Lists of Guantanamo Prisoners (Organized by Last Name, Citizenship, ISN, Date of Birth"

UPI. "Burma Plaintiffs to Appeal Dismissal of Unocal Suit." September 7, 2000.

Van der Zee, Bibi. "Global Injustices." *Guardian*, January 21, 2015.

Vann, Carole. "Suicides in Guantanamo: A Swiss Autopsy Reveals Troubling Facts." *InfoSud: Human Rights Tribune*, March 3, 2007.

Van Schaak, Beth. "Evidence Unsealed in Colvin v. Syria." *Just Security*, April 10, 2018. https://www.justsecurity.org/54653/important-sources-evidence-unsealed-lawsuit-syria-killing-marie-colvin-case/

Van Schaack, Beth. Interview by author, 2017, Stanford University.

Van Schaack, Beth. "Romagoza v. García: Proving Command Responsibility under the Alien Tort Claims Act and the Torture Victim Protection Act." *Human Rights Brief* 10, no. 1 (2002).

Van Schaack, Beth. "Syria Found Liable for the Death of War Correspondent Marie Colvin." *Just Security*, February 1, 2019. https://www.justsecurity.org/62459/breaking-news-syria-liable-death-war-correspondent-marie-colvin/

Verkaik, Robert. "BP Pays Out Millions to Colombian Farmers." *Independent*, July 22, 2006.

Vidal, John. "Lawyers Leigh Day: Troublemakers Who Are a Thorn in the Side of Multinationals." *Guardian*, August 2, 2015.

Voice of America. "British Finally Agree to Help Kenyans Injured by Their Munitions." July 25, 2002. https://www.voanews.com/amp/a-13-a-2002-07-25-52-british-67276632/268335.html

"Volkswagen 'Allowed Torture' under Brazil Military Rule." *BBC*, September 23, 2015. https://www.bbc.com/news/world-latin-america-34335094

Von Zielbauer, Paul. "Iraqi Inquiry Says Shooting Was Unprovoked." *New York Times*, October 7, 2007.

Voorhees, Bert. Interview by author, 2017, Skype.

Walker, Samuel. *In Defense of American Liberties: A History of the ACLU*. Carbondale: Southern Illinois University Press, 1999.

Watt, Steven. Interview by author, 2018, New York.

Weinstein, Henry. "Fight for Human Rights Ranges the World." *Los Angeles Times*, November 22, 2002.

Weinstein, Henry. "Marcos' Victims Settle Case for $150 Million." *Los Angeles Times*, February 25, 1999.

Weiss, Debra Cassens. "DC Lawyer Pursues Suit to Unmask Authors Who Changed Her Wikipedia Page." *ABA Journal*, September 16, 2013, http://www.abajournal.com/news/article/dc_lawyer_pursues_suit_to_unmask_authors_who_changed_her_wikipedia_page.

Weiss, Peter. Interview by author, 2017, New York.

White, Richard Alan. *Breaking Silence: The Case That Changed the Face of Human Rights*. Washington, DC: Georgetown University Press, 2004.

Wilkerson, Lawrence B. "Declaration by Lawrence B. Wilkerson in the Case of Adel Hamad." 2010.

Wilner, Thomas. "Columbia University Oral History Project." New York: Columbia Center for Oral History, 2009.

Winkler, Adam. *We the Corporations: How American Businesses Won Their Civil Rights* New York: W. W. Norton, 2018.

Wiwa v. Royal Dutch Petroleum Co., 226 F.3d 88 (2000).

Wong, Edward. "Following Up; Still Seeking Justice in a Brother's Death." *New York Times*, October 1, 2000.

Woods, Andrew. "Landmark Human Rights Trial Continues in Bowoto v. Chevron—Opening Statements and More." *Huffington Post*, May 25, 2011.

Woodward, Colin. "US Case Highlights Cuban 'Slaves' in Curacao." *Christian Science Monitor*, November 18, 2008.

Worldwide Movement For Human Rights. "Q&A on the Dabbagh Case: French

Judges Issue 3 International Arrest Warrants against Top Syrian Officials." May 11, 2018. https://www.fidh.org/en/issues/litigation/q-a-on-the-dabbagh-case -french-judges-issue-3-international-arrest

Worldwide Movement For Human Rights. "Syria, Iraq, Rwanda: Universal Jurisdiction Has Gathered Unprecedented Momentum in 2016." March 27, 2017. https://www.fidh.org/en/issues/international-justice/universal-jurisdiction/syr ia-iraq-rwanda-universal-jurisdiction-has-gathered-unprecedented

Yatron, Gus. "Declassified Letter to Honorable Ronald Reagan." 1983.

Yatron, Gus. "The Phenomenon of Torture: Hearings of the Subcommittee of Human Rights of the House Committee on Foreign Affairs." House of Representatives, Ninety-Eighth Congress, 1984.

"Yatron Will Seek Reelection to Seat for Ninth Term." *Morning Call*, January 10, 1984.

Index

American Declaration of the Rights and
　Duties of Man, 21
American Society of International Law, 45
Amesys, 137
amicus briefs, 81, 94, 111, 126
Amin, Idi, 26, 27
Amnesty International, 5, 19, 20, 23, 24,
　27, 38, 41, 42, 55, 91, 133, 135
Amsterdam, Anthony, 81
Anderson, Brian, 62
Anderson, David, 129
Anfalis, Amal Hag Hamdo, 141
Antioch Law School, 18
Anti-SLAPP, 103
Antonanzas de Barrosa, Norma, 30
Anvil Mining, 133
Aquino, Benigno Jr, 25
Aquino, Corazon, 25
Arabs, 72, 74, 76, 87
Aranowski, Amanda, 91
Arar, Maher, 73, 77, 78, 132
Araya, Gize Yebeyo, 135
Argentina, 22, 28, 29, 125, 138
Argor-Haraeus, 136
Argos, 138
Aristide, Jean-Bertrand, 13
Aristotle, 19
Ashcroft, John, 74, 75, 76, 78
Asia, Asian, 6, 16, 27, 52, 72, 74, 139
Assad regime, 45, 46, 143, 144
Associated Press, 82, 91
Asuncion, Paraguay, 18, 20
Atlanta, Georgia, USA, 5, 36, 37, 38, 42
attorney-client privilege, 93
Attorney General, 32, 73, 74, 75, 76, 102,
　105, 119
Austria, 143
Autodefensas Unidas Campesinas
　(AUC), 14, 118, 119, 120, 122, 123,
　138
Avila, Oscar, 149
Azmy, Baher, 89

Baach, Robinson & Lewis, 82
Baba Media Center, 143
Baghdad, Iraq, 99
Bagram Air Force Base, 88, 104
Baltasar Garzon International Founda-
　tion (FIBGAR), 127

Banadex, 118, 119, 122
Bangkok, Thailand, 14
Barak, Ehud, 15, 16
Bartlett, Chris, 93
Baudouin, Patrick, 137
Bay Area, California, 5, 36
Beeson, Ann, 99
Belgium, 125, 140
Bell Atlantic v. Twombly, 76
Belli, Melvin, 26
Ben Soud, Mohamed Ahmed, 104, 105,
　106, 107, 108
Benchoam, Debora, 28, 29
Benchoam, Rubin, 29
Benin City, Benin Republic, 109,
　153
Berlin, Germany, 126, 142,
Bernabeu, Almudena, 12, 44, 45, 46, 139,
　140, 141, 142, 144, 150
Biko, Steve, 129
Bill of Rights, The, 29, 32
Bisha Mine, 135
Bivens v. Six Unnamed Agents, 75, 78
black sites, 72, 77, 127, 146, 147
Blackwater USA, 101, 102, 103
Blank Rome, 106
Boeing, 100
Bonifaz, Jon, 54, 55
Bordaberry Arocena, Juan Maria, 161
Bork, Judge Robert, 82
Bosanski Samac, 42
Bosnia, Bosnian, 15, 22, 34, 36, 38, 39,
　42, 53
Bosnian War, 42
Boumediene v. Bush, 83
bounty hunters, 82
Bowoto v. Chevron, 7, 69, 70, 153
Bowoto, Larry, 64, 66
Brazil, 138
Breyer, Justice Stephen, 110
Brinkema, Judge Leonie, 96, 97
Britain/British, 128, 129. *See also* Great
　Britain; UK
British Columbia, Canada, 134, 135
British military, 128
Broder, Sherry, 26
Brodzinsky, Sibylla, 118
Bromley, Mark, 5
Brooklyn Navy Yard, 21